The Forms of
Historical Fiction

The Forms of Historical Fiction

Sir Walter Scott and His Successors

By Harry E. Shaw

Cornell University Press · *Ithaca and London*

THIS BOOK HAS BEEN PUBLISHED WITH
THE AID OF A GRANT FROM THE HULL MEMORIAL
PUBLICATION FUND OF CORNELL UNIVERSITY.

First published 1983 by Cornell University Press.
Second printing 1985.

International Standard Book Number 0–8014–1592–6
Library of Congress Catalog Card Number 83–5354

Printed in the United States of America

*Librarians: Library of Congress cataloging information
appears on the last page of the book.*

*The paper in this book is acid-free and meets the guidelines
for permanence and durability of the Committee on Production
Guidelines for Book Longevity of the Council on Library Resources.*

FOR JUDY JENSVOLD

Contents

Preface

Few intellectual developments in the last two hundred years have affected us more profoundly than the enriched sense of historicity which emerged in the late eighteenth century. In various ways, this historical sense informs the works of Herder, Ranke, and Marx—and the novels of Balzac, Tolstoy, and Scott. Though we may attempt to repudiate it, it is constitutive of our intellectual and moral worlds. Given such a situation, one might expect the historical novel to have attained a privileged place in the ranks of literature. Instead, the form suffers from neglect, even contempt.

This book proceeds from the conviction that the historical novel deserves a closer, more reasoned appraisal than it usually receives. Historical fiction merits such attention for a number of reasons, which include but transcend simple critical justice and the possibility of discovering new sources of esthetic pleasure. The problems historical novels have with history and we have with historical novels are potentially instructive. They can help to reveal limits in the esthetic forms we most prize—knowledge that matters for those who employ imaginative forms to make sense of the world. A clearer understanding of the workings of historical fiction can also clarify certain aspects of the nature of history itself, and of our situations as historical beings.

In all these areas, the novels of Sir Walter Scott, the first and arguably the greatest historical novelist in the modern sense, are exemplary, and they therefore have special prominence in this book. Scott's works are exemplary, first of all, in being neglected. Despite some stirrings of a Scott revival in recent years, the Waverley Novels remain the least-appreciated and least-read body of major fiction in English. For anyone who admires historical fiction, this situation stands as an affront and a challenge. But the current neglect of Scott also raises questions that transcend the history of taste. Is there something about his novels themselves, or about nineteenth-century historical fiction in general, which resists our favored modes of analysis? Is the relationship between Scott and the larger traditions of the novel more problematical than it may appear to be? Is critical suspicion of Scott to some extent justified, and if so, on what grounds? This book responds to these questions and others like them. By discriminating between different roles history can play in historical novels, it seeks to present a fruitful approach to Scott's novels and to nineteenth-century historical fiction in general.

This approach departs in certain ways from those employed, often to good effect, by others who have attempted to lift the historical novel from its present obscurity. The most significant attempt in this century to reassert the importance of historical fiction and of Scott did so by exploring the process by which history comes to human consciousness in art. If something of a Scott revival is afoot in the English-speaking world, this must in part be attributed to the translation of Georg Lukács's *The Historical Novel* in 1962. Lukács values Scott precisely because he embodies a critical moment in the development of our knowledge of history. Lukács has shed much light on Scott and on historical fiction generally, and I am greatly indebted to him. But the strength of his approach is also its weakness. His story of the development of historical consciousness finds its climax, not in the creation of increasingly rich historical novels, but in the emergence of works that can register the present as history. For Lukács's own purposes, this procedure is entirely justified and yields impressive results. But by shifting the focus away from historical fiction as a phenomenon in its own right, his developmental vision unavoidably reduces Scott in particular, and historical fiction in general, to the status of forerunners. It invites us to think of Scott perhaps as a John the Baptist, more likely as a pigmy on whose shoulders giants stand, and then to look beyond him.

Lukács has provided what is likely to be the definitive *historical* study of historical fiction. I treat historical fiction in terms that are primarily synchronic. I concentrate on the representational possibilities and limitations of historical fiction, as exemplified by Scott's novels as well as by certain other works in the European realist tradition. Such an approach is appropriate to nineteenth-century historical novels, because (as I indicate in my first chapter) they lack an independent history of their own. In larger terms, a dialectical tension between the synchronic and the diachronic is part of historicism itself, for historicism can lead to visions of emerging historical process like Hegel's, but it can also promote an appreciation of systematic cultural uniqueness and irreducible historical difference.

A synchronic treatment of Scott's novels is also a less paradoxical enterprise than it might seem. When he began writing novels Scott was in his forties and fully formed as a thinker and an artist. He produced good and bad novels throughout his career, and only with distortion can his works be made to fit a developmental pattern. My discussion reveals two moments when he engaged in significant though short-lived departures from his normal fictional practices, first by using his fiction primarily to explore contemporary concerns and later by making his protagonist the true center of two novels. These moments are unusual: except for the decline in his final works, such trends as exist in his career as a novelist are best explained on grounds other than personal growth or artistic development.

In my discussion of Scott, I have felt compelled to disagree with efforts to show that history is not his ultimate concern, or to assimilate his works too directly to the norms of the novelists who followed him. If Scott is really trying to do the same things in the same ways as his successors, he does them much less well and deserves obscurity. It is also important not to defend Scott by concentrating on a favored kind of Waverley Novel and forgetting that he created a number of different kinds of historical fiction. To be sure, certain Waverley Novels are better left in oblivion. But much of Scott's greatness lies in his variety. One of my objects has been to promote an awareness of this variety by describing in a systematic way the different kinds of novelistic structure in which it is embodied.

A discussion of historical fiction quickly extends into areas of daunting complexity and importance. I have tried to strike a balance between giving such issues the attention they deserve and producing a study focused on a manageable subject. Thus I deal in some detail with certain aspects of Lukács, but avoid the controversies that have swirled around his name and methods, particularly since his death. Lukács always appeared to have something to tell us about nineteenth-century realism, and the time may come when, instead of dismissing his attack on modernism by calling him a Stalinist or fetishist or closet bourgeois, we will respond to the moral challenge it presents, for all its shortcomings. I also avoid discussing the representation of history in novels set in the recent past or the present. I believe that the representational problems that shape historical fiction touch such works as well, but in ways complex enough to demand a much longer discussion than I can here provide. Finally, I discuss only certain aspects of the problem of whether history (or anything else) can be represented in fiction, and indeed of whether history can be known or experienced at all. Questions of historical epistemology and of the means by which the readerly texture of a novel can create a "history-effect" have considerable interest. They have already begun to be explored with fruitful results in studies of historical fiction and of Scott.[1] My focus lies elsewhere.

Depending on one's metaphysical presuppositions, stories about history may seem potentially true or false, or they may seem a set of essentially arbitrary constructs, reflecting the present if they reflect anything at all. Yet the works themselves remain. Charles Altieri has noted that "for the agents involved in particular practices, metaphysical standards of arbitrariness are irrelevant."[2] If this book promotes a sharper awareness of the "particular practices" embodied in Scott's novels, and of the problems and possibilities that Scott and his successors faced in their attempts to give history fictional form, it will have achieved its primary goal.

Despite the subject of my book, I shall not attempt a history of influences on its progress from the past to the present, but shall simply

1. See, for instance, Richard Waswo, "Story as Historiography in the Waverley Novels," *ELH*, 47 (1980), 304–30. After I had completed the present book, I had the pleasure of hearing Waswo deliver a rousing talk entitled "Scott and the Really Great Tradition" at the Aberdeen Scott Conference held in the summer of 1982, in which he attacked much the same set of critical presuppositions that I question in my first chapter.

2. Charles Altieri, "Culture and Skepticism: A Response to Michael Fischer," *Critical Inquiry*, 6 (1979), 351.

chronicle some debts. My debt to certain books, above all to the works of Georg Lukács, should be obvious enough, especially since I offer the tribute of vigorous disagreement to many of those whose writings have set the terms for present-day discussions of the subjects I treat. Debts to persons, though less obvious, are not less real. Early help came from Basil Guy, John Henry Raleigh, Ian Campbell, Martin Jay, and from Ralph Rader, generous in agreement and disagreement, the finest teacher I have known. More recently, Jean Blackall, Fredric Bogel, Jonathan Culler, Edgar Rosenberg, Daniel Schwarz, and Cushing Strout read and commented upon various parts of my manuscript, and my students at Cornell stimulated and challenged me as we tried to make sense of historical fiction.

During the early stages of this project, I was fortunate enough to spend a year in Edinburgh, where I was supported by a Fulbright-Hays Scholarship and a Traveling Fellowship from the University of California. Completion of the book was aided by grants from Cornell University. I appreciate this support. I also thank the editors of *Studies in the Novel* for allowing me to use in my discussion of *The Bride of Lammermoor* material that originally appeared in their pages. John Ackerman and Bernhard Kendler of Cornell University Press are model editors, and I appreciate their assistance. Finally, I acknowledge with pleasure a special debt to Walter Cohen and Laura Brown, who read and commented upon every page of this book save one, and who persuaded me to conclude.

HARRY E. SHAW

Ithaca, New York

A Note on Citations
of Scott's Works

Throughout, I cite passages from the Waverley Novels parenthetically in my text. I use the Dryburgh Edition, 25 vols. (London: Adam and Charles Black, 1892–94). I have checked all passages cited against the versions given in the "Magnum Opus" edition, 48 vols. (Edinburgh: Cadell, 1829–33) without finding any significant variants, except that the Dryburgh edition misspells the name of Montrose's castle. (I have corrected it.) In discussing Scott's prefatory material, I differentiate between Introductions and Notes written for the first editions of the novels, and the material Scott put together retrospectively for the "Magnum Opus" edition.

Abbreviations used in citing other works by Scott are as follows:

Journal   *The Journal of Sir Walter Scott*, ed. W. E. K. Anderson (London: Oxford University Press, 1972).

Letters   *The Letters of Sir Walter Scott, 1787–1832*, ed. H. J. C. Grierson, 12 vols. (London: Constable, 1932–37).

MPW   *The Miscellaneous Prose Works of Sir Walter Scott, Bart.*, ed. J. G. Lockhart, 28 vols. (Edinburgh: Cadell, 1834–36).

The Forms of
Historical Fiction

An Approach to the Historical Novel

WHAT IS THE HISTORICAL NOVEL?

When critics discuss literary groups and genres, they are usually doing more than indulging in the pleasures of the taxonomical imagination. Genres help us sense the lay of the literary land. They imply questions and sometimes answers: we see a forest, or at least clumps of trees, instead of trees. In other parts of life, we constantly make distinctions that are like generic distinctions in literary studies, and they matter. As we know, an attempt to correct social injustice may dictate very different actions depending on the groups it singles out for attention. Debates between microhistorians and macrohistorians hinge on the same problem; they also remind us that the time span we choose to think about has a significant impact on the conclusions we draw about a given topic. It may be true that in the long run, we are all dead, but such a perspective is more useful to a mystic than to a mercenary. When we experience a work of literature, we employ in a refined and complex way our general ability to see the world in terms of significant groups and patterns. Making sense of a work rests upon knowing what to expect from it, understanding how to take it in. This in turn implies that we have a sense of what sort of thing it is, how it works, what its rules are. Beyond that, generic assumptions allow us—indeed, force us—to focus on some things at the expense of others; they can make certain aspects of a text disappear or seem trivial. If I begin this book about Scott and form in the historical novel by asking about the generic status of historical fiction, then, my purpose is not merely to devise a set of labels. Questions of genre are questions of meaning and literary effect.[1]

What is the historical novel? In attempting to answer this question, it would seem advisable, before plunging into speculations about historiography and the nature of a truly historical outlook, to ask what sort of term "the historical novel" is in the first place. How does it differ from other groups of novels—the picaresque novel, the industrial novel, the sentimental novel, the eighteenth-century novel? Which is it most like? A simple but accurate answer is that the term historical novel denotes a kind of novel which can be differentiated from other groups of novels not in terms of a defining compositional technique (the picaresque novel), nor through its power to evoke a set of emotions (the gothic or sentimental novel), and certainly not in terms of the period in which it was written (the eighteenth-century novel). Instead, the principle of differentiation involves the milieu represented, which makes the closest parallel in our list the industrial novel. Though it seems fair to say that the industrial novel is a narrower category, it is the same sort of category as the historical novel.

A convenient way of extending this simple, intuitive notion that historical novels are works that in some way represent historical milieux is to speak in terms of fictional probability. A character or incident in a novel can be probable in either or both of two ways. We usually think of probability as involving fidelity to the external world that a work represents. Some eighteenth-century readers of *Clarissa* found Mrs. Sinclair's house in London improbable because they could not believe that such carefully contrived dens of iniquity actually existed. One might complain that Clarissa herself violates probability in this sense because she is too good to be true—we have never met anyone like her in the world in which we live. In the historical novel, anachronisms and mistakes of historical fact are responsible for breaches of

1. My discussion employs the notion of genre in a more extended way than its common use to identify certain large classes of works, such as epic, tragedy, or novel. I believe, drawing upon the work of Ralph W. Rader, that we make sense of works by intuitively classing them according to a whole range of increasingly specific distinctions, from the most general (literature as opposed to nonliterature) to the most specific (one work as opposed to another by a given author). For Rader's views on genre, see "The Concept of Genre and Eighteenth-Century Studies," in *New Approaches to Eighteenth-Century Literature*, ed. Phillip Harth (New York: Columbia University Press, 1974), pp. 79–115.

probability in this sense. But probability can also depend upon how consistently a work follows its own internal rules and patterns. Soliloquies in drama are probable in this second sense, but not in the sense of being faithful reproductions of the behavior we expect from our fellows in their everyday affairs. In general, the more stylized a work becomes, the more these two kinds of probability diverge; the more directly mimetic it is, the more they coalesce. Probability involves our sense of a novel's "fit," both the way it fits the world it imitates and the way its parts fit together to produce a unified whole. A novel's power to illuminate life and its intrinsic beauty as a formed work of art depend in large measure on its probability in both senses.[2]

The concept of fictional probability implies a way of defining historical fiction. We can say that while in most novels probability stems from our general ideas about life and society, in historical novels the major source of probability is specifically historical. Though many kinds of novels may incorporate a sense of history, in historical novels history is, as the Russian Formalists would put it, "foregrounded." When we read historical novels, we take their events, characters, settings, and language to be historical in one or both of two ways. They may represent societies, modes of speech, or events that in very fact existed in the past, in which case their probability points outward from the work to the world it represents; or they may promote some sort of historical effect within the work, such as providing an entry for the reader into the past, in which case the probability points inward, to the design of the work itself. In *Waverley,* Fergus MacIvor has both internal and external probability, while Edward Waverley's probability rests primarily on the way in which he furthers the novel's historical design. Fergus is a faithful composite picture of the Highland Jacobite nobility, providing a good external portrait of them and also representing the historical weaknesses that in Scott's opinion doomed their movement. Waverley, on the other hand, is the reader's entry into the novel. He functions primarily as a fictional device, allowing the historical import of the novel to be felt with maximum force. The idea of internal probability allows us to see why a work

2. W. J. Harvey, *Character and the Novel* (London and Ithaca, 1965; rpt. Ithaca: Cornell University Press, 1968), pp. 11–13, discusses these two kinds of fictional probability, which answer roughly to the New Critical terms "coherence" and "correspondence"; subsequent references to Harvey appear in my text.

can become more historical, not less historical, if it rearranges individual aspects of the historical record for the sake of demonstrating a larger pattern.[3]

Historical novels, then, are works in which historical probability reaches a certain level of structural prominence. This may seem an impotent and lame conclusion, objectionable on several counts. It is negative and minimal. It is vague in terms of what counts as historical. It creates distinctions of degree, not kind; and in particular, it does not indicate the kind of prominence history must have in the structure of a truly historical novel. In fact, these qualities are virtues. Because the definition is vague in terms of what counts as historical, it leaves open the possibility that history may mean different things in different works. The definition works in terms of differences of degree, not kind, but it should: the modern historical novel arose as part of the rise of historicism, which made a sense of history part of the cultural mainstream and hence available to novels in general, not simply to historical novels. But the definition's greatest strength is that it does not specify what role history must play in a novel's structure if we are to consider that novel a work of historical fiction. One of my main contentions is that we cannot make sense of historical fiction unless we recognize that history plays a number of distinctly different roles in historical novels. My second and third chapters will explore the three main functions history performs in the classical historical novel, and it will be necessary to create a further set of distinctions when we discuss Scott's works. A negative, minimal definition of historical fiction leaves the way clear for these necessary distinctions.[4]

3. The reader will notice in my account even a novel's internal probability ultimately serves referential, not self-referential ends: this might be a liability in dealing with some kinds of fiction but seems an asset in dealing with historical fiction.

4. Roland Barthes, "Historical Discourse," in *Introduction to Structuralism*, ed. Michael Lane (New York: Basic Books, 1970), pp. 145–55, defines a distinctive kind of historical discourse characterized by its production of a historical "reality effect." Whatever its other merits, such an approach cannot be used to solve the problem of defining historical fiction by discovering its basic representational means. As we shall see in Chapter 2, the structures that embody historical probability in historical fiction exist at all levels of generality, often at a level of allegorical abstraction very far removed from the concreteness or pseudo-concreteness of "historical discourse." Wolfgang Iser, *The Implied Reader: Patterns of Communication from Bunyan to Beckett* (Baltimore: Johns Hopkins University Press, 1974), pp. 81–100, discovers in *Waverley* a variety of historical discourse, with instructive results. Though he does de-

In most respects, historical fiction depends upon the formal techniques and cultural assumptions of the main traditions of the novel. Because of this dependence, it does not have a significant history apart from the history of the novel as a whole. What is often called the classical historical novel begins with Scott; but the important line of fictional development runs not from Scott to the historical novelists who followed him, but instead from Scott to such masters of European fiction as Balzac, Dickens, and even (so argues Louis Maigron) Flaubert.[5] The authors who produce the best historical novels after Scott tend, with the exception of Cooper and Tolstoy, to be masters of other kinds of writing, who enter the field with one or two attempts, as Dickens, Thackeray, and Hugo do. Georg Lukács is in my opinion essentially accurate in describing the history of the novel as a great stream from which tributaries branch off, only to rejoin and further enrich it in due course. Scott's works form such a tributary: he branches off from the eighteenth-century novel, discovers in artistic terms the rich significance of history, and then reunites with the mainstream of nineteenth-century fiction through his influence on Balzac, enriching it with new materials, insights, and techniques.[6]

Since they lack a history of their own, the most useful way to group historical novels historically is in terms of coherent movements of the novel as a whole, and of the esthetic and cultural presuppositions that underlie them. The realist novel, which begins with Richardson and finds its greatest achievement in the works of Eliot and Balzac and

---

fine one aspect of the immediate texture of Scott's writing, he neglects the larger structures that create a novel's meaning and effect, and he ignores the self-consciousness with which Scott employs, and we accept, various fictional conventions. For a critique of Iser on Scott, see Richard L. Stein, "Historical Fiction and the Implied Reader: Scott and Iser," *Novel*, 14 (1981), 213–31.

5. Louis Maigron, *Le roman historique à l'époque romantique: Essai sur l'influence de Walter Scott* (1898; new ed. Paris: Champion, 1912). An important recent attempt to reinstate Scott as a source of the realist novel is George Levine, *The Realistic Imagination: English Fiction from Frankenstein to Lady Chatterley* (Chicago: University of Chicago Press, 1981).

6. *The Historical Novel* (1937), trans. Hannah and Stanley Mitchell (London: Merlin, 1962). One general property of literature set in the past is that it can provide a privileged area for formal and thematic innovation. In his historical dramas, John Banks made the transition from Restoration tragedy to the sentimental drama of the eighteenth century: see Laura Brown, *English Dramatic Form, 1660–1760: An Essay in Generic History* (New Haven: Yale University Press, 1981), pp. 95–97. Shakespeare's history plays may well have served a similar function in his career.

Tolstoy, is such a movement. I shall call such works "standard" novels; the group of historical novels which derives its unity from its relationship with standard fiction then becomes "standard historical novels." These works form the subject of this book. They all employ the formal techniques of standard fiction, and in particular, they use the plotted action, which creates in the reader a pattern of hopes and fears for one or more protagonists, as their formal basis.[7] They also share with the standard novel a set of broad cultural assumptions that provide the grounds for their intelligibility and are the ultimate source of their "realism." The situation of historical fiction in our own century becomes more complex. As the novel in general changes, new forms of historical fiction emerge. But strong continuities with nineteenth-century forms also persist in such distinguished historical novelists as Marguerite Yourcenar or H. F. M. Prescott.[8]

I have suggested that no single quality of historical insight defines historical fiction. But since we have narrowed our sights to the standard historical novel, can't we say something more specific about the kind or kinds of historical vision they embody? We can indeed, but

7. The concept of the "plotted action," which I employ throughout, derives from Ralph W. Rader's extension and revision of R. S. Crane's "form of the plot," which Crane develops in "The Concept of Plot and the Plot of *Tom Jones*," in *Critics and Criticism: Ancient and Modern*, ed. R. S. Crane (Chicago: University of Chicago Press, 1952), pp. 616–23. According to Rader, the plotted action gives form to a novel by creating in the reader a dynamic pattern of hopes and fears about the fate of the protagonist: "the author pits our induced sense of what will happen to a character against our induced sense of what we want to happen to him, our hopes against our fears, in order to give the greatest pleasure appropriate to their resolution." For a fuller and more technical definition, see Rader, "Defoe, Richardson, Joyce, and the Concept of Form in the Novel," in *Autobiography, Biography, and the Novel*, by William Matthews and Ralph W. Rader (Los Angeles: William Andrews Clark Memorial Library, 1973), pp. 33–34.

8. Joseph W. Turner, "The Kinds of Historical Fiction," *Genre*, 12 (1979), pp. 333–55, produces an interesting typology of kinds of historical fiction in the twentieth century. He also briefly points out some of the problems inherent in the attempt to define historical fiction by differentiating it from historiography, noting that this procedure tends to reduce historiography to one single thing, and fiction to another single thing. In my view, a valid differentiation between historiography and historical fiction would require an exhaustive typology of subclasses of the two kinds of works. Even then, the complex set of resulting distinctions would almost certainly have to exist at a high level of generality, involving such matters as the cognitive claims of art and the truth values of statements in different kinds of discourse. Such speculations might have considerable general interest but would probably have little heuristic value for understanding individual works.

only within limits. The historian Herbert Butterfield and the literary critic Avrom Fleishman have both tried in different ways to define the quality historical novels share, and their discussions are useful here. Both define historical fiction by differentiating it from historiography. For Butterfield, historiography attempts to "make a generalisation, to find a formula," because it views history as "the whole process of development that leads up to the present." The historical novel, by contrast, attempts to "reconstruct a world, to particularise, to catch a glimpse of human nature." The task of the historical novelist is to render the unique "atmosphere" of an age in the past, to "recapture the fleeting moment." For Fleishman, by contrast, the historical novelist accomplishes something more like the task Butterfield sets the historian: "What makes a historical novel historical is the active presence of a concept of history as a shaping force." Both critics are clearly drawing on the achievements of historicism for their definitions, a procedure that seems entirely in order since the rise of the historical novel is bound up with the rise of historicism in general. But Butterfield invokes what we might call a minimal historicist vision; Fleishman, historicism at its most powerful and dignified.[9]

Identifying the historicity of historical novels with "the active presence of a concept of history as a shaping force" seems to have much to recommend it. Probably the most important aspect of the historicist view of the past is its recognition that history shapes human beings through specific and unique social mediations. This need not imply the view often attributed to Hegel—the idea that history is a vast teleological progression leading relentlessly toward one divine event—though such a belief is one of its extreme potentialities. It does involve a sociological sense of both past and present, a recognition that societies are interrelated systems which change through time and that individuals are profoundly affected by their places within those systems. The greatest modern critics of nineteenth-century fiction from a historical point of view, whatever their other differences, agree that the creation of this grasp of social-historical milieux is its principal achievement. For Erich Auerbach, it is the prerequisite for a fully serious treatment of everyday life; for Lukács, it involves a fundamen-

9. Herbert Butterfield, *The Historical Novel* (Cambridge: Cambridge University Press, 1924), p. 113; Avrom Fleishman, *The English Historical Novel: Walter Scott to Virginia Woolf* (Baltimore: Johns Hopkins University Press, 1971), p. 15.

tal discovery concerning the meaning of historical process itself. Both critics describe this development as the discovery of "the present as history," a phrase which derives ultimately from Hegel. In asserting that historical novels are defined by their sense of "history as a shaping force," Fleishman would thus appear to have rendered them an important service: he has acquitted them of the charge of portraying mere local color, finding in them instead the historical insights we associate with historicism at its most developed.[10]

But Butterfield, writing at a time when valuing historical particularity caused critics less embarrassment than it does now, is closer to the truth about the historical probability that serves as a basis for the standard historical novel. The problem with Fleishman's mode of definition is that it saves too much too quickly, giving historical fiction a cognitive dignity that is unearned. The works of Harrison Ainsworth betray no insight whatever into "history as a shaping force," but we unhesitatingly call them historical novels. Fleishman's discussion quickly slides from defining historical fiction to finding a criterion for "authentic" historical fiction, a separate issue for which his maximal kind of definition is entirely appropriate.

The recognition that human beings are part of a larger historical process is not the source of the distinctively historical probability that distinguishes standard historical fiction, though the best historical novels certainly convey it. The probability that distinguishes standard historical novels rests on a simpler notion—the realization that history is comprised of ages and societies that are significantly different from our own. We can call this idea the recognition of "the past as past"[11] (Ainsworth's fiction doesn't really measure up to this crite-

10. Since "historicism" has been given a pejorative meaning by certain writers (especially Karl Popper), let me make clear that I use the word to refer to the enriched sense human beings gained of history about the time of the French Revolution, involving a new awareness of the systematic otherness of societies in the past, and a new interest in the process by which the past becomes the present. Useful introductions to historicism include Isaiah Berlin, *Vico and Herder: Two Studies in the History of Ideas* (London: Hogarth, 1976), and Friedrich Meinecke, *Historism: The Rise of a New Historical Outlook* (1936), trans. J. E. Anderson (London: Routledge and Kegan Paul, 1972). For a useful discussion of the definition of historicism, see Maurice Mandelbaum, *History, Man, and Reason: A Study in Nineteenth-Century Thought* (Baltimore: Johns Hopkins University Press, 1971).

11. In my discussion, I am assuming that historical novels depict societies that are in fact different from our own. Now it is possible to write a historical novel that at-

rion either, but it is at least possible to recognize in his sensationalistic use of historical atmosphere a debased version of it, whereas any connection whatever with a notion of historical process or the present as history is in his case unimaginable.) The recognition of the past as past can lead to a sense of history as a process, and perhaps it ought to, but in fact it has not always done so in historical fiction.

By arguing that historical fiction need not view history as a process, I am parting company not only with Fleishman but with Lukács as well, though in a different way. For Lukács, the historical novel arises in the works of Scott when Scott discovers on an esthetic level that history is a process in which the past acts as the necessary precondition for the present. Unlike Butterfield or Fleishman, however, Lukács simply isn't interested in the problem of defining historical fiction, and given his distrust of "mere formalism," it is hard to see how he could be. He pursues instead the question of how the historical spirit comes to consciousness in literature. With more consistency than other writers who hold similar views concerning what is truly historical about historical novels, Lukács believes that historical fiction does not constitute a genre separate from the European realist novel as a whole. In his version of Marxist esthetics, a truly separate genre can arise only from a new vision of reality, and the truly historical novel shares (and in fact helped to create) the vision of reality we find in genuinely realistic novels. Historical fiction is thus part of a larger fictional genre, realist fiction, which is characterized by the mode of knowledge it embodies. This mode of knowledge provides, in the process he calls "preparatory esthetic processing," a necessary but not sufficient condition for the creation of realist fiction.[12]

My discussions of Lukács, Butterfield, and Fleishman have revealed

---

tempts to show just the opposite—that life is essentially the same in all ages. Anatole France's *Les dieux ont soif* is written from such a perspective. But even this sort of novel must at least show that life seems to be different, if only to refute that claim. The very notion of history implies change over time: the question that *Les dieux* raises is how important the areas are in which change occurs. For most historical novels, their importance is considerable.

12. Béla Királyfalvi, *The Aesthetics of György Lukács* (Princeton: Princeton University Press, 1975), pp. 104–5. Királyfalvi is a useful guide to Lukács's later works, but he generally gives references only to the Hungarian translations of Lukács. The passage here will be found in the original in Lukács, *Probleme der Ästhetik* (Berlin: Luchterhand, 1969), p. 765.

a number of fundamental differences among them, but they are united in believing historical fiction to be fundamentally a mode of knowledge. Such a view has its attractions. Who would want to deny that the best historical fiction can add to the richness of our sense of history, or that the structuring of history in great historical fiction may have cognitive value? Narrativist philosophers of history have recently argued with some persuasiveness that historical understanding itself may proceed according to the logic of narrative discourse, not of science.[13] But it seems important for a number of reasons to oppose the idea that historical novels, or even standard historical novels, embody a defining vision of history in more than a minimal way.

Such an idea can become quickly and narrowly prescriptive in practice, blinding us to the workings of novels that embody a vision of history we do not respect. It is tempting to say that works which embody a historical vision we find uninteresting or unacceptable, or that seem to have no historical vision at all, are not "really" historical novels. But it is more useful to discriminate between great and mediocre historical novels than to exclude imperfect works from the group—a procedure that logically tends to produce a group containing one and only one true member. A different consequence appears in Fleishman's criticism. As we have seen, he believes that historical novels are characterized by "the active presence of a concept of history as a shaping force." He is also interested in tracing the history of historical fiction in England, which of course implies that there is a significant history to trace. Each of these premises raises problems. Combined, they cause him to exaggerate and homogenize the level of historical consciousness in the works he considers. Only by doing so can he produce a developing tradition of English historical fiction.

The search for a specific way of perceiving history which defines historical fiction is in my view a local manifestation of the understandable but unacceptable desire to separate literary discourse from "scientific discourse" and thus to save for literature its own distinct significance. This view, which places great stress on differentiating be-

---

13. W. B. Gallie, *Philosophy and the Historical Understanding* (London: Chatto & Windus, 1964). For a discussion of the narrativist historians and their rivals, see Cushing Strout, *The Veracious Imagination: Essays in American History, Literature, and Biography* (Middletown: Wesleyan University Press, 1981), pp. 3–28.

tween true and false poetic modes, is most familiar as one of the cornerstones of the New Criticism as practiced by Cleanth Brooks and others. Lukács from his Marxist point of view has come up with a similar if somewhat more elegant procedure involving three levels of discourse—everyday speech, scientific discourse, and (mediating between the two on a whole series of intermediate levels) the language of literature. This is not the place to weigh the merits of such views extensively. I shall merely say that in my view "scientific discourse" in the sense required by Brooks and the others has been shown not to exist; their argument is based upon a false dichotomy. Literary works in general do not embody a distinct mode of knowledge, though they certainly can impart knowledge. Though literary works can have cognitive claims, they are in the first instance verbal constructions designed to create certain effects through the disposition of their parts.[14]

For our present purposes, the idea that historical fiction is a mode of telling the truth about history is objectionable chiefly because it does not account for the very different formal status that visions of history have in fact assumed in historical fiction. Such a definition excludes works we all call historical novels. Furthermore, if we adopt such a definition, we must conclude that most great nineteenth-century novels are historical novels, which renders the concept "historical novel" useless as a conceptual aid and falsifies the strong intuitive impression that leads readers to give the group a name in the first place.[15] In practice, such an emphasis also tends to exclude or preclude problems of artistic form and effect, operating as if historical novels conveyed unmediated historical doctrine. Finally, the idea that historical fiction is a mode of historical knowledge leaves as a com-

14. For Lukács's three levels of discourse, see *Die Eigenart des Ästhetischen*, 2 vols. (Berlin: Luchterhand, 1963), II, 11–192; and Királyfalvi, pp. 88–102. For an incisive critique of the New Critical distinction between poetic and scientific discourse, see R. S. Crane, *The Languages of Criticism and the Structure of Poetry* (Toronto: University of Toronto Press, 1953).

15. Fleishman, p. 15, notes and is properly suspicious of John Lukacs's assertion that "In the broad sense every novel is a historical novel," in *Historical Consciousness, or The Remembered Past* (New York: Harper, 1968), p. 118. In a certain sense, *Emma* and *Old Mortality*, which were both published in 1816, are also both "historical" for readers today, because they are implicated in the history of their own times. But an important difference remains between the degree to which a desire to depict history dominates their structures.

plete mystery what is surely the most striking fact about these works. Why do the finest historical novels, with the single exception of *War and Peace*, seem flawed when compared with the best standard fiction? The lack of a great tradition of historical fiction is remarkable. From a point of view that sees history as one kind, and potentially an intractable kind, of material to receive esthetic shaping, it may perhaps be explained.

THE PROBLEM WITH HISTORICAL NOVELS

My definition of historical fiction has been primarily negative. I have tried to show that historical novels do not constitute a strongly unified, independent genre. The most we can say is that there are groups of historical novels, united by their dependence on broader fictional traditions, which constitute significant objects of critical attention. The group with which I am concerned, standard historical novels, shares the conventions of the realist novel; they are also united, in a minimal way, by incorporating within their systems of fictional probability a sense of the past as past. But as a result of these unifying factors, historical novels have in common a third characteristic—a shared problematic, which (as my next chapter will show) assumes different degrees of prominence in different works, depending primarily on the end to which they employ history.

The historical novel raises in an acute form a question common to all mimetic works of art—the relationship of the individual to the general, of particulars to universals. Such problems tend to remain submerged in most literary works. Several things bring them to the surface in the historical novel. Because historical novelists depict ages significantly different from their own and may aspire to represent the workings of historical process itself, they are faced with the task of creating characters who represent social groups and historical trends. But creating such characters involves certain inherent difficulties. This is a major reason for the problem with historical novels.

Human beings live at a number of different levels of generality. They are individuals, with unique thoughts, feelings, and ideas; they are members of small social groups such as families; they are also members of larger groups, of cities, regions, nations, races; finally, they are human beings in the widest and most general sense, as opposed to the rest of nature. As we move up the scale from particularity to generality, we become interested in different characteristics of the same individuals. The higher we go, the more we focus on the general and representative at the expense of the specific and idiosyncratic. The question that faces mimetic works in general and historical novels in a particularly acute form is how much of the scale a literary work can represent. If such literary forms as the standard novel have evolved in such a way that they deal most successfully with one segment of the spectrum, while historical novels by their very nature must treat a broader or different segment, we might expect standard historical fiction to have had only partial esthetic success.

The problem I have raised was very much a part of the intellectual milieu from which the historical novel arose. At about the time when Scott was inventing the historical novel in its modern form, Hegel was at work on history in a different way. One way of approaching Hegel's philosophy of history is to see it as an attempt to solve just this problem, for the dialectic is a device that bridges the gap between particulars and universals. Whatever we think of Hegel's system as a solution, we can understand why the problem of the relationship between particulars and universals interested him. The discovery that past ages are crucially different from the present and from each other challenges radically the belief that any assumptions about human beings are universally valid. It is only natural that philosophers should attempt to solve this problem. Hegel, it is worth adding, believed that Scott's historical fiction provides no solution at all: it was for him all particularity, presenting merely a "detailed *portraiture* incorporating all the minutiae of the age, in which the deeds and fortunes of a single individual constitute the work's sole *futile* interest and *wholly particular* matters are all put forward as *equally important*."[16] Even Homer nods.

The issue at hand involves some of our most basic, irreducible, and unprovable beliefs about human existence. Questions about mimesis in art are ultimately questions about what we think is centrally im-

16. G. W. F. Hegel, *Lectures on the Philosophy of World History, Introduction: Reason in History*, trans. H. B. Nisbet (Cambridge: Cambridge University Press, 1975), p. 19. Hegel's attempt to create a system that sees history as universal but at the same time as utterly concrete and particular is stressed throughout George Dennis O'Brien's helpful *Hegel on Reason and History* (Chicago: University of Chicago Press, 1975).

portant about human beings. In the following pages, I intend to describe the ideological underpinnings of a variety of beliefs about mimesis in novels, and to indicate the reason for the choice I make among them. I hope that the position I take will recommend itself by its usefulness for understanding the workings of historical fiction. From what I have already said, it will be apparent that I have little of interest to offer those who believe that novels do not mirror external reality in any important sense.

I am familiar with two main views concerning the mimetic scope of prose fiction, and I want to describe their implications rather fully. The view that in my opinion characterizes most English-speaking criticism in this century locates the mimetic power of the novel at both ends of the human spectrum simultaneously.[17] It holds that good novels attempt to depict individual human beings in their mental complexity and spiritual depth; to the extent to which these novels succeed in doing so, they touch upon the most lasting, universal aspects of humanity in general. The intermediate levels involving society, nation, and history are either irrelevant or valuable only insofar as they reveal the universal through the individual. For convenience and despite the gracelessness of the term, we may call this an "individualist" view of the novel. This view often (though not necessarily) leads to a devaluation of interest in plot, that element of the novel which shows a character interacting with a larger social framework. Patterns of words and images instead become the central expressive techniques of the novel. When this tendency is carried far enough to imply an attack not merely on plot but on character, we begin to leave the realm of a mimetic conception of the novel altogether, and the possibility of representing society, much less history, as more than aspects of an individual vision diminishes to nothing.[18]

In sharp contrast to the individualist view of the novel is the idea that novels can represent the entire spectrum of human existence. This belief rests upon the assumption that there is a seamless connec-

17. Lionel Trilling would seem at least a partial exception to this trend, but the strenuousness of his effort to argue for the importance of "manners" in the novel itself testifies to the strength of the "individualist" view he is trying to broaden. He stresses the importance of historical difference in his last published fragment, "Why We Read Jane Austen," *TLS*, 5 March 1976, p. 251, col. 2.

18. Harvey, pp. 191–217, provides a useful discussion of "The Retreat from Character" and "The Attack on Character" in modern criticism of the novel.

tion between all levels of human existence. If any one level is presented clearly enough, it implies all the others. This is the view of Lukács. We can adapt his own terminology to call such a view "typicalist." For Lukács, great literature contains "typical" characters who concentrate within themselves all levels of human existence. If he is right about the novelist's ability to create typicality in literature, there should be no inherent formal problem in creating great historical fiction.

It is important to examine the ideas that underlie these two positions, and particularly what they presuppose about the meaning, or lack of meaning, of history. We may begin with a viewpoint that Aldous Huxley expresses succinctly and as a foregone conclusion in his essay on Piranesi:

> Any given work of art may be represented as the diagonal in a parallelogram of forces—a parallelogram of which the base is the prevailing tradition and the socially important events of the time, and in which the upright is the artist's temperament and his private life. In some works the base is longer than the upright; in others the upright is longer than the base.
>
> Piranesi's *Prisons* are creations of the second kind. In them the personal, private and therefore universal and everlasting upright is notably longer than the merely historical and therefore transient and local base. . . . His concern is with states of the soul—states that are largely independent of external circumstances, states that recur whenever Nature, at her everlasting game of chance, combines the hereditary factors of physique and temperament in certain patterns.[19]

Here we have most of the characteristics of the point of view I have called "individualist." There is the assumption that socially significant events and private life are sharply distinct, that the soul is "largely independent of external circumstances." Accompanying this belief is a suggestion that history is a mere flux, resulting from the chance workings of heredity. Finally, there is the striking and rhetorically deft opposition between "the personal, private and therefore universal and everlasting" on the one hand and "the merely historical and therefore transient and local" on the other. The "therefores" are what we need to attend to here, for with their help a paradoxical feat is performed:

19. Aldous Huxley, "Variations on *The Prisons*," in *Themes and Variations* (London: Chatto & Windus, 1950), pp. 199–200.

the most individual and personal elements in life become the most universal, while history becomes transient, local, and unimportant.

The explanation for this paradox is not far to seek, and Huxley is not alone in assuming its validity. Writing in another context, Hayden White usefully places Huxley in a long tradition of writers, starting fitfully in the nineteenth century and coming into its own only in the twentieth, who attack historicism and the historical consciousness in the name of "the essential contemporaneity of all significant human experience."[20] At issue here is the freedom and power of the individual. In asserting that history is transient and local, Huxley is defending the power of the individual to transcend his or her own time and thus escape being historically determined. Freedom has dwindled to the chance play of hereditary factors, but that seems preferable to the vision of human beings as mechanically determined products which writers like Huxley believe nineteenth-century historicism to entail. The elevation of the human soul into the realm of freedom and universality depends upon breaking the iron chain of necessity by reducing history to flux. Devaluing history becomes a moral act that asserts human dignity, freedom, and moral responsibility.

When an extreme form of the view of history as flux underlies the reading of a novel, it can prevent a critic from recognizing the representation of history at all. This tendency is apparent in Dorothy Van Ghent's essay on *The Heart of Midlothian*. In her analysis, Van Ghent decries Scott as a money-grubbing hack; she tries to rewrite his novel, wishing it were *Pride and Prejudice* or *Measure for Measure*. For her, there is simply no place at all in a serious novel for the predominant representation of the past as past. She considers Balzac a true artist because when he creates a historical milieu, it functions as a "spiritual symbol."[21] She has great contempt for Scott's protagonist, Jeanie

20. Hayden V. White, "The Burden of History," in his *Tropics of Discourse: Essays in Cultural Criticism* (Baltimore: Johns Hopkins University Press, 1978), p. 31.

21. Dorothy Van Ghent, "On *The Heart of Mid-Lothian*," in *The English Novel: Form and Function* (1953; rpt. New York: Harper, 1961), p. 123; subsequent references appear in my text. Van Ghent derives her notion of the "spiritual symbol" from Coleridge (some of whose comments on Scott she misinterprets at the end of her essay). I discuss the problem of Coleridgean symbolism in historical fiction extensively in Chapter 3. For a more recent study that belittles Scott by measuring his works against an inappropriate standard, see David Craig, *Scottish Literature and the Scottish People, 1680–1830* (London: Chatto & Windus, 1961), pp. 139–56, 166–88. Craig's conception of the novel derives from that of the Leavises.

Deans. In particular, she cannot see the point of Scott's careful depiction of Jeanie's rigidly moralistic upbringing as a member of a dying Calvinist sect, the Cameronians:

> The pressure placed on our actions by "conditions" is of the greatest dramatic and moral interest: it provided the most powerful source of ambiguity in ancient Greek tragedy, and it does so again today in the novels of Faulkner. But the "conditioning" of Jeanie Deans is not used as a source of ambiguity; it is, indeed, not *used* by Scott at all in the structure of the book. It is an element existing in the book; we are allowed to know and understand Jeanie's training in verbal scrupulosity; but we are not led thereby to penetrate into the complexity of our destiny as "conditioned" and yet morally independent creatures, as we are led to do by Sophocles and by Faulkner. Jeanie's Cameronian training is a mere bit of local color.   [p. 119]

According to Van Ghent, the depiction of social and historical circumstances in prose fiction is justified only if it leads us to explore such matters as the timeless ambiguity of the human condition. Scott's fascination with the fact that people like Jeanie Deans actually existed in the past is trivial; it neglects what Hayden White calls "the essential contemporaneity of all significant human experience." True artists build their novels around the individual. Van Ghent elsewhere remarks that Scott's central weakness is that he does not realize that the fictional character ought to be "an inwardly complex agent out of whose human complexity evolve the event and the destiny" (p. 124). The full implications of this statement for historical fiction are worth pondering.

It is only fair to add that as far as Van Ghent is concerned, her analysis of Scott does not imply a preference for probing the moral life of the individual instead of representing social and historical forces. Given the presuppositions she shares with Huxley, the historical setting of *The Heart of Midlothian* naturally appears to her to be what she derisively calls "local color," random antiquarian detail used to enliven Scott's plot. In a real sense she simply cannot see one side, the main side, of Scott's novel. Critical theories are lenses that are useful (and dangerous) because they exclude some things from view as a condition of focusing on others. Van Ghent's lens has, as we would have expected, reduced history to flux.

Van Ghent has little of value to tell us about Scott or the historical novel in a positive way. She is useful, however, in reminding us of what we cannot expect to find in a novel like *The Heart of Midlothian*. She is certainly right, for instance, to note a lack of psychological depth in the portrayal of Jeanie Deans. On the other hand, her critical tenets produce better results with many of the greatest English novels. This implies two things. First, we require a set of critical presuppositions different from hers if the historical novel is to come into focus for us; in particular, we need a more flexible conception of the place of character and the direct depiction of consciousness in fiction. But second, her success with some distinguished standard novels suggests that weaknesses in the historical novel itself may account in part for her inability to deal with it adequately.

Why does Van Ghent's lens have the curvature it does? To be fair, it requires the affront Scott poses to bring out so baldly her presuppositions about form in the novel. In her essays on other novelists, she makes some attempt to deal with a variety of cultural issues; as a "second-generation New Critic," she is interested in treating novels as something more than self-contained urns.[22] But for all that, we feel certain imperatives throughout her essays. In the last analysis, and often in the first analysis, she insists that contextual matters be mediated through individual interiority, depicted either directly or in symbolic form. Why this insistence on the primacy of individual consciousness as the grounds for literary structuring and thematics? Why must "the event" evolve from a character seen as "an inwardly complex agent"? What implicit criteria are at work here?

Van Ghent's notion of what novels ought to be and do is anything but idiosyncratic: it is based on a set of cultural presuppositions that inform the standard novel itself and render it intelligible. We can say that this set of presuppositions reflects bourgeois ideology and bourgeois individualism, so long as we use the terms with care. Both "bourgeois" and "ideology" are notoriously ambiguous and tendentious words, but I think we can make their difficulties work to our advantage. Here and throughout this book, I shall use "ideology" in a basically neutral sense, to refer to a culturally induced and shared set of beliefs through which we make sense of our world and act within

22. Daniel R. Schwarz, "'The Idea Embodied in the Cosmology': The Significance of Dorothy Van Ghent," *Diacritics*, 8 (1978), 72–83.

and upon it.[23] But I do not want to drop out the pejorative connotations of the word altogether. The notion of "ideology" as "false consciousness" can serve to remind us that world views are never neutral and value-free, and that thought often involves mystification. My use of the term "bourgeois" is similar. Primarily, I intend it to refer to a class and set of class values that are centrally implicated in the rise of realist fiction and its flourishing in the nineteenth century. At its most pejorative, the notion of "bourgeois individuality" becomes synonymous with "privatization," reminding us that Van Ghent's radical valorization of human interiority, which reflects a valorization implicit in standard fiction itself, can have the ideological effect of making readers ignore the social and historical realities around them. But at its best, bourgeois individualism and the ideology that surrounds it constitute a positive moment in the development of human consciousness. They have virtues we should be wary of relinquishing or denigrating, unless we are certain that they will be truly sublated, canceled but also preserved, in a higher form of consciousness and social practice. And they are valuable not least because they have enabled a particularly rich and fertile tradition of literary creativity. Van Ghent succeeds with many fine standard novels and fails with Scott, then, because she is working in a relatively uncritical fashion within the ideology that enables standard fiction. Her privileging of the "spiritual symbol" is another indication of her place in this tradition, which values the symbolic above the allegorical and the metaphorical above the metonymical.

Our discussion of the grounds of Van Ghent's strengths and weaknesses as a critic implies that the problem with historical novels is a special, extreme example of a problem with (some would say the glory of) standard fiction in general. To be sure, the novel is the form that most adequately depicts human beings in their full historical and social contexts: Lukács is right to consider it in this sense the most historical of genres. But though this is a real achievement, it is also a partial one. The novel has pitted interiority against social and histori-

23. Clifford Geertz, "Ideology as a Cultural System," in his *The Interpretation of Cultures* (New York: Basic Books, 1973), pp. 193–233, attempts to use "ideology" in a neutral way. For a survey of the various meanings of "ideology" in Marxist thought, see Raymond Williams, *Marxism and Literature* (London: Oxford University Press, 1977), pp. 55–71.

cal inclusiveness ever since Clarissa Harlowe revealed her soul in letters that gave a new concreteness to the depiction of a certain class at
a certain time in history.[24] A tendency toward absorption into the
self is always there, though it reaches a greater intensity in many
twentieth-century critics than it does in the nineteenth-century novels
they describe.

The notion that bourgeois individualism informs the standard novel
and guides its reception, I might add, explains why the distinction between "novels of the recent past" like *Vanity Fair* and "historical
novels" like *Henry Esmond* or *Waverley* seems intuitively clear,
though difficult to theorize. To the extent that we value bourgeois individualism and respond to its successful portrayal as the norm in the
novel, we will tend to interpret standard novels as centering on the
"timeless" individual unless we are positively prevented from doing
so by some anomaly in their form. In most novels of the recent past,
historical probability is present, but not in a strong enough way to
shift our perception of their form; in historical novels, it *is* strong
enough.[25] We can also understand our divided reaction to Scott's
own characterization in these terms. We need not explain away what
we register as central weaknesses in that characterization as resulting
simply from inappropriate expectations. This is part of the truth, but
not the whole truth. Because of the way in which many of Scott's basic fictional techniques were developed by other authors, his novels
seem to announce themselves and to some extent *do* announce themselves as part of the nineteenth-century bourgeois tradition in fiction
and may be judged accordingly.

Van Ghent's rejection of Scott and the artistic possibilities of the
historical novel is total. *The Heart of Midlothian* is not inferior in

24. I say Clarissa Harlowe, not Moll Flanders, on formal and ideological grounds.
Rader, "Defoe, Richardson, Joyce," demonstrates that Richardson's novels are plotted
actions and Defoe's are not. And Ian Watt, *The Rise of the Novel: Studies in Defoe, Richardson, and Fielding* (University of California Press, 1957), pp. 133–34,
seems to me right in suggesting that Defoe's works challenged in advance certain values central to the standard novel that followed him.

25. For the useful term "novels of the recent past," see Kathleen Tillotson, *Novels
of the Eighteen-Forties* (1954; rpt. London: Oxford University Press, 1961), pp.
92–93. I believe that the three uses of history in standard historical fiction which I
outline in Chapter 2 could be profitably used to analyze novels of the recent past as
well, since the two groups partially overlap in their formal problematic and their interest in history.

some ways to *Pride and Prejudice*, it is "essentially valueless" (p. 114). But the criticism of W. J. Harvey, who works from a set of assumptions comparable in many respects to Van Ghent's, suggests that a less drastic judgment is possible. Harvey does not deal with the historical novel directly, but he does consider the question of what levels of human existence can be successfully represented in prose fiction.[26] The partial success of *Germinal*, he believes, indicates that "many novels may approach if not achieve greatness by realizing through a host of background characters a sense of society in action" (p. 57). Harvey recognizes that Zola must keep his characterization schematic, since "more complex characterization or greater psychological subtlety would have compelled a different kind of interest, quite fatal to the book's distinctive achievement" (p. 58). But because this achievement demands that the novel lack a fully realized and individualized protagonist, Zola's novel cannot be truly great. Harvey would probably view historical novels in the same way.

Harvey draws his conceptual framework explicitly from Kant. It is not surprising that he should on the one hand speak of "the world of flux and historical relativity" (p. 19), while on the other hand stressing the dignity and importance of the individual. Harvey tells us that "most human beings will always elude or overflow the categories of *any* ideology" (p. 26), and he quotes with approval Robert Langbaum's notion that great fictional characters convey "the element we call *individual* because it eludes and defies classification . . . that unlit area behind the Aristotelian agent in sensing which we sense what we mean by the character's *life*" (p. 188). He dismisses the idea that beneath the flux of history lies an eternal human nature (and here he parts company with many critics who defend man's moral dignity against historical determinism). But he replaces the eternal human heart not simply with his own version of Kant's constitutive categories but also with a necessarily vague notion of eternal human mystery. The belief that human beings finally elude any of the categories that we use to describe them has for him important fictional implications:

> To load the protagonist [of a novel] with a great deal of generalized, representative value is always a tricky business since what we attend

26. Harvey does give a brief negative judgment of George Eliot's *Romola* (p. 30).

to in his story is the individual, the unique and particular case. It is *his* story and his alone. . . . We quickly feel uneasy if the protagonist is made to stand for something general and diffused; the more he *stands for* the less he *is* and we may soon end up with an allegorical figure, an Everyman. Of course, many protagonists are in a sense Everyman but only because they are in the first instance a particular man; if the protagonist is in some way a universal value or meaning, he is primarily a *concrete* universal. [pp. 67–68]

Generalized meaning ought in Harvey's view to be expressed through minor characters, who can function as the reader's "delegates" in a novel, provide "the comfortable recognition of the typical," and "bear the weight of a good deal of symbolic value" (p. 67). Zola's major characters are thus too generalized to be true protagonists: they are merely inflated minor characters. Much of Harvey's discussion is admirably attuned to the way in which standard novels operate. His brief introduction of the Hegelian concrete universal into his Kantian framework, however, raises more difficulties than it solves. If standard novels in fact can have protagonists who are concrete universals, then the representational problems Harvey so clearly identifies in Zola's novels ought not to exist, at least not as part of an inescapable trade-off between social and individual representation. Harvey's analysis reveals but then ignores the limits of mimesis in standard fiction.

Van Ghent and Harvey express two versions of the attitude toward social and historical mimesis in fiction which I take to be central to English-speaking novel criticism in this century. Van Ghent seems to believe that the distinctively historical part of human life is not a proper subject for art at all, because it is external and inessential. Harvey believes that history and society are important, but that too great an interest in representing them will necessarily flaw a novel. For both critics, human value and the proper sphere of art reside in the individual consciousness: it is either undesirable or impossible to represent the entire spectrum of human existence in any work. In practice, we must choose between the particular and the general. We should choose the particular, for if we dig deeply enough into the individual soul, we shall discover there the universal and eternal part of humanity.

If criticism based on bourgeois ideology has had only a limited success with Scott and the historical novel, it would seem natural to turn to criticism of a different ideological persuasion. The obvious choice is Lukács. For Lukács, the problem of social mimesis takes on significantly different contours because he approaches it with different assumptions. The critics whom we have discussed believe that human beings are at their most human as individuals and that history is without meaning, except in terms of the individual. For Lukács, human beings reach their fullest humanity not as isolated individuals but in society, and history is a process that can be objectively understood. Lukács does not believe that art should concern itself exclusively with that part of the spectrum of human existence which the "individualist" critic finds unimportant. In fact, Lukács describes Zola's novels in much the same way as Harvey does. According to Lukács, *Germinal* is faulty because it creates abstract pictures of general types at the expense of human particularity. Where Lukács differs from Harvey is in the extent of the human spectrum he thinks art can represent. For Harvey, Zola's defects are the necessary consequences of his virtues. For Lukács, they are mistakes, which reflect a bad esthetic theory.[27] The finest works of literature embody a quality that Lukács calls "realism." They are able to represent all levels of human existence at once, because history has an unfolding meaning to which all the particularities of daily life are ultimately related. This meaning is available to cognition, and also to esthetic intuition. Lukács's belief that history is a coherent process that can be represented in art provides the ultimate grounds for his judgment that realist art constitutes a mode of knowledge which provides "a different, but no less truthful picture of reality than does natural science."[28]

Realist fiction captures all levels of our experience by creating what Lukács calls "typical" characters. This is a pivotal concept for his discussion and for our own:

27. Lukács, *The Historical Novel*, pp. 171–250; see also "The Zola Centenary" (Moscow, 1940), in *Studies in European Realism* (1935–46), trans. Edith Bone (London, 1950; rpt. New York: Grosset & Dunlap, 1964), pp. 85–96. In preferring the royalist Balzac to the radical Zola, Lukács follows the lead given by Engels in his famous letter to Margaret Harkness (April 1888).

28. Georg Lukács, *Realism in Our Time: Literature and the Class Struggle* (1957), trans. John and Necke Mander (London, 1962, as *The Meaning of Contemporary Realism*; rpt. New York: Harper, 1971), p. 124.

What is the key to these "typical" heroes of literature? The *typical* is not to be confused with the *average* (though there are cases where this holds true), nor with the *eccentric* (though the typical does as a rule go beyond the normal). A character is typical, in this technical sense, when his innermost being is determined by objective forces at work in society. Vautrin or Julien Sorel, superficially eccentric, are *typical* in their behaviour: the determining factors of a particular historical phase are found in them in concentrated form. Yet, though typical, they are never crudely "illustrative." There is a dialectic in these characters linking the individual—and all accompanying accidentals—with the typical. . . .

The heroes of . . . schematic literature . . . altogether lack these features. They are not typical, but topical. Their features are prescribed by a specific political intention. I should add that it is always extremely difficult to isolate "typical" features. The typical hero reacts with his entire personality to the life of his age. . . . The characters produced by the schematists, on the other hand, are both above and beneath the level of typicality. The individual characterization is beneath it (whereas Natasha Rostova's "tripping step," say, or Anna Karenina's ball costume are unquestionably typical), whereas what is intended to establish their typicality may be irrelevant to their psychological make-up. This weakness is common, of course, to all naturalistic literature—Zola's "typical" characters have similar shortcomings.[29]

For Lukács, then, even the smallest detail describing a typical character is lit up with wide-ranging significance. In the view of Van Ghent or Harvey, the greatness of fictional characters resides in that region of the individual soul for which historical and ideological categories cannot account, "that unlit area behind the Aristotelian agent in sensing which we sense what we mean by the character's *life.*" For Lukács, such talk is mere obscurantism. In his view, the more significant an index of historical process a character is, the more humanly true and esthetically powerful he or she becomes.

29. *Realism in Our Time*, pp. 122–123. In his later work on esthetics, Lukács creates a special category of reality in which typical characters exist, the category of "specialty" as opposed to the individual or the universal. For "specialty," see Lukács, *Probleme*, pp. 539–789; Lukács, *Eigenart*, II, 193–266; and Királyfalvi, pp. 71–87. Fleishman (pp. 11–13) calls on Wilhelm Dilthey to resolve the same problem which "typicality" and "specialty" solve for Lukács. According to Fleishman, Dilthey believes that history can be made sense of only in terms of the shapes of completed human lives. Using this notion as the key to interpreting historical fiction throws too much emphasis on the role of protagonists, who often function primarily as narrative devices, not as symbolic expressions of an author's view of history.

I find Lukács's argument compelling. He has a profoundly moral view of literature, its function and importance; his esthetic system as a whole possesses a depth, coherence, and consistency that I can only suggest in a brief review of those aspects most relevant to my own interests. His analysis and use of the concept of "the present as history" are fundamentally important for any study of the relationship between history and literature. Furthermore, and this is not always recognized, his analyses of individual works are often brilliant and undogmatic. Nonetheless, I must dissent from his views at a fairly basic level and in a number of areas.

My most fundamental disagreement with Lukács involves his belief in the power of typical characters to represent all levels of man's social existence.[30] The difficulty here is that the idea of the "typical," like Harvey's borrowed "concrete universal," precludes a strong explanation of certain weaknesses in Scott and historical fiction in general of which Lukács's own discussion betrays he is aware. The problem with typicality in Lukács is a complicated matter, which can be approached in a number of ways—in terms of foreground and background, of "enactment," or of what we as readers need to bring to a work as opposed to what it dramatizes for us. I admire Lukács's boldness and consistency in telling us that in *War and Peace* Natasha's "tripping step" is "undoubtedly typical," but I do not quite believe him. The problem that I am pointing to tends to be harder to see in his comments about novels, the works his theories fit best; it is much more visible when he discusses lyric poetry. Lukács says—as he must, given his belief that the true subject of all art is man as a social being—that even lyric poetry describing simple natural beauty "betrays the position that the poet takes with regard to the truly great currents and battles of his age."[31] This assertion seems questionable. Two issues are involved here. The first is that there are surely some

---

30. For a discussion of the central place "typicality" holds in Lukács's intellectual system as a whole, see Rolf Günter Renner, *Ästhetische Theorie bei Georg Lukács* (Bern: Francke, 1976), pp. 67–80. Peter Demetz, *Marx, Engels and the Poets: Origins of Marxist Literary Criticism*, trans. Jeffrey L. Sammons, rev. ed. (Chicago: University of Chicago Press, 1967), pp. 133–38, discusses the source of this concept; both Demetz and Renner point out its kinship with the Hegelian "concrete universal."

31. Királyfalvi, p. 123; the passage appears in *Eigenart*, II, 640. In *Probleme*, p. 769, Lukács also asserts the larger cultural resonances of lyric poetry and remarks that Natasha's "tripping step" is just as evocative as any lyric metaphor.

areas of privacy in human existence to which the great currents and battles of an age do not penetrate, particularly in the brief lyric moment. That they do not so penetrate may have political and ideological implications and necessitate "symptomatic" analysis, but that is another matter. Beyond this lies another problem, raised by Lukács's formulation that lyric poetry *betrays* a poet's position about great social issues. In my view, we have a right to expect that a work of art will not only betray things but also enact them. As an object of cultural or historical analysis, a novel may passively betray a great deal about a society; as the producer of an esthetic response, it must play a more active role. It may be that if we come to a work with a certain theory about society in mind, it will provide evidence for our hypothesis. But we may also be interested in what issues or feelings a work actively dramatizes. In some details of a novel, historical content may be in the foreground, whereas in others it may drop so far into the background that it disappears. The process of determining what is in the foreground of a work is often difficult and controversial, but we must and in practice do engage in it whenever we make sense of a work of art. And in fact, this is a process which Lukács himself constantly engages in when his criticism is at its best. His celebrated distinction between realism and naturalism is meaningless except in terms of formal priorities and active literary enactment, for he values realism over naturalism precisely because he sees realism as a mode which actively grapples with and reduces to knowable order the phenomena of historical life.

I realize that in my critique of Lukács, I am privileging the category of the esthetic, and thus inviting the charge that I myself am complicit in the very bourgeois ideology whose effects I have deplored in Van Ghent.[32] I would reply that there are different degrees and modes of complicity, and that one can think of worse ideologies with which to be tentatively complicit if one wants to understand Scott and the standard historical novel. Beyond that, I am in fact simultaneously promoting and demoting the category of the esthetic. I am suggesting

32. Terry Eagleton, *Marxism and Literary Criticism* (London: Methuen, 1976), pp. 56–57, accuses Lukács himself of fetishizing the esthetic. He quite properly explains Lukács's value for the esthetic as a result of his residual ties with the German Humanist tradition, though he neglects to mention that precisely those ties account for some of Lukács's best criticism.

that there may exist important areas of human experience which cannot be easily dramatized in literary form; indeed, works of which we highly approve on esthetic grounds may even blind us to social, historical, and moral problems and responsibilities. They may, but they needn't—unless we mystify the esthetic by ignoring its equivocality as a category and equating it with the cognitive or the moral or the historical. Symptomatic readings, which uncover what a work of art betrays by its volubilities and silences, are important, but they do not exhaust what we can know and need to know about literary works. Indeed, symptomatic readings are likely to be misleading when they do not use esthetic readings as their points of departure.[33]

Let me repeat that I do not mean to deny Lukács's assertion that the great achievement of nineteenth-century realism was to enable prose fiction to encompass a broader segment of the scale of human existence than it had included before or has since. But there are limits to this achievement. If what we require is active representation, I think we are bound to conclude that even in the greatest realist fiction, characters cannot represent all levels of human existence at once. Lukácsian typicality cannot solve the problem with historical novels. The idea of "typical" characters can be very helpful, though, if we use it in a more modest way than Lukács himself does, to describe characters who actively represent that part of the spectrum of human existence where the individual and society meet. We can then make a useful distinction between characters who are historically "typical" in that they represent salient aspects of a historical milieu, and characters who are simply historically "probable" members of that milieu. Characters who are nothing more than historically probable can of course be placed in relation to the salient forces in their milieu, if it is depicted as a systematic whole. But they promote historical meanings indirectly if at all: they require symptomatic reading to gain substantial historical significance, whereas symptomatic reading would either extend, revise, or contradict the historical significance that is already central to typical characters.[34]

33. For "symptomatic" reading, see Louis Althusser, "From *Capital* to Marx's Philosophy," in *Reading Capital*, by Louis Althusser and Etienne Balibar (1968), trans. Ben Brewster (London: New Left Books, 1970), pp. 13–69.

34. For a concrete example of this distinction, see my comparison of Milnwood and the Baron of Bradwardine in the discussion of *Old Mortality*, Chapter 4. Another

For all his love of Scott, Lukács is suspicious of historical fiction. Much of his classic study *The Historical Novel* demonstrates that novel after novel is decadent and unsatisfactory. I do not quarrel with his negative assessment of many of the works he discusses or with his respect for Scott. I do disagree with his justification for these judgments. His underlying rationale becomes clear if we recall the distinction between "the past as past" and "the present as history." For Lukács, the proper function of historical fiction is to provide a representation of historical process which promotes the discovery of the present as history. He is not interested in the depiction of the past as an object in its own right: in fact, he tends to deplore it. In neglecting the problems involved in depicting the past as past, Lukács not only fails to account for the distinctive formal strengths and weaknesses of historical fiction, he also cuts himself off from recognizing the full esthetic situation from which the very sense of history he so admires arises in the best historical fiction.[35]

Basic judgments about historical fiction necessarily rest upon assumptions about the nature of history itself. If we believe that history is flux, it is likely that we will assign its representation in prose fiction a low priority. Our conclusions will be different if we believe that history is a coherent process with an emerging meaning available to artistic intuition and capable of being represented by esthetic means. Since I have scrutinized the underlying assumptions of others in this regard, it seems only right to indicate my own. My views stem primarily from work with literary texts, but they are supported and clarified by the speculations of Siegfried Kracauer concerning the nature of history and historical understanding.

I find two of Kracauer's ideas particularly useful: his belief that his-

---

"probable" character is the Laird of Dumbiedikes, whom I contrast with the "representative" Duncan Knockdunder in the discussion of *The Heart of Midlothian*, Chapter 5.

35. Lukács's theory of literature is by no means the "simple" reflection theory it is sometimes said to be, but it does not wholly escape a major problem inherent in all reflection theories—that the unmediated passivity of the metaphor of reflection itself tends to weaken the recognition that literary mimesis is an active, constructive process. For a discussion of the complexities of Lukács's reflection theory, see G. H. R. Parkinson, "Lukács on the Central Category of Aesthetics," in *Georg Lukács: The Man, His Work, and His Ideas*, ed. G. H. R. Parkinson (London: Weidenfeld and Nicolson, 1970), pp. 109–46. On the weaknesses inherent in the reflection metaphor, see Williams, p. 97.

tory is nonhomogeneous in structure, and a corollary principle that he calls the law of perspective. Kracauer points out that historians who work at different levels of human generality usually assume that in principle their work is theoretically compatible—that all the findings of microhistory will eventually lead up in a smooth and seamless way to the broadest, most inclusive generalities of macrohistory. Thus the macrohistorian Arnold Toynbee believes that his historical generalizations will ultimately mesh with the most detailed work on individual historical topics. Kracauer thinks that this faith is an illusion: "Toynbee's suggestion of a merger of the bird's-eye view [of macrohistory] and the fly's-eye view [of microhistory] is in principle unfulfillable. The two kinds of enquiry may co-exist, but they do not completely fuse: as a rule, the bird swallows the fly."[36] He describes this phenomenon in terms of a law of perspective. As we ascend progressively higher over the historical terrain, events and situations begin to blur and their full particularity is lost; different patterns emerge at different altitudes. This should not surprise us: that "macro realities are not fully traceable to the micro realities going into them—that interrelated events at low and higher levels exist, so to speak, side by side—is by no means an uncommon phenomenon. Most individuals behave differently in different dimensions of being" (p. 117). This "side-by-side" philosophy makes him interested in phenomena occurring on all levels of generality. He is not tempted to dismiss the historically particular as involving mere "local color," but instead defends the historical "collector" for redeeming aspects of the past from oblivion. Such a viewpoint is useful in dealing with an author like Scott, whose fiction is fundamentally informed by a desire to preserve the remnants of Scotland's past.

The ultimate justification for Kracauer's views is philosophical. It involves the relationship between particulars and universals, which he believes traditional philosophy has misconceived. Philosophers have assumed that "the highest principles, the highest abstractions, not only define all the particulars they formally encompass but also contain the essences of all that exists in the lower depths" (p. 130). But this is false: "philosophical truths do not fully cover the particulars logically subsumable under them" (p. 212). In a formulation I find

36. Siegfried Kracauer, *History: The Last Things before the Last* (New York: Oxford University Press, 1969), pp. 127–28; subsequent references appear in my text.

particularly useful, Kracauer asserts that "it is doubtful indeed whether the truths of the highest generality are capable at all of rousing the particulars they logically encompass. These extreme abstractions crystallize into statements so wide-meshed that the particulars— a series of historical events, or so—cannot but drop through the net" (p. 102).

Whatever we think of the ultimate validity of Kracauer's philosophy of history, it illuminates a critical problem inherent in writing historical fiction.[37] I am not entirely convinced that his "law of perspective" holds for all philosophies of history, though it surely underlines in a pointed and useful way a problem they must address. It may also not apply to all historical narratives, especially when their writers adopt the technique of running up and down the scale of human generality, as Edmund Wilson tells us Michelet does: "Michelet's skill at shifting back and forth between the close-up of the individual, the movement of the local group and the analytical survey of the whole, is one of the features of a technical virtuosity which becomes more and more amazing."[38] But I am convinced that standard historical fiction cannot enact all levels of human experience with equal success. Unlike Michelet, the standard historical novelist cannot create a texture that is primarily analytical and descriptive, and then particularize it through imaginative excursions into groups and individuals. Tolstoy may be reaching toward such a form when he writes the analytical chapters in *War and Peace*. But what a small proportion these comprise of his novel as a whole, and what scandal even they have caused among lovers of the standard novel!

Kracauer tells us that in historiography, the fly's-eye view and the bird's-eye view cannot coexist—usually, the bird swallows the fly. In standard historical fiction, the fly is just as likely to swallow the bird. When it does not, when fictional plots and characters are adapted to dramatize historical process, a price must be paid. As characters become translucent to allow historical processes to shine through them

37. Martin Jay, "The Extraterritorial Life of Siegfried Kracauer," *Salmagundi*, 31–32 (Fall 1975–Winter 1976), 49–109, points out that Kracauer's philosophy of history runs the risk of hypostatizing modern anomie and his own consciously chosen position as an outsider into a universal law of cognition.

38. Edmund Wilson, *To the Finland Station* (1940; rpt. New York: Doubleday, 1953), p. 18.

more clearly, they also tend to become thinner as representations of "inwardly complex" human beings.

Is there a problem with standard historical fiction? I conclude that there is.[39] When W. J. Harvey and Dorothy Van Ghent stress the primacy of the individual, they may or may not be enunciating an eternal truth, but they are indicating the area of life with which standard fiction is best equipped to deal. In standard novels, protagonists are characteristically at the center of things. Milieu, minor characters, and plotted action are there to illuminate them. This formal arrangement has many virtues, but it conflicts with the priorities of historical fiction. Historical fiction often employs characters to represent salient aspects of a historical milieu. In the greatest historical fiction, characters and narrative sequences elucidate historical process. But if historical novels attempt to use plot or milieu primarily for the sake of illuminating individual consciousness or moral choice, they risk blurring their distinctively historical focus. In historical fiction, character is likely to illuminate historical events and destinies, not to act as "an inwardly complex agent out of whose human complexity evolve the event and the destiny." It would be foolish to deny that this is a limitation, but historical fiction has its compensations. It is tempting to suppose that all important aspects of life can be fully explored by the literary forms we most admire. I believe that this is untrue, and that it is also wrong to assume that an area of life is trivial because it cannot be so represented. Because history matters, it is worth understanding the limitations of historical novels and then using this understanding to discover and enjoy their strengths.

39. John Maynard, "Broad Canvas, Narrow Perspective: The Problem of the English Historical Novel in the Nineteenth Century," in *The Worlds of Victorian Fiction*, ed. Jerome H. Buckley, Harvard English Studies, 6 (Cambridge: Harvard University Press, 1975), p. 242, recognizes the problem but does little with it, perhaps because of his impatience with generic distinctions. For him, the problem with the English historical novel turns out to be cultural cowardice about facing up to history, and works like *The Red and the Black*, which treat the present as history, solve whatever problems historical fiction poses. Peter K. Garrett, *The Victorian Multiplot Novel* (New Haven: Yale University Press, 1980), p. 16, believes that "the common and distinctive structural problematic of the major Victorian multiplot novels" involves the dialogue within them between social and individual perspectives. His use of Mikhail Bakhtin's notion of "dialogical form" enables some interesting readings, but it also tends to explain away structural problems and disregard the importance of the ideological contradictions with which they are associated.

My discussion has attempted to open the way for a new look at standard historical fiction and at Scott's novels, by suggesting the diverse and inherently problematical nature of these works. In the following chapters I hope to give a reasonably systematic view of the different ways in which they employ history and cope, or fail to cope, with the problems that result.

2

History as Pastoral,
History as a Source of Drama

Samuel Johnson was alive to the perils of approaching literary works with inappropriate demands. Realizing that anyone who read Richardson for the story would hang himself, he suggested that we read him "for the sentiment, and consider the story as only giving occasion to the sentiment." Johnson's remarks reveal an interest in the function and hierarchy of the parts that constitute artistic wholes; he recognizes the importance of determining whether one aspect of a work of art exists for the sake of another. I do not intend to suggest that we read all historical novels for the history, and consider the story as only giving occasion to the history, but in this chapter and the next one, I do want to take a close look at the different roles history has played in standard historical fiction.

Tzvetan Todorov asserts that there are two possible ways to arrive at generic groupings: "theoretical genres" stem from "a deduction of a theoretical order," whereas "historical genres" stem from "an observation of literary reality."[1] My interest in the uses of history in fiction is neither purely theoretical nor purely historical. Instead of at-

---

1. Tzvetan Todorov, *The Fantastic: A Structural Approach to a Literary Genre* (1970), trans. Richard Howard (Ithaca: Cornell University Press, 1975), pp. 13–15. In my view, the clearest way to discuss the inner logic of individual works and larger literary systems is in terms of the fiction of authorial intentions and the problems and choices that result from those intentions, and I do so throughout. Some such fiction, whether about authorial intentions, reader reception, or the self-sustaining, intrinsic properties of individual works or larger semiotic systems, necessarily underlies any attempt to discuss literary structure.

tempting to imagine all the possible ways in which history might enter historical fiction, I shall concentrate on the uses that have dominated artistic practice. But I also want to understand the logic behind their existence and functioning. I have argued that we cannot isolate a single historical vision that all standard historical novels share, except in a minimal way, but nothing prevents us from describing the various roles history plays in these works. My method will be to explore a few carefully chosen novels. Scott, the primary focus of my study, will play a major role here; I shall also draw some examples from French and Russian fiction, where certain tendencies exist in a clearer and more interesting form than they do in the relatively impoverished tradition of nineteenth-century English historical fiction after Scott.

The ways in which history has been employed in standard historical fiction fall into a small number of broad categories, which are not particularly recondite and have been individually recognized, implicitly or explicitly, by previous critics. My intention is to synthesize and extend the best of their insights. I shall argue that works of standard historical fiction have employed history in three main ways. First, history has provided an ideological screen onto which the preoccupations of the present can be projected for clarification and solution, or for disguised expression. I refer to this use as "history as pastoral." Second, history (here conceived of as inherently colorful and dramatic) has acted as a source of dramatic energy that vivifies a fictional story. Such dramatic energy can produce effects that are melodramatic and insubstantial, but it can also produce catharsis. Finally and obviously, history has acted as the subject of historical novels, in a variety of ways. These different uses of history often coexist in a given novel. But the sense we make of a historical novel, or of any character or scene within it, depends upon our conception of its purpose. We will have very different notions about the meaning of a Waverley hero and the novel he inhabits, for instance, depending on whether we believe that his primary purpose is to project and consolidate present-day values, or to go through a series of dramatic adventures, or to act as an instrument through which Scott expresses a view of history. Though all of these uses of history may coexist in a work, they are likely at any given moment to fall into a hierarchy in which one of them predominates, and adequate interpretation depends upon recognizing this hierarchy.

Why should these uses of history have dominated standard histori-cal fiction? Two kinds of answers come to mind. If we think in terms of literary and cultural history, it is clear that some novels were bound to use history as their subjects after the rise of historicism. Us-ing history as a source of drama seems an equally natural step, espe-cially because of the importance of creating dynamic movement in a plotted action. It is also not surprising that nineteenth-century society, which had recently learned to think of history in a new way and felt itself in crisis, used fiction to project its problems onto the past in the hopes of clarifying or solving them.

On a more theoretical level, we can follow Hegel in taking the rela-tionship between present and past in historical works to determine their modes.[2] There are then two main possibilities: modes in which present concerns predominate and modes in which an interest in the past predominates. The category of history as pastoral is clearly an example of a mode in which the past is used to serve the present. So is the use of history as a source of drama, though in a much narrower way: in such works, the past fulfills the need for an intense imagina-tive experience in the present. My final category, history as subject, covers those works primarily interested in the past. Of course a fur-ther theoretical possibility exists. What of works that balance past and present interests? I believe that in standard historical fiction, this possibility is rarely if ever actualized. In the novels that come closest to achieving such a balance, an interest in the past still predominates. The needs of the present are compelling; they are likely to upset the balance and hence require a strong historicist counterweight.

The wary reader will have noticed that my three uses of history im-ply a simpler distinction between more and less truly historical vi-sions. Whatever their other merits, novels that use history as pastoral or as a source of drama will lack the potentiality to be as richly and integrally historical as novels that find their subject in history. In the previous chapter, I pointed out the dangers of using a distinction be-tween true and false historicity as the basic tool in approaching his-torical fiction, but we can hardly escape such judgments altogether. I do not wish to produce a value-free account of my subject, but in-

2 G. W. F. Hegel, *Lectures on the Philosophy of World History, Introduction: Reason in History*, trans. H. B. Nisbet (Cambridge: Cambridge University Press, 1975).

stead to provide a mode of analysis in which value judgments do not immediately homogenize and distort phenomenological perceptions. Once we are able to recognize the different kinds of roles history plays in fiction, questions about the relative historicity of different fictional structures are inescapable and useful. An attempt to meet works on their own generic terms does not mean that we will consider equally valuable all that we find: to understand is not to forgive. I should reemphasize that a historical novel may well employ history in a variety of ways as it proceeds. We are looking for what the Russian Formalists might have called the historical "dominant" of a work; this does not imply excluding other kinds of historical intentions and effects, only putting them in their places.[3]

The need to decide which uses of history are present in a given novel, and which one predominates, involves some necessary complications, since historical novels are notoriously capacious, sprawling, and disunified. We will find ourselves discussing works that change intention as they proceed or have competing intentions throughout. This procedure need not be viewed with alarm or suspicion. What ought to make us suspicious are critical methods that find a hidden consistency and higher unity in works that have always seemed to readers very baggy monsters indeed, and my approach attempts to provide an alternative to such methods.

HISTORY AS PASTORAL

One of the most important ways in which the nineteenth century employed history is as pastoral. A wide variety of Victorian works in poetry and prose use history as a testing ground for social visions focused not on the past but on the present or future. In *News from Nowhere*, William Morris projects an idealized vision of the Middle Ages into a utopian future: he uses history as a quarry from which to select materials to build a society embodying values of which he approves. In *Idylls of the King*, Tennyson uses the Middle Ages in a similar way, though with little of Morris's conception of medieval society as an organic whole. One function of Arthur's England is to serve as a region where Tennyson can work out a quasi-allegorical vision of nineteenth-century England's moral degradation; at the same time, it

3. Roman Jakobson, "The Dominant," in *Readings in Russian Poetics*, ed. Ladislav Matejka and Krystyna Pomorska (Cambridge: MIT Press, 1971), pp. 82–90.

provides a repository of values against which to measure Victorian society and find it wanting. Tennyson is said to have done a good deal of research into Celtic customs in writing the *Idylls*, but we do not read them primarily as reflections of a past historical age, and we are right not to do so.[4] The past in such works takes on certain conventionally agreed-upon characteristics that make it a convenient screen upon which to project modern problems. History becomes a pastoral setting, with knights and yeomen replacing shepherds.[5]

Most authors of serious historical fiction care about the ideas, values, and problems of their own day; such a concern can energize their interest in the past. But this does not mean that they use history as pastoral in a dominant way in their works. It is naive to imagine that we can wholly escape bias in our attempts to make sense of the past, but hardly less mistaken to suppose that we cannot transcend our present concerns at all.[6] History as pastoral dominates only in works in which history takes a shape that serves primarily to elucidate the present. Bulwer-Lytton's historical novels are clear examples, despite the conscious intentions of their author. Curtis Dahl has persuasively demonstrated that although Bulwer thinks he is finding parallels between the past and present, "it is truer to say that he explains contemporary life by reading the political and social conditions of his own time into past eras and there commenting on them." Dahl believes

4. See Henry Kozicki, *Tennyson and Clio: History and the Major Poems* (Baltimore: Johns Hopkins University Press, 1979), for a demonstration of Tennyson's interest in the philosophy of history. What Tennyson actually did with this interest is another matter. Kozicki's reference to Tennyson's faith in "the idyl's ability to fuse past and present" and hence to make history a "palimpsest" (p. 60) recalls Dahl's description of Bulwer-Lytton's intention in his novels, mentioned below.

5. The idea of pastoral as I here employ it derives from a common way of describing the kind of Shakespearean comedy typified by *As You Like It*: an author moves certain problems into a less complex yet imaginatively richer setting for the purposes of expression and analysis. It should not be confused with other notions of pastoral, useful for other purposes, such as Leo Marx's "middle ground" between nature and civilization: see *The Machine in the Garden* (London: Oxford University Press, 1964).

6. The problem of whether history is knowable is complex, and I do not suppose that my brief assertions have solved it. All the arguments currently offered on both sides of the issue with which I am familiar are in my view necessarily circular in their logic: history is where you begin. The question of the moral and political consequences of deciding that history is unknowable is another matter, but answers to it are also not susceptible of proof. I provide a brief discussion of some of the reasons why I believe history to be knowable in the introductory section of Chapter 4.

that Bulwer inaugurated "the technique of using historical fiction as a means of commenting on current social, political, or personal problems."[7] Whether or not we rate Bulwer's influence quite so high, we can surely agree on the fundamental importance this mode of employing history assumes in the imaginative literature of Victorian England. The use of history as pastoral has its drawbacks. An author who looks determinedly enough for past analogues to present problems will find them, even if they are not there. History then becomes merely a screen, and historical difference vanishes. But despite such dangers, the use of history as pastoral in the right hands can help to produce major fiction.

Henry Esmond

One of the best historical novels in English, *Henry Esmond* employs history as pastoral with great richness. Thackeray uses the past as a ground on which he can project some of the cultural problems that occupy him in such earlier works as *Vanity Fair*. And on a less controlled, more personal level, reacting to history becomes a metaphor for coming to grips with memory itself. I shall discuss these two versions of history as pastoral in turn, but I must first deal with the novel's claims to employ history as its subject.

Esmond is a paradoxical work. Critics are sharply divided about its merits and even about its subject. Large claims have been made for it as a piece of historical fiction; and on the most obvious level, what could be more historical than a novel which successfully mimics even the style of the age in which it is set? Yet Lukács considers *Esmond* radically unhistorical in its viewpoint, and most critics find much to say about its "unsavoury plot" but little to say about it as history. To be sure, attempts have been made to discover a larger unity in the novel which would include both its love interest and its history. The

7. Curtis Dahl, "History on the Hustings: Bulwer-Lytton's Historical Novels of Politics," in *From Jane Austen to Joseph Conrad: Essays Collected in Memory of James T. Hillhouse*, ed. Robert C. Rathburn and Martin Steinmann, Jr. (Minneapolis: University of Minnesota Press, 1958), p. 62. Dahl shows that Bulwer's "semi-allegorical characterization" does not surmount what I have called the problem with historical novels: "Whenever the reader becomes vitally interested in a character, that character turns into an abstract force. Whenever the reader follows an abstract force, that force is confused by its being given individual personality" (p. 68).

usual tactic here is to talk of the novel as a Bildungsroman, which in a sense it is. But such attempts turn the odd, powerful, and unsettling love story into something abstract and antiseptic: we are informed that in marrying a woman whom he has earlier thought of as his mother, Esmond learns that "a realistic acceptance of the sometimes humdrum reality of the present is an essential characteristic of sane maturity."[8] Alternatively, the novel is said to enact a vision of cultural progress or historical relativism or escape from history altogether.[9] Such descriptions seem to me untrue of the experience which *Esmond* provides and unfair to Thackeray: his work is more powerful and disturbing than such schemas begin to suggest.

This is not to say that history is unimportant to Thackeray. An attitude toward English history emerges from the novel, and the rendering of period detail is painstaking and on the whole effective. Thackeray's handling of such matters is worth examining in some detail, if only to show that it does not dominate *The History of Henry Esmond.*

We may begin by defining the view of history as a political process that informs the novel. It is difficult to agree with Avrom Fleishman that *Henry Esmond* contains a "revolutionary force" which the author of *History and Class Consciousness* missed because of his class prejudices.[10] Despite Esmond's cynicism about history and historians

8. George W. Worth, "The Unity of Henry Esmond," *Nineteenth-Century Fiction,* 15 (1961), 346.

9. John Loofbourow, *Thackeray and the Form of Fiction* (Princeton: Princeton University Press, 1964), p. 164, believes that the linguistic texture of *Esmond* contains a series of modes that symbolize cultural changes from the Elizabethan age to the nineteenth century. Loofbourow shows that different styles exist in the novel, but he demonstrates no necessary connection between these styles and given periods of history, except of course for the obvious eighteenth-century element in the novel. John Sutherland, Introd., *The History of Henry Esmond* (Harmondsworth: Penguin, 1970), pp. 20–21, suggests that Henry's choice of Rachel over Beatrix figures the nineteenth century's attempt to wean itself from the glamor of the previous century.

10. Avrom Fleishman, *The English Historical Novel: Walter Scott to Virginia Woolf* (Baltimore: Johns Hopkins University Press, 1971), p. xvii. Fleishman believes that *Henry Esmond* is a great historical novel "by virtue, in part, of its movement beyond history" (p. 142) and that Esmond's withdrawal from "the emptiness of all life in history" (p. 142), which leads him to a belief in love as an absolute value, is in itself "an attitude toward history" (p. 144). Perhaps it is, but it is one which is more likely to promote abstract formulations about the meaninglessness of history than great historical fiction. Andrew Sanders, *The Victorian Historical Novel, 1840–1880* (London: Macmillan, 1979), takes a similar line.

and despite his disparaging remarks about Marlborough, the novel reflects a basically Whig point of view—that of a member of the middle classes in nineteenth-century England who may not like the four Georges personally, but who looks back on the Glorious Revolution as an obvious improvement on what preceded it. Concerning the comparatively trivial matter of who should occupy the throne after Queen Anne dies, Esmond is a Jacobite for love, but his ideas about the nature of kingship itself are essentially Whig even before he rejects the Pretender. Esmond considers divine right a "monstrous" doctrine, and the Jesuit Father Holt reacts to this opinion by saying "with a sigh" that he fears his former pupil is "no better than a republican at heart."[11] Similarly, in the midst of his Jacobite plotting, Esmond pays tribute to the "manly" Whig creed of Addison, admitting that he really ought to be on Addison's side (p. 416; Bk. 3, ch. 9). The "republican" aspect of the novel, its attempt to define a gentility based on personal worth and not simply on inherited rank, is mildly progressive, but hardly revolutionary. For all his protestations about individual worth, Esmond is glad to discover that he is, after all, the legitimate scion of a noble family. This discovery revolutionizes his view of himself and prepares for that ultimate expression of noblesse oblige, his external renunciation of his title.

The representation of such beliefs in *Esmond* owes something to Scott, though one sometimes feels that Thackeray thinks he is defying the Great Unknown when he is in fact borrowing a perception or a technique from him. (The best example of this tendency in Thackeray is *Rebecca and Rowena*, where Thackeray believes he is reversing Scott's evaluation of the heroines but in fact merely underlines it in cruder terms than Scott cares to employ.) Early in *Henry Esmond*, for instance, is a brief passage which must be an echo, conscious or unconscious, of *Waverley*:

> There was a German officer of Webb's, with whom we used to joke, and of whom a story (whereof I myself was the author) was got to be believed in the army, that he was eldest son of the Hereditary Grand Bootjack of the Empire, and heir to that honour of which his ancestors had been very proud, having been kicked for twenty generations

11. William Thackeray, *The History of Henry Esmond, Esq.*, ed. George Saintsbury (London: Oxford University Press, [1908]), p. 322 (Bk. 3, ch. 1); subsequent references appear in my text.

by one imperial foot, as they drew the boot from the other.   [p. 14;
Bk. 1, ch. 1]

The object of ridicule in this passage recalls the Baron of Bradwardine
in *Waverley,* who takes great pride in his family's hereditary duty of
removing the king's boots after battle, but the comparison does not
work to Thackeray's advantage. Scott allows us to see the silliness of
the Baron's pedantic dedication to antiquated customs; we see its destructive side as well, when Bradwardine blithely wills his property
away from the daughter he loves for the sake of an antiquarian definition of land tenure. But Scott also reveals the part such customs play
in holding societies together, and the measure of nobility inherent in
any sort of fidelity, no matter how quixotic.[12] The depth and gener-
osity of Scott's historical vision make Thackeray's satire in the "bootjack" passage seem superficial and obtuse. I don't think that we can
attribute its weakness simply to Esmond as narrator, for feudal dues
are just the sort of thing that Thackeray is often content to caricature
instead of understand. Such ironic dismissiveness implies a lack of interest in the stuff of history itself, in favor of ethical absolutes and the
analysis of individual emotions.

Some parts of *Henry Esmond* represent historical process with
greater sensitivity than the "bootjack" passage does. One such moment involves Father Holt and young Esmond, who still retains a naive enthusiasm for the Catholic Church:

> And when little Tom Tusher, his neighbour, came from school for his
> holiday, and said how he, too, was to be bred up for an English
> priest, and would get what he called an exhibition from his school,
> and then a college scholarship and fellowship, and then a good
> living—it tasked young Harry Esmond's powers of reticence not to
> say to his young companion, "Church! priesthood! fat living! My
> dear Tommy, do you call yours a Church and a priesthood? What is a
> fat living compared to converting a hundred thousand heathens by a
> single sermon? What is a scholarship at Trinity by the side of a crown
> of martyrdom, with angels awaiting you as your head is taken off?
> Could your master at school sail over the Thames on his gown? Have

12. A recent critic of the Waverley Novels who is fully aware of the central importance of fidelity in Scott is Francis Hart, *Scott's Novels: The Plotting of Historic Survival* (Charlottesville: University Press of Virginia, 1966). Hart compares *Waverley*
and *Esmond* on pp. 14–31, finding *Esmond* less historical than *Waverley.*

you statues in your church that can bleed, speak, walk, and cry? My good Tommy, in dear Father Holt's Church these things take place every day. You know St. Philip of the Willows appeared to Lord Castlewood and caused him to turn to the one true Church. No saints ever come to you." And Harry Esmond, because of his promise to Father Holt, hiding away these treasures of faith from T. Tusher, delivered himself of them nevertheless simply to Father Holt, who stroked his head, smiled at him with his inscrutable look, and told him that he did well to meditate on these great things, and not to talk of them except under direction. [p. 39; Bk. 1, ch. 3]

This passage encapsulates a significant transition in British social history. Tusher's idea of religion is less noble than Esmond's, but its practicality will clearly prevail over Esmond's half-comic idealism, which has had to stretch its claims absurdly and thus betrays its inner exhaustion and irrelevance to the times. Thackeray's satire is sharp: he even takes a leaf from the book of his *bête noire*, Swift, in talking of statues that can "bleed, speak, walk, and cry." But our admiration for Esmond's artless, charmingly youthful faith prevents us from feeling here the brittleness that so often accompanies Thackeray's parodies. The last sentence is the masterstroke, with its unexpected turn at the end, which illuminates Father Holt with merciless precision. How small his scheming appears in comparison with his little pupil's faith! Yet the Jesuit has his own dignity, for his manipulation is so deft, so understated, so final.

What allows this passage to succeed? First, there is the narrator, whose innocence is crucial. In his uninformed credulity, young Esmond is like one version of the Waverley hero, but he can only maintain this quality when he is young and inexperienced, particularly in a first-person narrative. Thackeray also relies upon his reader's possessing stereotypes of eighteenth-century Anglican worldliness and Jesuitical scheming. Historical fiction often succeeds in making its characters reveal their historical significance when the author draws upon traditional views of history, either to refresh them or to play against them.

If Thackeray were writing another kind of novel, he might have maintained this kind of representation to the end, but in fact he does not do so. By the end of the book, Father Holt has become simply an object of wry amusement, a man who cannot quite live up to his self-imputed omniscience, who never quite gets his details right, and whose schemes are absurd. This may tell us something about Esmond's *Bildung*: it is to my mind an unpleasant example of a son's rejecting his father. But it tells us precious little about the decline of Catholic influence in England or the failure of the Jacobite movement. The treatment of Father Holt in the final scenes follows the probabilities that guide *Esmond* as a whole, for nearly everything in the novel exists primarily to illuminate Esmond's character. Even actual historical figures act as foils to set off Thackeray's hero. Esmond helps to write one of Addison's poems, while showing a moral sensitivity to war which leaves Addison himself behind. He indulgently comments on Steele's weaknesses. Swift makes a fool of himself in front of Esmond, who later reduces him to silence. The Duke of Hamilton begins by insulting Esmond, only to end by acknowledging that to be allied to him is an honor. The Pretender makes a similar mistake and a similar discovery. The course of history itself makes the same point, as the Pretender loses his crown for chasing after Beatrix when he should be listening to Esmond, and Esmond decides that since Beatrix has stooped to the Pretender, she is not worthy of him. The use of actual historical figures to ennoble Esmond in this compulsive way suggests a set of structural priorities very different from those of a novel centrally concerned with exploring history.[13]

On one level, the treatment of these historical figures stems from a wish, predictable in any period, to settle accounts with the age that preceded it. Esmond's hatred of Swift has a palpably Victorian ring to it, as do his virulent attacks on Beatrix for being sexually sullied and his complaints about the debased and debasing view his eighteenth-century contemporaries have of women. Such critiques defiantly assert modern values by projecting them into the past and finding the

---

13. Georg Lukács, *The Historical Novel* (1937), trans. Hannah and Stanley Mitchell (London: Merlin, 1962) pp. 201–4, rightly complains about Esmond's reduction of historical figures such as Swift to the dimensions of their private lives, but he is not interested in discovering the purpose of this reduction, seeing it instead as a symptom of what does interest him, a narrowing bourgeois vision of history. Wolfgang Iser, *The Implied Reader: Patterns of Communication in Prose Fiction from Bunyan to Beckett* (Baltimore: Johns Hopkins University Press, 1974) pp. 121–35, provides some general explanations for why such reductiveness might take place, but his attempt to show that Thackeray's vision of history is in its way just as historical as Scott's seems to me unconvincing.

past wanting by comparison: they use history as pastoral. But the novel also contains a more interesting kind of projection, which is less reassuring. Readers from George Eliot to the present have commented on the unsavory feel of a work in which Esmond ends by marrying a woman he has consistently called his mother. J. Hillis Miller goes a step further in demonstrating how deeply Oedipal structures inform the novel, showing Esmond to be an Oedipus who never comes to know himself as such.[14] I believe, however, that Thackeray is at least as interested in examining sexual stereotypes as he is in attacking Esmond's pride. In *Esmond,* Thackeray self-consciously projects certain stereotypes onto the past as a way of questioning their validity and revealing their bases, pushing this inquiry even further than he does in his depiction of Amelia in *Vanity Fair.* Esmond himself feels toward women an illuminating mixture of idealization and hatred, and the repression of direct sexual feelings in the narrative is matched by the perverse forms they take just under the surface.

The famous scene depicting the reunion of Esmond and Rachel at Winchester Cathedral is a case in point. The scene proceeds through a series of equivocations on Rachel's part, as she half-reveals and half-conceals her guilty love for Esmond. He in turn decodes yet does not decode the message she is sending him, taking immense pride in having awakened the passionate love of the mother of the family in which he has been raised, while at the same time speaking of that love in only the most ethereal and bodiless of terms. In a moment that would approach comedy were it not for the powerful emotions surrounding it, he offers to take her away with him to the New World (a fantasy that in the end of the novel becomes reality), seemingly in the role of his mother and yet with her passion intact. At the close of this implicit analysis of the incestuous feelings that lie behind the idealization of woman as mother and goddess, Thackeray reveals that he knows very well that he is reducing certain conventional notions to their unsavory constituent parts. Here is how Rachel confesses her "guilt" and Esmond responds:

> "Be silent! let me say all. You never loved me, dear Henry—no, you
> do not now, and I thank Heaven for it. I used to watch you, and

14. J. Hillis Miller, *The Forms of Victorian Fiction* (Notre Dame: University of Notre Dame Press, 1968), pp. 17–25; 97–104; for a modification of this argument, which stresses the novel's radical irony, see his *Fiction and Repetition: Seven English Novels* (Cambridge: Harvard University Press, 1982), pp. 73–115.

knew by a thousand signs that it was so. Do you remember how glad you were to go away to college? 'Twas I sent you. I told my papa that, and Mr. Atterbury too, when I spoke to him in London. And they both gave me absolution—both—and they are godly men, having authority to bind and to loose. And they forgave me, as my dear lord forgave me before he went to heaven."

"I think the angels are not all in heaven," Mr. Esmond said. And as a brother folds a sister to his heart; and as a mother cleaves to her son's breast—so for a few moments Esmond's beloved mistress came to him and blessed him. [p. 215; Bk. 2, ch. 6]

There are equivocations throughout the passage worthy of attention, but I want to focus on the chiasmus in the description of Rachel's coming to and blessing Esmond. Who is acting here? The brother-sister description gives the active role to Esmond, while the mother-son gives it to Rachel, where according to the final words in the passage it belongs. I cannot think that the blur here is inadvertent. If we ask why the description of the brother and sister is out of step with the rest of the vignette, the answer seems clear: it would be indecorous to make a sister, and particularly *this* "sister," take the more active role. Rachel's powerful sexual feelings toward Esmond can be admitted at this point, even in symbolic and sublimated form, only if the magic word "mother" is there to neutralize them. But the very exactness with which Thackeray's language obeys these cultural taboos, and thereby allows the different images they create to collide with one another, reveals them *as* taboos and accordingly makes us seek the content they are designed to conceal. The way in which, despite all his efforts, Thackeray's metaphors blur makes us wonder what he and his metaphors have to hide. Our general uneasiness with the relationship between Esmond and Rachel becomes thematized as an uneasiness with the cultural metaphors that prove the only way to express and suppress the content of that relationship. We begin to wonder whether the feelings here gain their intensity from the very conventions by which their direct expression is occluded. In Rachel, the "Goddess" of Castlewood, we see the Angel of the House unmasked.

Thackeray's double-edged use of history as pastoral is an important aspect of *Esmond,* but it does not exhaust the ways in which the novel employs history, or the resonances of its unsavory love story. To pursue these matters further, I want to return to the novel's trivialization of historical causes and figures, which turns Swift into a cranky bully, Steele into a pathetic drunkard, and the failure of Jacobitism into an entirely contingent event caused by the weakness of a Frenchified "boy" who thinks of himself as a king but lacks a hundredth of Esmond's own "true" nobility. If we look at *Esmond* as a sequel to *Vanity Fair* in general, and not simply in its exploration of sexual stereotyping, one explanation of this debunking is clear. Thackeray is employing the eighteenth century, and a political movement that Scott had made vital and glamorous even in its defeat, as he had less systematically used the Napoleonic period in *Vanity Fair*—to demonstrate the vanity of life. But there is more to his use of the past than that.

It is possible to argue that Esmond's trivialization of causes for which men were willing to fight and die itself constitutes a view of history. Some readers have been impressed by the surprisingly modern philosophy of history which they believe *Esmond* expresses. For them, *Esmond* is a great novel because it plays out in fictional form the implications of the utterly relativistic view of history suggested by the "perspective-glass" passage explaining Esmond's dislike for Marlborough:

> A word of kindness or acknowledgement, or a single glance of approbation, might have changed Esmond's opinion of the great man; and instead of a satire, which his pen cannot help writing, who knows but that the humble historian might have taken the other side of panegyric? We have but to change the point of view, and the greatest action looks mean; as we turn the perspective-glass, and a giant appears a pigmy. You may describe, but who can tell whether your sight is clear or not, or your means of information accurate?   [p. 244; Bk. 2, ch. 10]

We can hardly doubt that relativism had its attractions for Thackeray, particularly in his darker moments: we need only to recall his celebrated comment that Tom Jones and Blifil are equally selfish.[15] Nonetheless, the perspective-glass passage is a misleading guide to the

15. "To Robert Bell," 3 September 1848, Letter 503, *Letters and Private Papers of William Makepeace Thackeray*, ed. Gordon N. Ray, II (Cambridge: Harvard University Press, 1945), 424. Even the comparison of Tom Jones and Blifil makes in context a point that is more morally affirmative than epistemologically nihilist. In it, Thackeray is reminding us that we all share the vice of selfishness: he is attacking pharisaic pride, not suggesting that all human actions are equally base.

novel as a whole, if it is taken to imply a philosophy of history.[16] When Esmond criticizes Addison for writing a poem that celebrates one of Marlborough's victories, he attacks him not on relativistic grounds but because he believes that the poem falsifies the ascertainable and morally inescapable truth, by ignoring the horrors of war. The perspective-glass side of the novel reflects not a coherent vision of history but a set of personal feelings about individual memory. These feelings generate scenes with an emotional intensity Scott rarely achieves, but they also help to create the radically unhistorical nature of the novel when compared with Scott's works.

Thackeray's excursions into historical relativism result from a fear of illusion and betrayal which surfaces continually in his novels. In *Esmond* this feeling is perhaps most memorably expressed by the narrator's description of the failure of Rachel's first marriage: "Who does not know of eyes, lighted by love once, where the flame shines no more?—of lamps extinguished, once properly trimmed and tended? Every man has such in his house. Such mementoes make our splendidest chambers look blank and sad; such faces seen in a day cast a gloom upon our sunshine" (p. 115; Bk. 1, ch. 11). No doubt such feelings were brought to a boil by Thackeray's own sufferings in the Brookfield affair,[17] but he had expressed them powerfully several years before he quarreled with the Brookfields, as these two passages from *Vanity Fair* indicate:

> There was a picture of the family over the mantle-piece, removed thither from the front room after Mrs. Osborne's death—George was on a pony, the elder sister holding him up a bunch of flowers; the younger led by her mother's hand; all with red cheeks and large red mouths, simpering on each other in the approved family-portrait manner. The mother lay under ground now, long since forgotten—

16. Fleishman, pp. 142–43, uses the perspective-glass passage in this way. Thackeray's treatment of Marlborough is usually used as the strongest evidence for his supposed historical relativism. John Sutherland, *Thackeray at Work* (London: Athlone Press, 1974), pp. 66–73, shows that Thackeray's vacillations about Marlborough were caused by his uneasy awareness that ancestral piety for General Webb had led him to falsify the historical record. Sutherland is able to show that Thackeray invented the novel's editorial apparatus (the footnotes and introduction) in an improvisatory fashion, partially for the same reason.

17. For the Brookfield affair, see Gordon N. Ray, *The Buried Life: A Study of the Relations Between Thackeray's Fiction and his Personal History* (Cambridge: Harvard University Press, 1952).

the sisters and brother had a hundred different interests of their own, and, familiar still, were utterly estranged from each other. Some few score of years afterwards, when all the parties represented are grown old, what bitter satire there is in those flaunting childish family-portraits, with their farce of sentiment and smiling lies, and innocence so self-conscious and self-satisfied.

Have you ever had a difference with a dear friend? How his letters, written in the period of love and confidence, sicken and rebuke you! What a dreary mourning it is to dwell upon those vehement protests of dead affection! What lying epitaphs they make over the corpse of love! What dark, cruel comments upon Life and Vanities! Most of us have got or written drawers full of them.[18]

"Lying epitaphs," "bitter satire"—here is the core of Thackeray's sense of the past. When they appear, Esmond's forays into historical relativism serve as attempts to neutralize the mocking, frightening powers of memory. This fear of memory informs the most powerful scenes in the novel, those in which Rachel turns upon and vilifies the bewildered, distraught Henry. Only later does he learn that the power of her anger depended upon the intensity of her guilty love for him. That this intensity of feeling will never quite be recaptured seems clear from the muted ending of the novel, even though Rachel is said by her daughter to have preserved her powerful jealousy intact. The individual's past is never what it seems at the time when it is experienced as the present, and can never be recaptured in its full intensity, even if it is later understood. With this emotional basis, Thackeray's attack on public history in the novel becomes a defensive degradation and self-protection, rooted in a fear of the ironies fostered by our illusions about our past and present lives.

Memory in *Esmond* contains much that seems placid, beautiful, and enduring—moments of touching lyric beauty. But behind such moments there always lurks the fear of disruption, dissolution, and reversal: the very lyricism with which they are described is a stay against such confusion. Throughout the novel, Thackeray is fascinated by the way in which human beings tame and neutralize the past by constructing and reconstructing it. Few readers can have missed

18. William Thackeray, *Vanity Fair: A Novel without a Hero,* ed. Geoffrey and Kathleen Tillotson (London: Methuen; Boston: Houghton Mifflin, 1963), pp. 222–23, 342.

the studied imprecisions of remembered fact scattered throughout the novel, in which we see various characters altering the past because they need to stabilize it or connect it with the present in a certain way. Rachel is continually doing this, often in a semihysterical manner, but she is hardly alone. A particularly rich example involves Steele's recollections of a scene by his father's coffin. He first mentions the scene as part of an attempt to comfort the child Esmond by proving the genuineness of his concern for him:

> "That was the first sensation of grief," Dick said, "I ever knew. I remember I went into the room where his body lay, and my mother sat weeping beside it. I had my battledore in my hand, and fell a-beating the coffin, and calling papa; on which my mother caught me in her arms, and told me in a flood of tears papa could not hear me, and would play with me no more, for they were going to put him under ground, whence he could never come to us again. And this," said Dick kindly, "has made me pity all children ever since. . . ." [p. 70; Bk. 1, ch. 6]

Steele later recalls the same incident for a different purpose, as he excuses Frank Esmond's insensitivity to his father's death by commenting that "grief touches the young but lightly, and I remember that I beat a drum at the coffin of my own father" (p. 178; Bk. 2, ch. 2). Steele's apparent confusion about the incident has been taken to exemplify Thackeray's interest in epistemology, but I believe it has another kind of significance. Thackeray's source for the scene, *Tatler* *181* (which he refers to elsewhere and may have expected the reader to know), is significant here. To begin with, it reveals that Steele's two descriptions of the scene in *Esmond* are not essentially inconsistent with one another:

> The first sense of sorrow I ever knew was upon the death of my father, at which time I was not quite five years of age; but was rather amazed at what all the house meant, than possessed with a real understanding why nobody was willing to play with me. I remember I went into the room where his body lay, and my mother sat weeping alone by it. I had my battledore in my hand, and fell a beating the coffin, and calling "Papa"; for I know not how I had some slight idea that he was locked up there. My mother catched me in her arms, and transported beyond all patience of the silent grief she was before in, she almost smothered me in her embrace, and told me in a flood of

tears, papa could not hear me, and would play with me no more, for they were going to put him under ground, whence he could never come to us again. She was a very beautiful woman, of a noble spirit, and there was a dignity in her grief amidst all the wildness of her transport, which, methought, struck me with an instinct of sorrow, which, before I was sensible of what it was to grieve, seized my very soul, and has made pity the weakness of my heart ever since.[19]

Thus it turns out that the drumming on the coffin *is* a sign of a certain kind of insensitivity, not a mark of grief; sorrow penetrated Steele only by reflection, from the grief of his beautiful mother. Yet the two versions of the scene in *Esmond* do *seem* inconsistent as we read the novel: they begin to fill with different contents a moment of slight indeterminacy in Steele's text, the moment when he beats the coffin ("I had some slight idea that he was locked up there"). Why? A look at the *Tatler* essay as a whole provides an answer. *Tatler 181* begins with a gently ironized description of how the narrator decides to spend an evening remembering dead friends. At first he is embarrassed by his lukewarm feelings, but then his memory of his father's funeral supervenes, with its arresting picture of his mother's grief; he then recalls "the beauty, innocence, and untimely death, of the first object my eyes ever beheld with love" (p. 352), in a passage filled with eloquent exclamations of sorrow. But he breaks off, as an invitation to drink a case of wine with his living friends brings him back to the present, with reassuring bathos.

Steele's essay is about the power we have to evoke memories, and the power they have over us when we evoke them. The bathetic ending, and the irony that makes itself felt in the essay's opening paragraphs and intermittently thereafter, are measures of defense against memory, less extreme than but not different in function from Thackeray's own defensive degradation of the past. *Tatler 181* tells

19. *The Tatler*, ed. George A. Aitken (London: Duckworth, 1899), III, 350; subsequent references appear in my text. Elaine Scarry, "*Henry Esmond*: The Rookery at Castlewood," *Literary Monographs*, 7, ed. Eric Rothstein and J. A. Wittreich, Jr. (Madison: University of Wisconsin Press, 1975), 1–43, argues that *Esmond*'s studied imprecisions are meant to have epistemological force, making us realize that truth itself is unknowable. One problem with this sort of argument from inconsistency is that it has little specific explanatory power: it predicts only that a work must have a certain number of inconsistencies, not what they should be or where they should occur. It also becomes difficult to differentiate between significant ambiguities and simple authorial slips.

us, in a passage *Esmond* echoes, that "the mind in infancy is, me-
thinks, like the body in embryo, and receives impressions so forcible,
that they are as hard to be removed by reason, as any mark with
which a child is born is to be taken away by any future application"
(p. 350). But future applications are necessary and inevitable. In
Esmond, we see Steele working over a vivid, painfully equivocal
memory for the purposes of containment and control—in this case,
by turning it into an illustration for moral discourse which alters and
diffuses its significance. Such reworking of memory occurs constantly
in the novel, and especially in the narrative voice itself. Are the judgments Esmond as narrator makes those of the past or those of the
present? Our uncertainty on this point opens up rich possibilities for
Esmond to remold the past, as present purposes and judgments im-
perceptibly infiltrate past actions. This process occurs, for instance,
whenever he mentions a character about whom he has reason to be
highly ambivalent, Rachel's first husband Lord Castlewood, the man
who acts as his protector but who also knowingly acquiesces in
usurping his rightful title. Esmond consistently calls this person his
"benefactor" (see, for instance, p. 175; Bk. 2, ch. 2), even after the
point in the narrative when he learns of the usurpation. And in the
midst of describing Castlewood's boorish treatment of Rachel and his
scarcely less attractive drunken remorse for the rift between them,
Esmond refers to him as "my honest Lord Castlewood" (p. 75; Bk. 1,
ch. 7), or as his "kind, manly friend and protector" (p. 129; Bk. 1, ch.
12), or as his "generous patron" (p. 154; Bk. 1, ch. 14). There is
some irony in this language, and also a good deal of covertly self-
congratulatory condescension, but isn't there also anxiety and guilt?
These honorifics tend to come particularly fast whenever Castlewood
shows signs of still loving Rachel, but given the part Esmond as narrator must now know he played in making a reconciliation between
them impossible, they seem backhanded compliments. His incongru-
ous praise attempts to distance a source of guilty memories, so that
they will not disrupt the present.

The power of memory in *Esmond* evokes constant countermeasures
because it is so strong that it poses a threat to the stability of personal
identity itself. This threat makes Esmond's own egotism explicable.
His objectively enacted fantasies of omnipotence, his need to assert
his superiority to everyone around him—these are understandable if

extreme reactions to a world in which the integrity of the self is constantly undermined by the disruptive power of memory. To the extent that we as readers feel this threat, ironic condescension toward Esmond and his predicament becomes impossible, and Thackeray has accomplished what he accomplishes in *Vanity Fair*: he has robbed us of a superior view of his characters by making us believe that their world is our world as well.

What, then, are the functions history plays in *Henry Esmond*? The second half of the novel, with its accounts of Esmond's military life, shows that Thackeray has some interest in the eighteenth century as chronicle and spectacle; the novel as a whole betrays an interest in certain representative historical types (such as Father Holt) and in the course history has taken to produce Thackeray's present. But Thackeray's primary interest in history lies elsewhere. He uses history as a pastoral setting onto which to project cultural concerns in a complex, double-edged way. *Esmond* allows the nineteenth-century reader to feel superior to certain aspects of the past, but covertly shows the limits and dangers of certain contemporary beliefs as well. Yet the history that matters most to Thackeray is personal history; the process he cares most about is the process of individual memory, which he views as a threatening, disruptive force. His treatment of public history ultimately serves as a metaphor for this fear of private memory. Thackeray's various uses of history as pastoral help to produce a novel of remarkable power. But that power is gained at the expense of other virtues possible in historical fiction. *Esmond* necessarily elides an important range of human experience, that part of the spectrum of human existence in which history centrally occurs and Jacobitism, or even pulling off a king's boots, is anything but trivial. *Henry Esmond* is nonetheless a great and disturbing work. For that very reason, it seems important to find ways of describing it that neither distort nor inflate its historical element. We need a method that allows us to understand what Thackeray's radically unhistorical depiction of a character like the Pretender adds to the kind of historical novel he is writing.

Guy Mannering and *The Antiquary*

Scott was passionately interested in the problems of the society around him, and we might well expect this interest to color his treatment of the past. How important is the use of history as pastoral in his novels? I believe that he kept his interest in current social issues under strict control when he was writing imaginative literature. He greatly disliked the use of history for modern purposes in works purporting to be about the past, particularly if he disagreed with the viewpoint thus expressed. In an early article on Godwin's *Life of Chaucer*, he drily observes: "It seems to have been his rule, that if it be difficult to think like our ancestors, it is very easy to make them think like ourselves," converting them into mouthpieces for our own tendentious views (*MPW* XVII, 72). Not everyone would agree that Scott himself escaped this tendency. On the publication of *The Abbot* in 1820, some saw the novel as a defense not of a sixteenth-century queen of Scots but of a nineteenth-century queen of Great Britain, Queen Charlotte, then in the midst of that extraordinary exercise in stupidity and bad taste, the divorce proceedings brought against her by George IV.[20] Taine accuses Scott of peopling the past with his contemporaries, and he is not alone in making this charge. The most subtle attempt to see the Waverley Novels as a projection of contemporary values into history is Alexander Welsh's *The Hero of the Waverley Novels*. My own view is that the Waverley Novels are the highly self-conscious products of a writer who generally put into them, and kept out of them, what he intended, which did not include, except in certain well-defined areas, anachronistically imposed values or ideas or problems. What may seem importations of the present into the past can be more usefully explained as attempts to represent lines of historical continuity, or to eke out gaps in the historical record, or to provide an entry point into the past for the modern reader, or to juxtapose the values of the modern world and those of the past within the action of his fiction, this latter practice reflecting his preference for the "dramatic method" of presenting material through action and speech instead of through authorial comment.[21] On a more general level, Welsh's claim that Scott's novels project his own values onto the past is in my opinion more than adequately countered by Lukács's claim that Scott's class status and ideology allow him his best insights into the workings of historical process.[22]

20. *Letters*, VI, 309. An equally erroneous report also circulated at the time, that a mob had attacked Abbotsford because they believed Scott to be on the king's side.

21. For Scott's use of the "dramatic method," see Frank Jordan, Jr., "Walter Scott as a Dramatic Novelist," *Studies in Scottish Literature*, 5 (1968), 238–45.

22. Alexander Welsh, *The Hero of the Waverley Novels,* Yale Studies in English,

Scott's contemporary political and social concerns make themselves felt most directly in his two early novels of the recent past, *Guy Mannering* and *The Antiquary*.[23] These works are as loosely organized as anything Scott ever wrote. They are also greatly prized by Scott's admirers, especially his Scottish admirers. In part, this popularity results from the freedom with which Scott uses his plot as a string on which to hang scenes of a past that still lived on in men's minds when the novels were published. Edinburgh's golden age and the rural society of the Borders provide Scott in *Guy Mannering* with two of his best-loved characters, Pleydell and Dandie Dinmont, neither of whom has much to do with the plotted actions of the novel in which he appears.

But the popularity of these novels when first published and their continuing interest for us today do not result entirely from the charming genre-pictures they contain. Both works explore a range of social concerns that the French Revolution and its aftermath had brought vividly to light for Scott and his contemporaries. It is impossible to overestimate the importance of the Napoleonic Wars in forming Scott as a moral being and a thinker about society and history. J. G. Lockhart reminds us of how great an influence the struggle against the

---

154 (New Haven: Yale University Press, 1963). At the root of the disagreement between Welsh and Lukács is, I believe, a difference in ontology. Welsh complains that Scott "did not greatly contribute to the 'protest on behalf of value' that Alfred North Whitehead discovered in the romantic movement—the perception of a concrete, unified, thing-in-itself" (p. 137). Lukács would find the perception of the mere thing-in-itself the basis not of realism but of *naturalism*, of an intoxication with the fragments of a world one can no longer understand. This stance toward life Lukács would find nicely illustrated by Welsh's approving description of what happens to the hero of *The Charterhouse of Parma* at the field of Waterloo: "Past Stendhal's hero the action at Waterloo sweeps in total confusion, a turmoil of impression and fragmented reality. . . . Stendhal thrusts his hero into a world of flux. . . . The public event . . . threatens . . . to expand and diminish without end . . . to overwhelm the account of itself by its enigmatic proportions" (pp. 28–29). There are further signs of this difference in Welsh's more recent *Reflections on the Hero as Quixote* (Princeton: Princeton University Press, 1981): see especially pp. 161–66, where he faults Lukács's reliance on teleology as a foundation for significance in art and life.

23. In the Introduction to the first edition of *The Antiquary*, Scott asserts that "*Waverley* embraced the age of our fathers, *Guy Mannering* that of our own youth, and the *Antiquary* refers to the last ten years of the eighteenth century" (p. v). The reader will notice that I have allowed a dominant place to history as pastoral (or, in *St. Ronan's Well*, to history as a source of drama) only in works by Scott that are not, properly speaking, historical novels.

French had on Scott's poetry. *The Lay of the Last Minstrel* was written while Scott was on maneuvers with the cavalry unit he helped raise in response to the threat of French invasion; *Marmion* was partly intended to boost public morale in the struggle against Napoleon; and *The Vision of Don Roderick* was also indirect propaganda for the war effort. This influence also extends to the novels. Scott was no less the bard of the Napoleonic Wars in *Guy Mannering* and *The Antiquary* than he was in *Marmion,* for both novels have much to tell us about social cohesion and patriotic unity.[24]

Guy Mannering is a more unified and powerful novel than *The Antiquary.* We feel the influence of the Scottish ballads strongly in *Guy Mannering,* and this may account for the greater strength of its design. The homecoming of Bertram is particularly impressive. Scott is uncharacteristically successful in making us share the dim recollections that fill Bertram's mind when he enters Ellangowan Castle for the first time since early childhood. And the upsurge of half-feudal, half-communal feeling which occurs when his tenants recognize him as their rightful lord is moving and persuasive. At least for the moment, we share Scott's evident conviction that due social subordination brings forth the best in both social inferiors and superiors.

Yet in the end, Scott's solution to the problems of class and authentic nobility in *Guy Mannering* is too easy. Bertram does not earn the warm feelings with which he is regarded by the peasantry. His father's misuse of his social status is ritually expiated, but its implications are not really faced. The negative aspects of class subordination are too neatly and easily defused by Scott's creation of an evil social climber, the attorney Gilbert Glossin. We may not like Glossin, but there is really more to say for the wish to change the social status quo than that it is tasteless and probably based on greed.[25]

In his next novel, *The Antiquary,* Scott probes the problems of so-

24. J. G. Lockhart, *Memoirs of the Life of Sir Walter Scott, Bart.,* 2d ed., 10 vols. (Edinburgh: Cadell, 1839), II, 210; III, 62, 319.

25. Robert C. Gordon, *Under Which King? A Study of the Scottish Waverley Novels* (Edinburgh: Oliver and Boyd, 1969), p. 26, notes the significance of the settings in *The Antiquary* and *Guy Mannering*: in *Waverley,* "history's decision on the Jacobites was public and immutable, but in the relatively isolated areas of Scotland where the two later novels are set, Scott's conservatism had its way and the forces of the past enjoyed some measure of success." Gordon also objects to Scott's treatment of Glossin in *Guy Mannering* (p. 34).

cial class and national solidarity in greater depth. This results in an even more disunified novel than *Guy Mannering*. The hero of *The Antiquary* is surely the weakest and least interesting protagonist in the Waverley series. But his weakness may be the sign of another kind of strength: Scott's refusal to create a central character who mythically "solves" the problems he wishes to explore. *The Antiquary* is in many respects a puzzling and unsatisfying work, but it has an interest that does not depend on such triumphs of individual characterization as Edie Ochiltree or the Antiquary himself. In terms of the amount of class protest and strife to which Scott is willing to give a hearing, *The Antiquary* marks a special moment in his career.

Looking for the influence of the Napoleonic Wars in *The Antiquary* soon becomes, to borrow a line from Nabokov, like looking for the imagery of large mammals in *Moby Dick*. The novel ends with an orgy of anti-French patriotism, enshrining the moment when the Scottish people rose to the defense of Great Britain as a whole, in response to a false alarm of French invasion in 1804. This was a story Scott loved to tell. It represented for him the final healing of the scars left by the Fifteen and the Forty-five and their brutal aftermath.[26] Another outlet for anti-French, anti-Jacobin enthusiasm is provided by the ritual casting out of a foreign villain, the German swindler Dousterswivel. He cannot be probably portrayed as a Frenchman living in Scotland, since the novel is set during the Napoleonic Wars. He is, however, accused of being a spy in the pay of the French. Even a translated tale from the German which Lovel reads during the picnic at the ruins of St. Ruth's Priory has Napoleonic overtones; it can be read as a final jibe at Jeffrey and the Whigs for their wish to promote peaceful coexistence with Napoleon. The townspeople in the tale take great umbrage when a wandering friar tries to warn them against the evil demon who inhabits a nearby forest. The demon's subsequent victim, Martin Waldeck, defends him louder than all the rest, asserting that he is anything but a threat to them. Waldeck's own ruin is the ironic sequel to his misplaced security.

When Waldeck defends the Demon of the Hartz Mountains by reminding his fellow townsmen that "the demon is a good demon. He lives among us as if he were a peasant like ourselves" (p. 158; ch. 18),

---

26. Scott discusses the false alarm in a lengthy note he wrote for the Magnum Opus edition of the novel: this note appears on pp. 419–20 of the Dryburgh edition.

he raises the issue in which we can feel the influence of the Napoleonic Wars most deeply in *The Antiquary*—the question of class relations. Every reader of the novel will remember the scene in which the
antiquary Monkbarns congratulates the fisherman Saunders Mucklebackit on being able to work on his boat the day after his oldest son
Steenie has drowned, and Mucklebackit replies in an unforgettable
way:

> "And what would ye have me to do," answered the fisher, gruffly,
> "unless I wanted to see four children starve, because ane is drowned?
> It's weel wi' you gentles, that can sit in the house wi' handkerchers at
> your een when ye lose a friend; but the like o' us maun to our wark
> again, if our hearts were beating as hard as my hammer." [p. 307;
> ch. 34]

Commentators sometimes forget that Monkbarns is not merely being
obtuse and intrusive here. He sees that Mucklebackit needs to speak
and be spoken to, and he provides him with the opportunity to un-
burden himself. Nonetheless, the class challenge in his remark cuts
deep, even though it is partly withdrawn when Saunders adds:

> I am a plain-spoken man, and hae little to say for mysell; I might hae
> learned fairer fashions frae my mither lang syne, but I never saw
> muckle gude they did her; however, I thank ye. Ye were aye kind and
> neighbourly, whatever folk says o' your being near and close; and I
> hae often said in thae times when they were ganging to raise up the
> puir folk against the gentles—I hae often said, ne'er a man should
> steer a hair touching to Monkbarns while Steenie and I could wag a
> finger; and so said Steenie too. And, Monkbarns, when ye laid his
> head in the grave—and mony thanks for the respect—ye saw the
> mouls laid on an honest lad that likit you weel, though he made little
> phrase about it. [p. 308; ch. 34]

The balance here between a sturdy pride that scorns to ape the upper
classes, and honest affection and social solidarity between men of different classes, is skillfully created.

Saunders Mucklebackit's outburst against Monkbarns is the culmi-
nation of a series of similar confrontations throughout *The Antiquary*. The Mucklebackit family seems expressly designed to bring
out class conflict, for there is an explosion every time they meet one
of their social betters. The class basis of these discords is rendered

particularly clear by the contrast between genteel English and the thick Scots in which the Mucklebackits express themselves. When Saunders first appears in the novel, he is busy helping to rescue Sir Arthur Wardour, his daughter, and the beggar Edie Ochiltree, all of whom are stranded on a ledge above the incoming tide, but he finds time to say that the rescue would be easy if only Monkbarns would get out of the way. When the family next appears, Saunders's wife Maggie reminds Monkbarns that it is all very well for him to be pleased that the smuggling trade has been suppressed and the price of liquor has gone up, but for the poor, in their cold and squalid huts, cheap alcohol is not the needless luxury it is for the rich. Monkbarns, in keeping with his role as a moderating force in the novel, admits the justice of her observations. There is more to come. On the day of Steenie's funeral, the Earl of Glenallan appears at the Mucklebackits' cottage to learn unexpected news concerning his past from Saunders's aged mother, who orders her son and daughter-in-law to leave while she speaks with the nobleman. Saunders tells him to come some other day, suggesting that he may not be a lord at all and that no one will find it worthwhile to listen to anything he has to say. Finally, he declares that he won't leave his hut on the day of his son's funeral either "for laird or loon, gentle or semple" (p. 295; ch. 32). The great scene with Monkbarns occurs directly afterwards, for Saunders in fact leaves, out of respect for his mother instead of deference for an earl, and begins to work on his boat.

Elspeth Mucklebackit, the former servant of the Glenallans whose genteel airs her son Saunders refuses to imitate, has her own contribution to make to the dialogue between classes in *The Antiquary*. She lends a historical perspective to the problem. Elspeth's Gothic memories of past misdeeds bring history into the novel in a way which Scott's contemporaries immediately recognized as anachronistic, but which allows Scott to raise an important question.[27] Loyalty between classes is necessary, if only to fight off the French, but what sort of loyalty shall it be? Elspeth's catalogue of the crimes she happily committed as a Glenallan retainer rules out blind feudal loyalty as an

---

27. For a contemporary complaint about the improbability of the Glenallan tragedy, see John O. Hayden, ed., *Scott: The Critical Heritage* (New York: Barnes and Noble, 1970), pp. 104–5.

acceptable answer. She recalls the good old days when nobles were nobles and servants were servants: "They were stout hearts the race of Glenallan, male and female, and sae were a' that in auld times cried their gathering-word of 'Clochnaben'; they stood shouther to shouther. Nae man parted frae his chief for love of gold or of gain, or of right or of wrang. The times are changed, I hear, now" (p. 302; ch. 33). Indeed they are, and for the better. As we shall see, the loyalty of an Edie Ochiltree is no less real for being less blind and lawless. The strength of this repudiation of old patterns of loyalty may seem surprising in Scott, but it is in keeping with the rest of the novel. Monkbarns actually defends the French Revolution, which is to be sure in Scott's mind something quite different from the threat of Napoleonic hegemony. Lord Glenallan may view the Revolution "with all the prejudiced horror of a bigoted Catholic and zealous aristocrat," but Monkbarns likens it to "a storm or hurricane, which, passing over a region, does great damage in its passage, yet sweeps away stagnant and unwholesome vapours, and repays, in future health and fertility, its immediate desolation and ravage" (pp. 319–20; ch. 35).

Edie Ochiltree plays a role in *The Antiquary* like that of the Mucklebackits. When he is stranded on the ledge above the sea with Sir Arthur and Isabella Wardour, and they are all in danger of drowning, Sir Arthur offers him wealth and comfort if only he will save them. Edie replies with a dignified moral rebuke: "Our riches will be soon equal" (p. 63; ch. 7). Later in the scene, Sir Arthur's frantic attempts to save himself and his daughter finally wear out Edie's patience, and he says to the baronet, "haud your tongue, and be thankful to God that there's wiser folk than you to manage this job" (p. 69; ch. 8). Edie has earned the right to say these things, for he endangered himself in the first place by attempting to warn the Wardours of the storm that is now threatening them, and in the end he helps to rescue them. The scene on the rock ledge provides an epitome of the novel's treatment of class differences, as people of different classes join together, whatever their sources of annoyance with one another, in the face of an external threat, provided here by nature and in the larger scheme of the novel by the French. Scott allows the lower classes in *The Antiquary* to have their say because they have shown in the recent past that, when it matters, they can be trusted. Edie's last contradiction of Monkbarns is appropriately an expression of patriotic support for the society in which he lives. Monkbarns jocularly suggests that Edie's martial spirit against the French is surprising, since as a beggar he has so little to fight for. Edie replies with some warmth: "*Me* no muckle to fight for, sir? Isna there the country to fight for, and the burnsides that I gang daundering beside, and the hearths o' the gudewives that gie me my bit bread, and the bits o' weans that come toddling to play wi' me when I come about a landward town?" This is convincing, sincere, and also very reassuring for the landowners of Great Britain, and Monkbarns states the novel's political and social moral in response to Edie's outburst: "Bravo, bravo, Edie! The country's in little ultimate danger when the beggar's as ready to fight for his dish as the laird for his land" (p. 401; ch. 44). The patness of this answer is annoying; what saves it from seeming intolerably smug is the extent to which Scott has tried to give social discontent a hearing in *The Antiquary* as a whole.

Guy Mannering and *The Antiquary* arise from a special period in Scott's life and in the life of Europe, but a crucial event separates the two works. *Guy Mannering* appeared a few days before Napoleon landed at Cannes on March 1, 1815, in an unsuccessful bid to regain his empire. Scott had thought of writing *The Antiquary* before then and had signed a contract for it in January 1815, but the actual writing began in December 1815, several months after Waterloo; the novel itself appeared in May 1816. We are fortunate enough to possess a record of the events of those years from Scott's own hand, the "History of Europe, 1814," which he wrote for the *Edinburgh Annual Register* in the summer of 1816. This "History" has much to tell us about the differences between *Guy Mannering* and *The Antiquary*, as well as about the shape of Scott's early career as a novelist.

The period after the first defeat of Napoleon seems to have been a euphoric time for Scott. Looking back on it elicited from him a paean of praise for modern British civilization worthy of Macaulay at his most aggressive, in a description of the visit which the allied monarchs made to London after their victory:

> The glory of the land was now before them. It consisted not in palaces and public buildings,—not in collections of that which is most

valuable in art and science,—in these Britain was far exceeded by her ancient rival and enemy, the country which they had just conquered;—it was in the general welfare and happiness of the community, displayed in fields cultivated to the uttermost, houses of every description, from the villa to the cottage, filled with all of use, and even of ornament, which suited the owners,—it was in those increasing villages, whose rising streets seemed yet too limited for the number of the inhabitants,—in those groups of healthy peasants and artizans, whose numbers, as well as their neat and orderly appearance, had an air of perpetual holiday,—it was that throng of a metropolis, in which none seemed to want employment, and yet all to have the means of enjoyment and relaxation,—it was in the bustle of seaports, and the hum of marts,—it was, above all, in the conduct of the inhabitants, who could preserve real good order amid apparent license, that the sovereigns recognized the beneficial effects of those equal laws and liberal principles of government which have placed Britain so high among the nations. We are well assured that amid the immense concourse which assembled with shout and jubilee to witness their presence at Ascot races, the Emperor of Russia . . . exclaimed to those who stood by him, "In what other country dared the government to permit such an assemblage, without forces sufficient to over-awe and controul [*sic*] them in case of uproar?" The full security and confidence reposed in the good sense and correct feeling of the people must have appeared the more surprising, as, to the eye of strangers, their blunt and tumultuous expressions of joy and of welcome approach in themselves to the very verge of license. In fact, the English common people on such occasions resemble the tides on many parts of their coast—fierce and tumultuous in appearance to the inexperienced spectator, but which, without some unusual and agitating cause, do not pass their natural limits, or encroach upon the land.[28]

The closing passage of the "History" looks back on this happy moment with disillusionment, anxiety, and wistful regret:

---

28. "History of Europe, 1814," in *The Edinburgh Annual Register for 1814,* Edinburgh Annual Register, 7 (Edinburgh: Constable, 1816), pt. I, pp. 350–51. Scott's immediate reaction to Napoleon's first fall is mirrored in his letters, where he expressed joy, some vindictiveness against Napoleon himself, and great pride in the British nation (see *Letters,* III, 428–29, 440–42, 446–48, 449; XII, 418–19). His delight was soon complicated, however, by a sense of "vacancy," a "stunning sort of listless astonishment and complication of feeling, which, if it did not lessen enjoyment, confused and confounded one's sense of it" (*Letters,* III, 450). This feeling was caused by the sudden removal of Napoleon as a center of attention and anxiety, and by disappointment in his ignoble surrender (*Letters,* III, 451).

The year 1814 . . . will be long distinguished in the history of Europe. . . . Neither will the sensations which we have felt during this remarkable era be ever erazed [sic] from the minds on which they were so vividly impressed. Other events succeeded in the subsequent year, even more striking in themselves, not of less deep influence upon the course of human affairs, and certainly more flattering to our feelings as Britons. But these succeeded to an unexpected convulsion, the recollection of whose unexpected fury will long make us feel like men who tread on the surface of a volcano. The victory of Waterloo, and the second capture of Paris, agitating, affecting, and interesting, as far as it is possible for human events to be so, had not power again to lull us into the pleasing delusion, that war was vanished from the earth, and that contending nations might in future hang the trumpet in the hall, and vie only in the arts of commerce and of peace. The eyes which wept for joy at the first restoration of the Bourbons, cannot look upon their second re-establishment without painful and anxious apprehensions, concerning the stability of their throne.[29]

Even the euphoria of Waterloo cannot bring back the simple confidence Scott had felt at Napoleon's first abdication. The effect of this shock on Scott was, I believe, complex. In the short term, it led him to look at the strengths and weaknesses of class relations in his own country in greater depth than he had done before, and the result was *The Antiquary*. The final assessment remained positive, but the vision of social solidarity was not easily achieved. In the long run, after the shock had been registered and dealt with in *The Antiquary*, the results were rather different, especially since, with the external threat of Napoleon finally removed, internal dissension in Britain grew with economic adversity. To "tread on the surface of a volcano" is in the long run a tiring business, likely to create rigidity in the most flexible of us, after our initial excitement at finding ourselves in such a situation has died down. In the novels following *The Antiquary*, Scott did not often give lower-class dissatisfaction the dignity it assumes in the Mucklebackits or in Edie Ochiltree. Some of the same sentiments are expressed, but the characters who express them are much less sympathetic.[30]

29. "History," pp. 366–67.

30. With the middle class it is different. They are consistently the class with whom Scott sides. In *The Bride of Lammermoor*, for instance, the cooper John Girder gets, as we shall see, reasonably sympathetic treatment for his wish to rise in the world; lower-class protest, however, is embodied in the horrible chorus of witches in the

I would argue, then, that the social and political developments of the time make *The Antiquary* a turning point for Scott. His interest in contemporary politics never weakens. Nor does his belief that certain aspects of the present and the past, like the French Revolution and the Great Rebellion in England, mirror each other in instructive ways, *mutatis mutandis*. But before *Guy Mannering* and after *The Antiquary*, he does not use his fiction primarily to explore current problems, as a comparison with Bulwer-Lytton's genuinely projective works quickly reveals. For all their love of Scott, the Victorians were generally and from their point of view rightly annoyed that his novels did not construct a politically and morally useful past. Clearly enough, we are as usual dealing here with a matter of degree and structural prominence. A number of recent studies explore the contemporary resonances of *Old Mortality*, the novel about revolution Scott began shortly after finishing the "History of Europe, 1814."[31] No doubt Scott's current concerns sharpened his awareness of how certain kinds of political processes work, and colored his evaluations of the actors and causes involved, both in *Old Mortality* and in his later novels. But to admit this does not imply that such concerns dominate *Old Mortality* and the novels that follow it. After *The Antiquary*, which is set almost in his own day, Scott reenters the past, discovering ways of using history in which his contemporary social concerns are not so much projected as sublimated, not ends but means. In the novels that follow *The Antiquary*, Scott uses his sensitivity to class interaction and social conflict as a powerful instrument for understanding and depicting history.

HISTORY AS A SOURCE OF DRAMA

In the works I have been discussing, history functions as a device for exploring a variety of contemporary concerns, from cultural problems

---

novel. The more sympathetically portrayed gravedigger (borrowed from *Hamlet*) does not begin to counteract the impression left by these hags. A lower-class wish to bring back the good old days, like the one expressed by old Alice, is of course another story, for part of Scott sympathized completely with such feelings.

31. Peter D. Garside, "*Old Mortality*'s Silent Minority," *Scottish Literary Journal*, 7 (1980), 127–44; Angus Calder, Introduction to *Old Mortality* (Harmondsworth: Penguin, 1975), pp. 9–11. Graham McMaster, *Scott and Society* (Cambridge: Cambridge University Press, 1981), finds in all of Scott's novels precisely the covert fixation on contemporary issues I deny them.

to individual emotions. A simpler and perhaps more familiar use of history in fiction makes it a vehicle for promoting fictional effects. One reason why Scott's novels were so popular in his own day is that fiction containing a tincture of history can fulfill the demand for literature that instructs instead of merely delighting. But history in fiction usually acts as more than a source of sufficient respectability to allay inner or outer censors. By setting a novel in the past, popular romancers from Ainsworth to the present have offered their readers a world in which life is more intense, passions simpler, men braver, women more beautiful than they appear to be today. This might be thought of as employing history as a kind of pastoral, too, but there is a difference between using history as a screen on which to project present concerns, and using history to intensify a fictional story's imaginative force. *Henry Esmond* uses history as pastoral, but it does not draw its imaginative vitality primarily from a dramatic quality that author and readers impute to life in the past. The idea that the past is intrinsically more dramatic than the present is something Thackeray debunks: the Pretender turns out to be a silly French boy, his attempt to gain the crown a simple farce.

The use of history as a source of dramatic energy is not limited to the debased and escapist form it often takes in popular literature. We can see it at work in Balzac's first signed novel, *Les Chouans,* as well as in Dickens's *A Tale of Two Cities* and Scott's only novel of contemporary manners, *St. Ronan's Well.*

Les Chouans

Balzac's *Les Chouans* is an interesting novel for the student of form in historical fiction, because it begins in the manner of Scott but soon becomes something quite different. Balzac's initial interest in representing and analyzing clashing historical forces gives way to his use of those forces to lend dignity and power to a love story.

Since *Les Chouans* is not well known, a brief summary of its plot may be helpful. The novel depicts the failure in 1799 of the last royalist rising against the French revolutionary government. It opens with an ambush of government troops by the Chouans, who are ferocious guerrilla fighters living in Brittany. This encounter serves to characterize the opposing forces and their leaders, the revolutionary soldier

Colonel Hulot and the émigré Marquis de Montauran; it also shows that the government will be hard put to quell the uprising with regular troops, because of the impassable terrain the Chouans inhabit. Accordingly, the Paris authorities dispatch a female spy, Marie de Verneuil, who is accompanied by the sinister government agent Corentin. Unfortunately for her mission, Marie and the Chouan leader Montauran fall in love during their first encounter. In the remainder of the novel, Marie oscillates between love for and hatred of Montauran, because the machinations of her fellow spy Corentin and others sometimes make it appear that Montauran is trifling with her for political advantage. Corentin ultimately tricks her into a jealous rage in which she lures Montauran to her house, which is then surrounded by soldiers. Too late, Marie discovers that Montauran has been true to her. The couple are married and spend the night together, but the next morning they both die as they attempt to escape.

The most important fact about the form of *Les Chouans* has become something of a critical commonplace; one would be surprised if it had not. Maurice Regard puts the matter succinctly when he comments that after Marie and Montauran meet, "a tale of unforeseeable love invades what had been a war novel and takes over the foreground. Henceforth, we clearly see, the war against the Chouans is no longer Balzac's main concern."[32] What such an account neglects is

32. Honoré de Balzac, *Les Chouans*, introd. and ed. Maurice Regard (Paris: Classiques Garnier, 1964), p. xxvi; subsequent references appear in my text; translations are my own. Compare Marion Ayton Crawford, who comments in the Introduction to her translation of the novel (Harmondsworth: Penguin Classics, 1972) that "the end of the love story is irrelevant to history" (p. 22) and speaks of "the different kinds of character and fundamentally different kinds of story in *The Chouans*" (p. 18). D. R. Haggis, in the article referred to in my next footnote, makes the same general point and gives references to further comments along similar lines (p. 54). Pierre Barberis, "Roman historique et roman d'amour: Lecture du *Dernier Chouan*," *Revue d'histoire littéraire de la France*, 75 (1975), 289–307, attempts to historicize Marie and her grand passion. I believe that a reading along similar lines, concentrating on the way in which the *reader's* passion is directed by the story, might be a valuable supplement to my own approach, but I am not persuaded that the novel succeeds in making the vicissitudes of Marie's love story a "homologue" of historical contradictions in the direct, schematic way Barberis suggests. Jeffrey Mehlman, *Revolution and Repetition: Marx/Hugo/Balzac* (Berkeley: University of California Press, 1977), p. 120, provides a discussion of the politics of "vision" in the novel; along the way, he notes that "there is an undeniable pressure in the text on the part of both Balzac and his characters to transform the historical-political drama into a love story interpretable in terms of individual passions."

how and why this change of emphasis occurs and what effect it has on the novel's form.

In its opening section, *Les Chouans* reflects Balzac's admiration for Scott's historical fiction in a number of ways.[33] There is an extended description of the post chaise of Brittany, the Turgotine, which recalls the loving depiction of mail coaches at the beginning of *The Heart of Midlothian*. The carefully delineated natural settings also owe something to Scott, though probably more to Cooper. Above all, the depiction of character in the early part of the novel draws on techniques developed by the Author of *Waverley*. In this section, Balzac creates figures who are interesting because they represent historical forces. When he describes the initial confrontation between Hulot and Montauran, for instance, Balzac's deepest debt to Scott does not involve the detailed physical resemblance between Montauran and Claverhouse, who appears in *Old Mortality*.[34] What matters most is the way in which Montauran is intended to represent the Old Regime:

> The spirit and animation of the young leader's bearing was military, in a way that strove to give warfare a certain poetry of form. His elegantly gloved hand flourished a sword that blazed in the sun. His look expressed elegance yet at the same time power. His exalted sense of duty, the severity of which was relieved by the charm of his youth and his noble manners, made this young émigré a gracious image of the French nobility. He contrasted vividly with the old soldier Hulot, who, standing four paces from him, was for his part the living image of the powerful republic for which he fought; his blue uniform with its shabby red underside and loose, blackened epaulettes gave a good picture of its character and the disadvantages under which it currently labored.   [pp. 48–49]

From such a description, with its sharply opposed emblematic figures, we might expect the novel to focus, as many of Scott's novels do, on a period of historical transition. In fact the novel shifts focus. The representation of these two opposing historical forces remains an impor-

33. D. R. Haggis, "Scott, Balzac, and the Historical Novel as Social and Political Analysis: *Waverley* and *Les Chouans*," *Modern Language Review*, 68 (1973), 51–68, explores Scott's influence on *Les Chouans*. The only point in this excellent article which seems to me strained is its comparison between the exceptional Marie and the mediocre Waverley.

34. This resemblance, like the many other echoes of Scott and Cooper in the novel, is noted by Regard.

tant but increasingly isolated strand in the novel, involving at its most successful Hulot, his soldiers, and the Chouan peasants.

Hulot succeeds as a historically representative figure for the same reasons that many of Scott's characters succeed. He remains basically the same throughout the novel: his uprightness, military severity mixed with decent kindness, and characteristic "tic" involving knit eyebrows are constants. Because his beliefs, his ideals, even his consciousness itself are inextricably bound up in a public code of action, we feel that the external depiction of character typical of Scott does full justice to him, not simply as a historical representative, but as a man.

Balzac treats Hulot's soldiers in a similar way, as we can see in a scene in which they argue about the significance of the compass emblem inscribed at the head of a letter from Napoleon to his armies. One soldier thinks that the compass must be a symbol of some sort, while another believes that it illustrates a problem concerning artillery trajectories. The argument ends in this way:

> "It's a symbol."
> "It's a problem."
> "Want to bet?"
> "What?"
> "Your German pipe."
> "Done."
> "By your leave, sir, ain't this a symbol and not a problem?" La-clef-des-cours asked Gérard, who, rapt in thought, was following Hulot and Merle.
> "It's both," he said gravely.
> "The adjutant is joking with us," replied Beau-pied. "That paper says that our Italian general is now consul, which is a very high rank indeed, and that we are all going to get coats and shoes." [pp. 81–82]

This passage suggests, with an unobtrusiveness reminiscent of Scott, what the aftermath of the French Revolution means to illiterate men like these. It would be easy to collapse it into an ironic revelation that despite all the highflown patriotism of Bonaparte's rhetoric, which the soldiers after all cannot read, they are really motivated by simple, petty materialism. But this is not the effect Balzac achieves. (The scene has another layer altogether, involving the officers' response to Napoleon, which I shall put aside.) Instead, we see the half-comic but none-theless admirable awakenings of curiosity among a group of men who otherwise might share the animalistic unreflectiveness of the Chouan peasants. Because of our sense of the concrete mediations through which the awakening humanity of these soldiers is evolving, we recognize that bringing shoes to them, and thus setting them one step further from the Chouans with their clumsy wooden sabots, is not the least noble task of the Revolution they are defending.[35]

Balzac also plants the Chouans firmly in history. They, like Hulot, can be adequately presented in terms of public codes and actions, such as their ruthless massacres or the primitive retributive justice they mete out to disloyal comrades. Balzac's "sociological" side comes out clearly when he depicts them. We learn what their fields are like and how their odd gates work; we observe the houses they inhabit, the food they eat, the patois they speak, the clothing they wear. And we have a sense of how all these externals shape their mental life, particularly in the mixture of opportunism, primitive superstition, and ignorance that is their religion. In conveying the strangeness of these people, Balzac succeeds very well; indeed, influenced by Cooper or rather by the European perception of Cooper's Indians, he succeeds perhaps too well. Balzac revels in their possessing "a terrible ferocity, a brutal stubbornness but also an utter fidelity to their word; a complete lack of our laws, our customs, our clothing, our new money, and our language, but also a patriarchical simplicity and heroic virtue which make this rural people, even poorer in abstract concepts than the Mohicans or the other redskins of North America, just as great, crafty, and rugged as they" (p. 24). A "complete" difference between a lower and a higher stage of society does not exist for Scott, and makes difficult the depiction of organic historical development. But it does give the Chouans a splendid exoticism and endows their clash against the revolutionary army with explosive energy. This difference between Scott and Balzac may partly result from the greater placidity of modern British history: Hugo, as we shall see, shares Balzac's interest in clashing dichotomies. But it also goes hand in hand with a shift of interest that leaves the historical depiction of the Chouans increasingly stranded from the novel's mainstream.

35. Balzac's political beliefs in this novel are complex and shifting; this scene mirrors the progressivism apparent in his Introduction to the Third Edition (1845).

After the initial skirmish between the Chouans and the Revolutionary soldiers, a pair of characters arrive on the scene who divert the
novel into a new course. The heroine, Marie de Verneuil, makes the
most obvious difference, her presence transforming Montauran the
émigré general into Montauran the passionate lover, who by the end
of the novel is arranging skirmishes and endangering his men not for
the sake of restoring the monarchy but as a means of obtaining inter-
views with his beloved. Now to many readers this change in the novel
must come as a distinct improvement, and it certainly gives Balzac the
opportunity to write in veins that Scott never could command.
Edward Waverley's "wild feeling of romantic delight" (p. 139; ch.
22) in the presence of Flora MacIvor seems insubstantial compared
not even to the most passionate moments Balzac creates, but to a
mere description of the way in which Montauran looks at Marie during a coach ride. Montauran "luxuriated in each movement of her
eyelids and in the alluring, rhythmic movement of her bodice as her
breathing rose and fell. Sometimes the flow of his thoughts made him
try to find a consonance between the look in her eyes and a minute,
scarcely perceptible change in the curve of her lips," and so on—a bit
rich for some tastes, but very fine in its way (p. 135). But from the
point of view of depicting the historical forces at work in the
Chouannerie, this is pure distraction.

The way in which Marie's watchdog Corentin disrupts the initial
antithesis between the republican Hulot and the royalist Montauran
is more subtle. Although they are both employed to destroy Montauran, Marie and Corentin are in other respects miles apart. Corentin embodies an inhuman, corrupt, and mechanical life, which we
come to associate with Paris, whereas Marie lives in a realm of passionate emotions in which questions of political manipulation for social advancement have no place. However deep their other political
and ideological differences may be, the other main characters all line
up with Marie and against Corentin in this respect. In the final chapter, for instance, Hulot expresses his disgust at Corentin's sordid
schemes, and Corentin walks away thinking with a sneer that Hulot is
one of those "honnêtes gens" who will never succeed (p. 405). Our
reaction to Corentin at such moments is meant to be exactly that
which Marie expresses earlier in the novel. "You have a withered
heart, Corentin," she tells him. "The kind of calculations that fasci-

nate you may work for external events, but not for human passions. Perhaps that's why you fill me with such repugnance" (p. 334). Marie is right: at one point, Corentin condescendingly explains to Hulot that human emotions are cogs a skillful operator can manipulate to serve that vast machine, the state.[36] The imagery here may be appropriate for the industrial society France has not yet quite become, but Balzac does little to vivify any such associations in the novel as a whole: Blake's dark satanic mills, not Dickens's Coketown, provide the proper literary parallel here. Corentin thus draws the focus of the novel away from the specific historical moment with which it was originally concerned, as well as from the aristocratic versus democratic values it originally juxtaposed. He introduces a polarity quite different from the one that pits a doomed if heroic past against a present based on the changes made by men like Hulot and Napoleon. The issue of corrupt public life versus elevated private emotions need not be and increasingly in the novel is not historical in the sense that the initial opposition between Hulot and Montauran is.

The essentially timeless problems that Corentin represents evoke an unhistorical counter image at the novel's climax. Until this point, the clergy of Brittany have been depicted as self-interested obscurantists who play on popular superstition to fan the fires of civil unrest. Suddenly, at Marie's wedding to Montauran, another kind of priest emerges:

> This wedding which was about to be consecrated two feet from the marriage bed, this hurriedly raised altar, this cross, these vessels, this chalice carried secretly by the priest, this scent of incense spreading itself under cornices where only the aroma of meals had ever been present before, this priest who wore only a stole under his cassock, these votive candles burning in the drawing room—all formed a scene which completes the picture of those times, sad to remember, when civil war overturned the most sacred institutions. Religious ceremo-

36. This explanation occurs on page 327. In the revisions to *Les Chouans*, which Balzac made as he was writing *Père Goriot*, Corentin becomes increasingly distasteful and mechanical. In one remarkable passage, he loses even the attractiveness of pursuing Marie because of honest lust, which is replaced by that quintessentially *Goriot* quality, social ambition—see the Garnier edition, p. 527, for the earlier version of this passage, which appears in its final form on p. 328. The inner logic of these revisions eventually results in Balzac's making the Chouans more heroic in the Complete Works of 1845: see, for instance, the revisions to pp. 23–24 of the Garnier edition.

nies then had all the grace of the early mysteries. Children were bap-
tized in the same rooms where their mothers still groaned. As in the
old days, Our Lord came, in simplicity and poverty, to console the
dying. Young girls took their first communions in the room where
they had played the evening before. . . . The priest who preserved in
this way the ancient rituals as long as he could was one of those men
who were faithful to their beliefs at the height of the storm. His voice,
unsullied by the oath which the Republic required, spread words of
peace above the tempest.   [pp. 397–98]

The issue here is not whether such priests actually existed, but what
part this particular priest plays in the total economy of Balzac's fiction and why he appears when he does. Balzac tells us that this scene
"completes" the portrait of the times he has been describing. In fact,
it draws a new picture of them. We hear in the narrator's voice a sudden nostalgia for a time of purer, simpler, and more intense emotions,
a time that escapes the modes of historical and social analysis he had
used to describe the Chouannerie in the novel's opening section. Balzac now wants to annex to these events a powerful, mythic quality,
the "grace of the early mysteries." For all its ill effects, the Chouannerie represents a time when life was simpler and purer, when men
and women were free from those qualities which contract the human
spirit in modern society and which Corentin expresses so fully. In the
grip of his desire to escape the realities which Corentin represents,
Balzac creates a picture in which the Chouannerie becomes not an episode in history during which the forces of reaction make a final attempt to turn the clock back, but a transcendent moment during
which the Savior himself seems to return to the earth in his purity and
meekness.

I do not wish to press too hard on this moment of nostalgia. It can
also be explained more simply, as a local attempt to increase the novel's drama. Everywhere in his final scenes, Balzac is looking for ways
of giving added pathos and grandeur to the tragic deaths of his hero
and heroine. But even at this level we can see the importance of the issues Corentin represents. His base fascination with power in public
life is the perfect foil for the timeless love that has become Balzac's
subject.

"Love is the only emotion which will brook neither the past nor the
future" (p. 152), the narrator tells us at one point in Les Chouans. By

the end of the novel, what began as its subject, the historical clash between the Chouans and the Republic, has become a means of adding
power and dignity to Montauran and Marie's tragic love. Regard
seems to me to go too far when he says that the initial conflict between Hulot and Montauran "is a prelude which creates a savage,
danger-filled atmosphere necessary to lift us to the emotional level of
the events which follow" (p. xxvii). For surely the skirmish that opens
the novel is primarily intended, as we have seen, to represent clashing
historical forces. But his statement nicely illustrates the way in which
the form of the novel changes: in retrospect, the scene also has the
function he describes. Regard's comment perfectly illustrates a larger
theoretical point which is central to my argument throughout this
study. It shows how the meaning of one part of a novel depends upon
our sense of the intention governing the work as a whole and changes
when our sense of the work's overall purpose changes.

In a review written shortly after *Les Chouans* appeared, Balzac uses
Guillaume-Guillon Lethière's historical painting *Brutus* to describe an
important way in which historical fictions can affect readers. He believes that Lethière "wished to reproduce ancient Rome in its entirety,
and . . . Brutus, condemning his sons to death, was merely the most
appropriate means to arrange the founders of the eternal city at the
period he had chosen." The composition seems to use the ancient
buildings and the crowd as a means of focusing on its ostensible subject, but when we withdraw from the picture, we think not just of
Brutus and his sons but of "the great city, its senators, its palaces, and
its people; and the painter's aim is fulfilled—he has made you know
Rome."[37] One could hardly ask for a better description of one way
in which historical fiction can affect us. Coming to know a milieu
separated from us in time can add great richness to our experience of
historical fiction. It is a gift which I associate most vividly with
Cooper, perhaps his greatest gift, though with him we come to know
not buildings and crowds but natural topography, above all the lake
called Glimmerglass in *The Deerslayer*.

37. "Du roman historique et de *Fragoletta*" (1831), in *L'oeuvre de Balzac*, ed.
Albert Beguin, XIV (Paris: Le Club Français de l'Art, 1952), 956–57. This is a review
of a historical novel by Balzac's friend Henri de Latouche; the novel appeared in 1829
and stole some of the thunder from *Les Chouans* at the time. For a discussion of the
correspondence between Balzac and Latouche as they were composing their novels,
see Regard's Introduction, pp. x–xxiii.

Balzac's description of how *Brutus* affects us has an ironic applicability to *Les Chouans,* at least in terms of my own reaction to the novel. What linger in my memory are not the main characters but the Chouans and the thick earthiness that blends them with the fields they till and the animals they tend. But everything about the structure of the novel suggests that this is not the reaction Balzac intends, that the selectivity of my own historicist memory is thwarting his fictional purposes. If he in fact intended his love story primarily to give us a picture of Brittany in 1799, he chose a remarkably inefficient and distracting device. The ruthlessness with which Scott habitually subjects his love stories to the demands of historical representation provides a significant contrast. I believe that in the actual process of reading *Les Chouans,* in which it is difficult to ignore most of the concluding two-thirds of the work, our reaction reverses the process by which Balzac believes we experience *Brutus.* We first attend to milieu; we then increasingly shift our focus toward the love story, as the Chouannerie's explosive power becomes attached to it and history acts as a source of drama, not as the novel's subject.

A Tale of Two Cities

In *Les Chouans,* one kind of historical novel becomes another. In *A Tale of Two Cities,* different uses of history coexist from the beginning. Dickens is fascinated by the French Revolution and its rituals—by the Carmagnole and the guillotinings that have lived in the public imagination ever since his novel appeared. Yet his moralistic and schematic treatment of the Revolution's course suggests that complex historical processes are not his central concern.[38] His novel seems ill adapted to deal with history as a subject, but it uses history with great skill both as pastoral and as a source of drama.

Dickens uses history as pastoral, in that he brings the Revolution to consciousness, not so that we can experience it as a complex totality

38. Gordon Spence, "Dickens as Historical Novelist," *The Dickensian,* 72 (1976), 25, is dissatisfied with Dickens's reduction of the French Revolution to the opposition between the Defarges and the Evrémondes. Sanders, p. 93, notes the novel's greater allegiance to "private resolve than . . . public action." Albert D. Hutter, "Nation and Generation in *A Tale of Two Cities,*" *PMLA,* 93 (1978), 448–62, shows that the novel correlates politics and certain aspects of the Freudian family romance; he states that in the process "Dickens distorted the reality of the French Revolution" (p. 453).

or understand its workings, but so that contemporary fears of lower-class unrest can be expressed and then laid to rest.[39] He achieves this purpose partly through the narrator's direct warnings that if people are crushed, they will revolt, which sound stern but also imply that if people are not crushed, they will not revolt—that with intelligence and good will, social problems can be solved. But the main way in which he achieves this end is formal and in a sense magical. The novel functions as an incantation that raises the specter of revolution and then dispels it, through the creation of a grand, simple, repetitive pattern of exhumations and burials.[40]

A few examples of this pattern will suffice for our present purposes. Dr. Manette begins it, by being unexpectedly "recalled to life." It is important to recognize that his return is not entirely welcome. Mr. Lorry and even Lucy Manette find that his reappearance fills them with uneasiness, even dread. Here, for instance, is Lucy's reaction to Mr. Lorry's news that her father is still alive:

> A shiver ran through her frame, and from it through his. She said, in a low, distinct, awe-stricken voice, as if she were saying it in a dream,
> "I am going to see his Ghost! It will be his Ghost—not him!"[41]

In the remainder of the novel there are a series of attempts to lay to rest the ghostly part of Dr. Manette. When it rises for the last time in

---

39. Critics are divided on the importance they assign in *A Tale* to the threat of lower-class rebellion in England. Nicholas Rance, *The Historical Novel and Popular Politics in Nineteenth-Century England* (London: Vision Press, 1975), pp. 83–101, considers Dickens's fear of revolution central, as does John P. McWilliams, Jr., "Progress without Politics: *A Tale of Two Cities*," *Clio*, 7 (1977), 19–31, and (to a lesser extent) Lee Sterrenberg, "Psychoanalysis and the Iconography of Revolution," *Victorian Studies*, 19 (1975), 241–64. Spence, p. 29, believes that such fears are there in the novel, but are not its "governing factor." William Oddie, "Dickens and the Indian Mutiny," *The Dickensian*, 68 (1972), 14–15, states that "the *Tale* clearly does not refer to the dangers of revolution in England." McWilliams, p. 23, cites a letter of 1855 in which Dickens compares the current state of England to that of France directly before the Revolution; it is also worth noting that fearing lower-class unrest or rebelliousness is not the same as holding the considered opinion that a revolution is imminent.

40. Both McWilliams, p. 29, and Robert Alter, "The Demons of History in Dickens's *Tale*," *Novel*, 2 (1969), 139, note the importance of ritualistic action in *A Tale*.

41. *A Tale of Two Cities*, The Oxford Illustrated Dickens (London: Oxford University Press, 1949), p. 24; Bk. 1, ch. 4; subsequent references appear in my text.

his long-lost written denunciation of the entire Evrémonde family, this "Ghost" necessitates Carton's sacrifice to lay it to rest. The logic of these burials and exhumations is one of magic or dreams, not of reason; it depends upon patterns, imagistic relations, and the use of religious myth. As a minor example of Dickens's skill in handling these elements, let me cite a single way in which he associates the destruction of Carton with the burial of Manette's threatening, ghostly side. One of the attempts to bury that aspect of Dr. Manette early in the novel comes when Mr. Lorry persuades the Doctor to give up the old workbench he had used when he made shoes in the Bastille. When Manette leaves for a short trip, the bench is destroyed:

> On the night of the day on which he left the house, Mr. Lorry went into his room with a chopper, saw, chisel, and hammer, attended by Miss Pross carrying a light. There, with closed doors, and in a mysterious and guilty manner, Mr. Lorry hacked the shoemaker's bench to pieces, while Miss Pross held the candle as if she were assisting at a murder—for which, indeed, in her grimness, she was no unsuitable figure. The burning of the body (previously reduced to pieces convenient for the purpose) was commenced without delay in the kitchen fire; and the tools, shoes, and leather, were buried in the garden. [p. 195; Bk. 2, ch. 19]

Two pages later, Carton requests that Darnay and Lucy allow him to visit them from time to time, thinking of him as a "piece of furniture, tolerated for its old service, and taken no notice of" (p. 197; Bk. 2, ch. 20). Like the workbench with which he is thus associated, Carton will eventually have to be destroyed. His execution completes in a definitive way the pattern we have been tracing and at the same time transforms it. With his death, he buries Darnay's ancestral guilt, the threatening specter that returned to life with Dr. Manette. But by charging Carton's death with religious associations, Dickens makes it a new kind of unburying in the novel, a religious "resurrection" that returns Carton to the purity of his boyhood: "Long ago, when he had been famous among his earliest competitors as a youth of great promise, he had followed his father to the grave. . . . These solemn words, which had been read at his father's grave, arose in his mind . . . 'I am the resurrection and the life, saith the Lord . . .'" (pp. 297–98; Bk. 3, ch. 9). Thus Dickens is able to exorcise the threat of guilt and revolutionary violence from both parts of the pattern of burial and exhumation.

Carton's comic counterpart is Jerry Cruncher. With Cruncher, the social aspect of Dickens's ritual exorcism of the French Revolution is considerably more obvious than it is with Carton. At the opening of the novel, he is one bourgeois stereotype of the lower classes—dirty, ignorant, irreverent, and violent. He beats his wife for praying, an activity he refers to as "flopping down." A body snatcher or "Resurrection-Man" himself, Jerry at the beginning of the novel looks forward to grooming his son for the trade. But living in Paris during the Terror teaches him that he had better mend his ways, and he decides to earn his living by burying dead bodies, not by resurrecting them, as he tells Mr. Lorry when that gentleman discovers the nature of his former work:

> Upon that there stool, at that there Bar, sets that there boy of mine, brought up and growed up to be a man, wot will errand you, message you, general-light-job you, till your heels is where your head is, if such should be your wishes. . . . let that there boy keep his father's place [at Lorry's bank, where Jerry worked during the day], and take care of his mother; don't blow upon that boy's father—do not do it, sir—and let that father go into the line of the reg'ler diggin', and make amends for what he would have un-dug—if it wos so—by diggin' of 'em in with a will, and with conwictions respectin' the futur' keepin' of 'em safe. [p. 292; Bk. 3, ch. 9]

By the end of the novel, Jerry has lost even his antipathy toward religion: "My opinions respectin' flopping has undergone a change, and . . . wot I only hope with all my heart as Mrs. Cruncher may be a flopping at the present time" (p. 346; Bk. 3, ch. 14). Cruncher's change of heart is a comic version of Carton's sacrificial transfiguration at the close of the novel.[42] Both do not really explain the French Revolution. Instead, they project an attitude toward it and toward

---

42. Sylvère Monod, "Some Stylistic Devices in A Tale of Two Cities," in Dickens the Craftsman: Strategies of Presentation, ed. Robert B. Partlow, Jr. (Carbondale: Southern Illinois University Press, 1970), pp. 168–69, notes that most readers have not found Jerry a particularly successful example of Dickensian comedy. Perhaps this is because he plays so integral a part in the novel's symbolic structure and hence lacks the freedom of Dickens's best comic figures.

lower-class rebelliousness in the present, "solving" their threatening aspects by putting them into an esthetically conclusive form. The not inconsiderable part of Dickens which positively delights in creating scenes of destruction is a great help to him here, for the more chaos he can fit into his larger pattern without destroying it, the stronger the esthetic and ideological impact of the pattern will be.

In *A Tale*, history acts as a pastoral setting, to allay fears of lower-class revolution for Dickens's contemporary readers. But the novel contains another use of history: it employs history as a source of dramatic power to vivify a timeless story. Balancing the various motives that underly the novel is a complex business. I believe, however, that the use of history as a source of drama proves strong enough to determine the shape of the novel as a whole, while the use of history as pastoral operates more on a subliminal level.

A Tale of Two Cities is ultimately about the sacrifice of Sidney Carton, and Carton's character and actions have at base little to do with the French Revolution as a historical phenomenon. Dickens shows where the heart of his novel lies when he allows it to end with the unhistorical Carton's taking the place of Charles Darnay as sacrificial hero. Because of his connections with France and England, the old and the new regimes, Monsieur the Marquis and the daughter of one of his victims, Darnay might have played a role like that of Edward Waverley, if *A Tale* had been written by Scott. But the problem his replacement Carton represents is personal, not historical. He is one of a familiar series of male lead characters in Dickens, the man without a will. It is possible to imagine a historical novel in which Carton's lack of will could be given a specifically historical coloring or explanation, though I have already suggested that there are inherent problems in dealing with the depths of men's souls in historical fiction. But in fact, Dickens makes no attempt whatever to connect Carton's inner malady with the historical side of the novel or indeed to explain it in any way at all: his sadistic and overbearing employer, Stryver, provides a further expression of the problem, but not an explanation of it. Similarly, Dickens uses the historical setting of *A Tale* not to explain Carton's problem, but to give cathartic power to its resolution.

The final paragraphs of *A Tale* present in the form of a prophetic speech Carton's vision of the future as he is about to be guillotined. Taken as a whole, the way in which the speech progresses encapsulates in an almost diagrammatic way the relationship between history and Carton's sacrifice. The first paragraph recalls the historical actors in the novel:

> I see Barsad, and Cly, Defarge, The Vengeance, the Juryman, the Judge, long ranks of the new oppressors who have risen on the destruction of the old, perishing by this retributive instrument, before it shall cease out of its present use. I see a beautiful city and a brilliant people rising from this abyss, and, in their struggles to be truly free, in their triumphs and defeats, through long long years to come, I see the evil of this time and of the previous time of which this is the natural birth, gradually making expiation for itself and wearing out. [p. 357; Bk. 3, ch. 15]

Even if this were all that Carton says, it would not represent the culminating moment in a vision intent on depicting historical process, though it does help the work's secondary purpose of laying the Revolution to rest.[43] The primary effect of the paragraph lies elsewhere. It serves as a rhetorical device, which is the reason why many readers find it and the speech as a whole offensively facile. Dickens uses Carton's rhetoric to heighten our wonder at the sublime sacrifice he is about to make. Our anger at revolutionary injustice is transmuted into pity for its victims through this reminder that the evildoers will be punished, every last one of them. Similarly, we are struck by Carton's magnanimity, his ability to imagine a great future for the nation that is about to execute him.

As Carton's speech proceeds through four more paragraphs, the controlling use of history in the novel asserts itself ever more strongly. His vision narrows from a utopian view of France in the future to a series of pictures of the individuals who are the reason for his sacrifice. He sees Dr. Manette, Darnay, Lucy, her children, and even her grandchildren blessing him for what he has done. Finally he sees himself become a legend:

---

43. Fleishman, pp. 122–23, takes the first paragraph of Carton's speech as evidence that the novel expresses an exalted vision of historical process. I have already noted that a disadvantage of Fleishman's mode of defining historical fiction ("What makes a historical novel historical is the active presence of a concept of history as a shaping force"—p. 15) is that to explain the obvious fact that a work like *A Tale* is a historical novel, and a powerful one at that, he must discover in it this sort of significance.

I see that child who lay upon her bosom and who bore my name, a man winning his way up in that path of life which once was mine. I see him winning it so well, that my name is made illustrious there by the light of his. I see the blots I threw upon it, faded away. I see him, foremost of just judges and honoured men, bringing a boy of my name, with a forehead that I know and golden hair, to this place— then fair to look upon, with not a trace of this day's disfigure- ment—and I hear him tell the child my story, with a tender and a fal- tering voice.

It is a far, far better thing that I do, than I have ever done; it is a far, far better rest that I go to than I have ever known.   [p. 358; Bk. 3, ch. 14]

Carton's final speech, beginning with a vision of France transformed but ending with the picture of Lucy's grandchild listening to a story, epitomizes the most important way in which Dickens employs history in *A Tale.* The sacrifice of Carton is rendered imaginatively powerful by the French Revolution, just as the tale which Lucy's grandchild hears gains poignancy from being told on the very spot where Carton suffered. In depicting this sacrifice, Dickens uses the powerful emo- tions he has generated by re-creating one of the nineteenth century's collective nightmares to intensify our reaction to a character who functions not as a symbol of historical process, but as the focus for our timeless hopes and fears.

History as Drama in Scott

Scott's fascination with the complexities of history makes it un- likely that he would produce many novels or even many scenes which use history primarily to vivify a timeless tragedy, as do Balzac in *Les Chouans* and Dickens in *A Tale.* The use of history as an energizing force pervades Scott's works, but it is nearly always subordinated to other historical purposes. Scott's most striking use of history as a source of dramatic energy occurs precisely where we would expect it, not in one of his historical novels, but in his novel most firmly set in the present. In *St. Ronan's Well,* he attempted a novel set at a con- temporary Scottish spa, though with misgivings about whether he possessed "the exquisite touch which renders ordinary common-place things and characters interesting."[44] In the end, I think most readers

44. *Journal* (14 March 1826). Scott uses the phrase to describe Jane Austen. He shows similar misgivings in his retrospective Introduction to the novel.

would agree that he lacked this touch. The best things he provides in its place come from history. Probably the most valuable part of the novel is its background depiction of the processes at work transforming the region in which it is set and the family with which it primarily deals. A rather more dubious legacy involves the main characters, and above all the heroine, Clara Mowbray, whose Gothic fate gains forcefulness from evocations of the past, especially in a scene in which the portraits in the family gallery look down upon her and shudder at her impending doom. The scene has its effectiveness, but the view of the past which vivifies it departs from Scott's characteristic historical vision. Instead of dialectical subtlety, we have simple, terrible, unexplained fatality. To be sure, the simplification here is functional, for it helps to give Clara her dramatic force. And the novel is in the end Clara's; its more subtly portrayed background never meshes convincingly with the foreground she occupies.

St. Ronan's Well does not reflect Scott at his best. Its weakness shows how little Scott can do when, having set a novel in the present, he finds himself dealing primarily with individuals, not with history; it also reveals more general limitations inherent in giving a dominant structural place to the use of history as a source of drama. Such a use of history, to be sure, avoids certain problems. There is little danger that present concerns will swamp the past completely, as often happens when history is used as pastoral: an author using history as a source of drama is much more likely to indulge in exoticism than to press an identification between present and past. The problem of representing the entire spectrum of human experience in history also largely disappears, as the focus falls on individual characters and on a sense of history as power and movement. When in *Les Chouans* Balzac shifts from using the past as his subject to using the past as a source of drama, he is moving from a problematic to an unproblematic form, and he obtains a strong ending for his novel. But as always in historical fiction, he pays a price for strengthening his action in this way, as does Dickens in *A Tale of Two Cities.* Many of the formal strains that the depiction of history usually causes in historical fiction are absent in *A Tale,* which is in fact less "baggy" than most of Dickens's nonhistorical works. But words like "sentimental" are hard to avoid when we think of the novel's effect as a whole, however powerful we may find it. Most readers are likely to feel, with some justification, that the use of the past as a source of drama produces the least dignified kind of historical fiction. In the next chapter, we will consider works in which the problems inherent in representing history in fiction are much more evident, but which at their best achieve a level of historical insight denied to novels employing history in less strenuous ways.

3

History as Subject

The novels I discussed in the previous chapter use history in a variety of ways—to explore contemporary political and social concerns, to express and resolve personal feelings, to give energy to a love story. But in none of them does history serve as the primary subject. It is possible to analyze them as if they were principally concerned with embodying visions of history, but if we do so, we falsify the experience they are intended to convey. In *Henry Esmond*, for instance, the depiction of the Pretender is puzzling in its inadequacy as history, but intelligible as an expression of Thackeray's personal terror at and consequent defensiveness before the past. Similarly, we would simply have to write off large portions of *Les Chouans* if we believed that Balzac intended to depict a historical moment instead of a timeless love story throughout the novel. In making historical depiction subordinate to other ends, the novels we have discussed are typical of most standard historical fiction after Scott, particularly in England. I now want to concentrate on works in which our esthetic pleasure flows from representations of and meditations upon history itself. Such novels as Anatole France's *Les dieux ont soif*, George Eliot's *Romola*, Victor Hugo's *Quatrevingt-treize*, and Leo Tolstoy's *War and Peace* all concern themselves centrally with history, whether this means representing historical milieux or great historical figures or the workings of historical process itself. In these works and others like them, the mimetic problems inherent in historical fiction which were the subject of my first chapter are fully apparent.

Historical novelists whose works center on history are usually not content to give a panoramic view of an age. They wish to understand, evaluate, and sometimes to rebel against or accommodate themselves to what they have presented. They are faced, in other words, with the problem of giving not only shape but meaning to history. One way in which this can be done is by inserting essays, brief or long, into a novel, but many authors are not satisfied with this solution. They wish to use their plotted actions and characters to dramatize directly the meaning they have discovered in historical process. Because of the state of literary theory and practice during the period in which the works with which I am concerned were written, this dramatization is likely to depend upon characters and scenes that function as historical symbols.

The symbol has been a central and powerful literary technique from the Romantics to our own day. But my earlier discussion of historical mimesis casts doubt on the adequacy of symbols to represent all levels of human existence at once, and particularly to represent those levels that are most characteristically historical. For critics who hold what I have called an "individualist" view of literary mimesis, such as Dorothy Van Ghent, the demand that novelistic characters function as "spiritual symbols" quickly becomes a way of downgrading and sometimes eliding history altogether, in favor of the universal human qualities to be found in the depths of the human soul—"the personal, private and therefore universal and everlasting" aspects of life, as Aldous Huxley puts it. Critics who work in the Hegelian tradition and have a genuinely historical interest in the "concrete universal" pose a more serious challenge to the view that symbolism has grave limitations for historical mimesis. I have already given a critique of a powerful literary category based on Hegelian identity theory and the concrete universal, Lukács's notion of "typicality": let me merely add here that Lukácsian typicality, because of its inherently social nature, looks very different indeed from the kind of representation which Anglo-American criticism has traditionally viewed as symbolic.[1] I

1. For Hegelian identity theory and the Frankfurt School's critique of that theory, see Martin Jay, *The Dialectical Imagination: A History of the Frankfurt School and the Institute of Social Research, 1923–1950* (Boston: Little, Brown, 1973). For a cri-

would also claim that making analogies to earlier literary practice—such as Dante's "figural" representation—is beside the point, because one consequence of the rise of historicism is precisely to make representation like Dante's no longer ontologically plausible, however esthetically satisfying. The historicist interest in the unique, irreducible elements of historical life makes achieving symbolic universality of any kind intensely problematical. Erich Auerbach expresses one consequence of the historicist vision when he asserts that in literature "the universally human or poetic factor . . . can only be apprehended in its particular historical forms, and there is no intelligible way of expressing its absolute essence."[2] The use of symbols, in the Coleridgean sense in which I am employing the term, tends to rely on capturing just such an absolute essence. Symbols can do many things, but they are unlikely to preserve the evolving web of concrete social relations which constitutes historical existence, as the inadequacy of such a metaphor as "web" itself suggests.

Instead of arguing further on a theoretical level, I propose to look at a number of novels that attempt, with varying degrees of success, to give shape and meaning to historical process, all but one of them by primarily symbolic means. My first two examples, *Les dieux ont soif* and *Romola*, are works in which symbolic representation helps to impoverish the depiction both of history and of human complexity as well. My next example, *Quatrevingt-treize*, is a powerful and successful work; in discussing it, I shall try to discover the conditions and limitations of its success in creating powerful historical symbols. I shall then turn to the greatest historical novel, *War and Peace*, for an alternative mode of depicting historical process, one that does not depend primarily on symbols and hence sets the stage for my exploration of Scott's historical fiction in the remainder of this book. Throughout, my discussion focuses on the use of fictional characters to represent history, and the chapter closes by examining character in the Waverley Novels.

---

tique of Jay's stress on "non-identity theory," see Fredric Jameson, *The Political Unconscious* (Ithaca: Cornell University Press, 1981), p. 52, n. 29.

2. Erich Auerbach, *Literary Language and Its Public in Late Latin Antiquity and in the Middle Ages* (1958), trans. Ralph Manheim (Princeton: Princeton University Press, 1965), p. 13.

Les dieux ont soif

In *Les dieux ont soif*, Anatole France recreates the milieu of the Reign of Terror during the French Revolution and gives some sense of the larger historical processes at work in the period. But he depicts public life and historical process only to show their unimportance. A minor scene from the novel illustrates his belief in the primacy of unchanging human passions throughout history. At the height of the Terror, Julie, the wife of an unjustly imprisoned aristocrat, disguises herself as a man to avoid molestation or suspicion in her daily visits to a garden outside her husband's prison in hopes of catching a glimpse of him. In due course she becomes aware that a kindly older man is observing her; once, as it begins to rain, he benevolently offers her a place under his umbrella. Then comes a moment typical of the novel:

> Julie, in her misery and solitude, was touched by the gentleman's discreet sympathy. . . . She told him sweetly, in her clear voice, that she accepted his offer. But at the sound of that voice and warned, perhaps, by her subtly feminine odor, he quickly retreated, leaving the young woman at the mercy of the downpour. She understood and could not help smiling, despite her worries.[3]

Throughout *Les dieux*, we feel that the same old passions persist, even under the nose of the Terror itself, and that they are what really matter.

A similar scene demonstrates one way in which France seeks to embody historical forces. He is describing a group of Parisians waiting in line for food made scarce by the dislocations caused by the Revolution. His view of history is perfectly mirrored in the way some members of the crowd degrade the patriotic song "Ça ira" to describe the way in which man's physical desires "go on":

> At each word, at each act, at each posture capable of setting off the off-color humor of the amiable French people, a group of young libertines [*libertins*] sang "Ça Ira," despite the protests of an old Jacobin,

3. I translate from *Les dieux ont soif* (1912; rpt. Paris: Le Livre de Poche, n.d.), p. 200; subsequent references appear in my text.

who was angry that anyone should compromise with such jokes the republican faith in a future of justice and happiness. . . .

Suddenly a whiff of overpowering rottenness came from a sewer, and many were seized with nausea. . . . A rumor circulated with constantly changing words, full of anguish and terror. One person asked if there were some sort of animal buried there, or perhaps some poison put there malevolently, or more likely one of the victims of the September Massacres, a nobleman or priest, had been forgotten in a neighboring cellar. . . . The Parisians feared the vengeance of those aristocrats who, dead, had the power to poison them. [pp. 53–54]

This scene contains an element that Julie's encounter with the gentleman lacks. The stench from the sewers is clearly symbolic, in a way things in *Esmond* or *Les Chouans* never are. Exactly what it symbolizes is another question. Lukács seems to believe that the stench symbolizes the persistence of old-style property relations, which are poisoning the Revolution. This scene is presumably a source for his comment that France "has no objection to the method of terror as such; he sees, however, an insoluble contradictoriness in the social aims of the Jacobins: the 'liberty, equality and fraternity' which had been fought for with such heroism and sacrifice by the best of them leads to increasing misery for the liberated working masses, as long as the economic basis of capitalism remains unshaken."[4] I believe that the novel provides little evidence to support this interpretation. In my opinion, the stench is more likely to represent the base realities of man's nature, which cannot be eradicated by executing members of an offending class, and to which political leaders like Robespierre succumb in an exaggerated fashion precisely because they ignore them— "Ça ira." But there may be no way of deciding with certainty. France's objective narration leaves the matter vague, perhaps purposely so—the point is to give a feeling that some larger force controls these Parisians, but to avoid pausing long enough to consider what that force is and whether it is reducible to individual passions. The vagueness here also reinforces the novel's chief source of pathos—its vision of human beings as victims, threatened by history, by other people, by their own desires.

In other parts of the novel, France seeks to represent historical process by giving certain characters symbolic overtones. The heroine,

4. Georg Lukács, *The Historical Novel* (1937), trans. Hannah and Stanley Mitchell (London: Merlin, 1962), p. 258.

Elodie, is a typical Parisienne but also a symbol for France itself, as she falls in love with the Jacobin Gamelin, admires him first for his clemency and then for his murderousness, and finally settles on a more moderate lover after Gamelin has been executed with Robespierre and the Terror has ended. Giving her this symbolic resonance demands a high degree of stylization and tends to reduce her depiction to a series of operatic gestures: thus she describes the way to her bedroom to successive lovers using exactly the same words. Despite their slickness, such techniques are reasonably effective in giving *Les dieux* a larger historical dimension of a kind. But France's depiction of Elodie has little else to recommend it. It interferes with the psychological realism we might expect in another kind of novel and in doing so exemplifies the difficulty of uniting a central interest in depicting historical process with creating characterization in depth. We might excuse this lack of psychological depth as necessary in the kind of novel France has chosen to write, were the vision of history it helps to produce more convincing. But it is not. If one is going to reduce history to individual emotions, one ought at least to depict those emotions in a way that seems humanly true. But France fails in this, because of the very superficiality of depiction which allows us to accept Elodie as a woman and a historical symbol at the same time. Upon reflection, we realize that although we may accept her as a fictional convention, we do not believe in her either as an adequate picture of a human being or as an adequate symbol of the spirit of France during the French Revolution. We know that Elodie's mindless, fickle sensuality does not adequately represent the human qualities that made the French Revolution occur in the first place. And the historical vision she reflects—that history involves a wavering public opinion driven partly by base human desires and partly by deep, dark forces that remain conveniently unknowable—is just as inadequate. If we believed in Elodie as a person, we might believe in the larger vision she represents. But because of the patness with which France merges her role as a portrait of the typical Parisienne with her role as a symbol of historical process, we believe in neither. France's vision of historical process can seem striking when it is merely a hint, a suggestion at the edge of our focus. But when our vision rests upon it directly in the person of Elodie, it is less impressive. Elodie as a symbol reveals more than France intends.

Romola

France's failure in *Les dieux* might seem simply the result of his reductive attitude toward history. Why bother to write about history at
all, if it's so trivial, and if life in the past is only superficially different
from life in our own day? Of course there are answers to this philistine question. An author might feel the need to demythologize the
past, or might believe that the unchanging human essence reveals itself more clearly at certain times than at others. Yet the question has
a point: any author who writes historical fiction without a positive interest in historical particularity is assuming a number of liabilities
without having access to their compensating virtues. But more is at
stake in the failure of *Les dieux* than the question of France's attitude
toward history. The limits of creating characters who function as historical symbols reveal themselves just as clearly in novels that view
history with the utmost seriousness. George Eliot's *Romola* is such a
novel.

Until very recently, *Romola* has passed largely unappreciated. Most
readers have considered this novel of Renaissance Florence a heap of
lifeless period details, organized around a heroine whose character
and problems have more to do with the nineteenth century than with
the fifteenth. Quite a different picture emerges from Felicia Bonaparte's recent study, which discovers in *Romola* a complex, learned
symbolic structure designed to realize "Eliot's epic intention to explore the historical confrontation, and to trace the influence on Western civilization, of the pagan and Christian cultures in their antholog-
ical forms."[5] Let me say at once that in my view Bonaparte has
revealed, with great skill and remarkable scholarship, Eliot's intention
in *Romola*. She shows with clarity and nuance, for instance, that
Romola's husband represents a vision of the Greek heritage, that her
brother represents a vision of Christianity, and that her attempt to
thread a path between the two meditates upon the fusion of pagan
and Christian elements in the spiritual heritage of modern Europe.
Bonaparte certainly knows what Eliot intended to do in *Romola*, but
her assumption that Eliot perfectly succeeded in realizing her intention, which reverses the nearly unanimous judgment of critics from

5. Felicia Bonaparte, *The Triptych and the Cross: The Central Myths of George
Eliot's Poetic Imagination* (New York: New York University Press, 1979), p. 80.

Eliot's day to our own, is cause for uneasiness. To say that the novel is really an epic or really poetic and hence will be misread if it is judged as a realist novel won't in my judgment quite do. Such a tactic might seem to reflect a reasonable insistence on the importance of approaching works with proper generic expectations; in this case, however, it subverts the historical foundations of genre altogether by its assumption that poetic, epic/mythic, and novelistic forms can all be made to coalesce, in a simple and unproblematic way, by authorial or critical fiat. Bonaparte's attempt to find in *Romola* a successful poetic novel constitutes a kind of Hegelian identity theory run wild, without dialectic, contradiction, or levels of mediation to give it credibility. The wish to make disparate kinds and levels of reality coalesce in a giant synthesis is surely present in Eliot herself, or at least in one side of Eliot, the side that yearns for heroic fulfillment, for St. Theresas, not Dorothea Brookes. But it is one thing to accept Eliot's choice to end a novel like *The Mill on the Floss* with a moment of mythic fulfillment, and quite another to imagine that such a representational mode could have guided the work as a whole, or could be fully realized in *Romola*.

Bonaparte has discovered precisely why *Romola*, though a significant work in many respects, fails as historical fiction—why its central characters seem anachronistic, why its historical detail seems heavy and unfunctional. Her analysis does not so much contradict earlier judgments of the novel as provide an explanation for them. *Romola*'s abstract schematization of cultural forces and its lifeless depiction of historical milieu are two sides of the same coin, providing yet another example of the principle that standard novels cannot depict all levels of human experience simultaneously. To use Siegfried Kracauer's terms, the schema on which Eliot has chosen to base her novel is too general and abstract to "rouse" to life the particularities that the other side of her artistic personality leads her to put in the novel, and that the standard novel as a form itself tends to demand. There appears to be a fundamental ontological contradiction here. Standard novels, especially as written by George Eliot when she is at her best, give a picture of reality which implies the importance of everyday life as lived; but the kind of symbolism on which *Romola* is based implies the unimportance of such particularity, stressing instead the large abstract movements of the cultural *Geist*. Ways around this contradiction might be found, but the chief artistic failing of *Romola* is that Eliot does not recognize that this problem exists and hence feels no need to deal with it.

The symbolic structure underlying *Romola* also goes far toward explaining the novel's palpable anachronism. The shift of focus away from representing social interactions leaves a vacuum, and it is only natural that Eliot's own contemporary concerns should rush in to fill it.[6] Such a result is furthered by the general assumption of an essential congruence between disparate realities upon which the novel as a whole is based. This is not to say that Eliot mysteriously loses her ability to depict social interaction in *Romola*: the novel in fact provides acute and persuasive insights into Florentine political life. But the pressure of the novel's dominant intention consistently shifts the focus elsewhere.

Eliot develops the relationship between her chief fictional character, Romola, and her chief historical character, Savonarola, in a revealing way. Scott might have created an indirectly illuminating or a merely causal connection between these two characters. Eliot does neither. Instead, she equates the two in terms of her own deepest moral concerns as a writer of the nineteenth century. When toward the end of the novel, Romola looks back at her decision to leave her husband, she makes a discovery that the novel invites us as readers to share: "It flashed upon her mind that the problem before her was essentially the same as that which had lain before Savonarola—the problem where the sacredness of obedience ended, and where the sacredness of rebellion began."[7] But the problems simply aren't the same, because of the utterly different ideological contexts in which they exist. Romola's problems are interesting, but they are conceived of in entirely nineteenth-century terms and ought not to be merged with Savonarola's. By pushing the identification of Savonarola and Romola too far, Eliot underlines the tenuousness of the connection between Romola's prob-

---

6. Among the many critics who have noted that Eliot in *Romola* projects nineteenth-century problems onto the past is W. J. Harvey, *The Art of George Eliot* (London: Chatto & Windus, 1961), p. 114.

7. *Romola*, ed. J. W. Cross, Cabinet Edition (Edinburgh: Blackwood, n.d.) II, 273. Eliot herself makes the same point in a slightly weaker way in a letter to Richard Holt Hutton, 8 August 1863, *The George Eliot Letters*, ed. Gordon S. Haight, IV (New Haven: Yale University Press, 1955), 97: "The great problem of her [Romola's] life . . . essentially coincides with a chief problem in Savonarola's."

lems and the historical setting onto which they are projected. The identification of Savonarola and Romola is one of many indications throughout the novel that Eliot has not achieved the dialectical richness of a novel like *Middlemarch*, but has instead yielded to her strong impulse toward heroic representation of timeless truths centering on the individual. And as happens so often in such cases, these "timeless" concerns turn out to bear a strong resemblance to the time-bound concerns of the author who imagines them.

Our discussion of *Romola* implies that, whatever Eliot intended it to be, it is probably best read as yet another example of the use of history as pastoral in English historical fiction. By treating it as such, in spite of itself, we confirm Curtis Dahl's opinion that this mode dominates Victorian historical fiction.[8] *Romola* has considerable interest if seen as an attempt by a great moralist to examine certain ethical and cultural concerns by projecting them onto the past. It is nevertheless likely that those who value Eliot precisely when she resists her impulse toward the epic, poetic, and heroic will return to *Middlemarch* for a vision of historical existence infinitely more rich and compelling than that adumbrated by the symbolic abstractions of *Romola*.

Quatrevingt-treize

George Eliot's wish to write a "poetic" historical novel may not have been successfully realized in *Romola*, but it suggests a means of pursuing further the question of the powers and limitations of symbolic representation in historical fiction. No great English poet attempted a historical novel during the nineteenth century; in France, the situation is different. The relevant figure is Victor Hugo. In *Quatrevingt-treize*, Hugo turns his immense powers to the task of creating in prose fiction a historical vision that will redeem the past and future of his country. *Quatrevingt-treize*, like *Les Chouans*, has as its subject one of the monarchist uprisings that took place in Normandy and Brittany after the French Revolution. One indication of the different role history plays in the two novels is that whereas Balzac chooses to write about the revolt of the Chouans, a last gasp

8. Curtis Dahl, whose work on Bulwer-Lytton I discuss in the introductory section of Chapter 2, lists *Romola* among his examples of works that project present concerns into the past.

of royalist reaction, Hugo concerns himself with the Vendée, an earlier, more important revolt. Balzac finds an out-of-the-way corner of history in which to set his story; Hugo seizes upon the historical mainstream.

Les Chouans and *Quatrevingt-treize* also differ markedly in their forms. After its introductory section, *Les Chouans* becomes a straightforward single-protagonist action, built around Marie de Verneuil. The pattern that dominates *Quatrevingt-treize* does not emerge so quickly. Instead, Hugo uses a technique like the one we find in Dickens's most sprawling works, creating a series of seemingly unconnected lines of action which converge at the climax of his novel. Hugo's narrative presence is even stronger than that of Dickens; this is one reason why we feel from the beginning that his novel's disparate elements will eventually be made to cohere. But *Quatrevingt-treize* also possesses from the beginning a less obvious source of unity, which is best approached through considering the ways in which different parts of the novel represent historical process and convey historical meaning.

Quatrevingt-treize contains two kinds of historical mimesis. Much of the novel uses allegorical characters to depict the duel between revolution and monarchism. Detaching themselves from this sort of depiction are quite different scenes, which have great emotional power and which seem to mean nothing more than the experiences they depict; they seem released from history and indeed from time itself. I want ultimately to argue that both kinds of novelistic texture in fact represent attempts by Hugo to convey the same vision of historical process. But first I shall clarify this duality of texture by considering the novel's greatest scene, "The Massacre of Saint Bartholomew."

The "Massacre" occurs late in the novel. When we reach it, the ideological structure of the work has become clear, and we recognize it in the physical setting of the episode. Lantenac, the representative of royalism, is besieged in a feudal tower by Cimourdain, who represents the Revolution. Thrown over the gorge separating the revolutionary forces and the feudal tower is a bridge-chateau which has as its main room a library and which has been shut off from both forces, except that the royalists command the means to destroy it. And they threaten to do so, if attacked, for they have locked inside it three children stolen from the revolutionary soldiers. The allegory is obvious:

the future, represented by the children, is threatened by the murderous collision of revolution and reaction. The opposition between revolution and royalism which dominates much of the novel has by this point been largely superseded by an opposition between both and the future. The narrator has informed us a few pages earlier that Cimourdain and Lantenac, because of their opposed inflexibility, are "to a certain extent the same man":

> The bronze mask of civil war has two faces, one turned toward the past, the other turned toward the future, but both are equally tragic. Lantenac was the first of these faces, Cimourdain the second; yet the bitter smile of Lantenac was covered with the shadow of night, while on the fated face of Cimourdain there fell the first rays of dawn.[9]

One indication that their political opposition masks a more fundamental similarity is that neither man will hesitate to destroy the records of the past in the library, if only he can triumph in the present. This heedlessness of time as process makes both men dangerous to future generations. Gauvain, who is a revolutionary general but also Lantenac's nephew and is thus clearly intended to be a mediating figure, wishes to avoid destroying the records. All three characters are obviously intended to represent historical forces, but they do so in a way that we describe as "allegorical" when we use the term more or less pejoratively, to refer to characters or objects that have slight intrinsic interest and need to be translated into other terms to gain real significance. The mechanical quality of Hugo's allegory and the thinness of the characters involved in it are indications of the problems involved in the use of fictional characters to embody directly a larger historical meaning, problems we have already met in France and Eliot.

The "Massacre" itself is different. In it, the three captive children, oblivious to their danger, "massacre" a priceless tome containing the apocryphal Gospel of St. Bartholomew, by ripping it to pieces. Hugo's genius is evident in the tone he creates to describe this un-

9. I translate from *Quatrevingt-treize*, ed. and intro. J. Boudout (Paris: Classiques Garnier, 1963), p. 314; subsequent references appear in my text; roman numerals refer to Boudout's excellent introduction. As the quotations will have indicated, Hugo ranks the Revolution somewhat higher than the reaction even in the process of substantially equating them from the perspective of the future.

likely event. He makes us feel the venerable qualities of the book as an artifact, though not as a piece of religious exposition. We also feel the incipient brutality of its destroyers:

> The appetite for destruction exists. . . . To tear into pieces history, fables, science, miracles false and true, Church Latin, superstitions, fanatical beliefs, to shred an entire religion from top to bottom—this is quite a task for three giants, and even for three children. [pp. 344–45]

"Et même pour trois enfants"—the phrase captures Hugo's indulgent, wondering love for the child as animal and angel; elsewhere in the passage, he coins the term "anges de proie" to describe them. Overwhelming any regret for the destruction of an irreplaceable artifact is a love for the children's naive power. They partake of a radical innocence in which seeming destructiveness is the sign of an energy that creates a higher beauty, the beauty of life itself. The hallmark of their inflexible opposite, Cimourdain, is "refoulement"—repression. The massacre ends in this way:

> Georgette picked up from the floor one of the pages, stood up, leaned against the window which came up to her chin, and began to shred the large page into little pieces.
> Seeing this, Renée-Jean and Gros-Alain did the same. They gathered and ripped, gathered again and ripped again, throwing the pieces through the window as Georgette had; and, page by page, crumbled by these eager little fingers, nearly all the old book flew away in the wind. Georgette thoughtfully gazed at these swarms of little white pieces of paper as they dispersed themselves on each gust of wind, and said:
> "Butterflies."
> And the massacre ended by vanishing into the clear blue sky. [pp. 345–46]

In the final lines, Hugo's style nicely reinforces the feeling that the massacre represents a triumph of life. Inanimate becomes animate through the connotations of the words that I have translated as "fly away" ("s'envoler" refers to a bird's taking wing) and "swarms" ("essaim" is primarily a swarm of bees or other insects).

Concrete, unreflective immediacy is the mode of the scene. There are implicit connections with the more schematic portions of the novel, but these connections stay mainly submerged. The comparison of the three children's destructiveness to that of three giants, for instance, recalls the three political giants of an earlier scene, Robespierre, Danton, and Marat. Further, seen in the context of Michelet's *History of the French Revolution*, a work with which Hugo was much occupied during the composition of *Quatrevingt-treize* and which his novel supports in some ways but tries to refute in others, the children's action gains a rather specific meaning. Michelet believed that the crime of the Old Regime was a crime primarily against children. The Old Regime enslaved each succeeding generation through the economic inheritance of property (which leads to inequality and injustice) and the religious inheritance of original sin (which leads to docility before injustice).[10] The destruction of the apocryphal gospel is an expression of the incipient anarchism that Hugo and Michelet share: it symbolizes a utopian vision of a new generation, freeing itself from the enslaving inheritance Michelet describes. But for all this, we do not react to the scene as embodying the sort of allegory so often created by the novel's main characters. The connections between the massacre's feeling of immediate actuality and the novel's allegorical structure remain on a tacit level. Hence the editor of the Garnier edition of *Quatrevingt-treize* remarks that "one understands Flaubert's taste for this episode, inserted carelessly and picturesquely in the midst of a novel about the French Revolution" (p. 344, n. 2). To say that Georgette's butterflies have a meaning in any way separable from what they immediately are would be to sap the sources of their imaginative strength and the power of the episode as a whole. The scene, we feel, is symbolic, not allegorical, remembering Coleridge's definition of symbols as "consubstantial with the truths, of which they are the *conductors.*"[11] It fully embodies the kind of symbolism that, I have argued, *Les dieux* and *Romola* lack.[12]

10. Jules Michelet, *History of the French Revolution*, trans. Charles Cocks, ed. Gordon Wright, Classic European Historians (Chicago: University of Chicago Press, 1967), pp. 28–30, 49–59. On Michelet's anarchistic vision of history mentioned below, see Hayden White, *Metahistory: The Historical Imagination in Nineteenth-Century Europe* (Baltimore: Johns Hopkins University Press, 1973), pp. 161–62.

11. Samuel Taylor Coleridge, *The Statesman's Manual*, in *Lay Sermons*, ed. R. J. White (Princeton: Princeton University Press, 1972), p. 29.

12. Jeffrey Mehlman gives a brilliant reading of the novel which draws on Derrida and Lacan in *Revolution and Repetition: Marx/Hugo/Balzac* (Berkeley: University of

Does this mean that Hugo, because of his greater command of poetic language, has solved the problem inherent in giving symbolic representation to historical process in a novel? The answer must be yes, but only momentarily. The scene, after all, is one among many in a long work, and the conditions responsible for its success are special and self-limiting. The choice of children as the actors here is brilliant, not least because instead of depicting their inner lives, Hugo can draw on cultural stereotypes of timeless childhood. With children, certain parts of the spectrum of human generality can be more easily elided than with adults. The three "angels of prey" can become symbols of human energy as it informs historical process, whereas one thing that makes Romola an unsuccessful cultural symbol is precisely Eliot's moral intelligence, which leads her to depict Romola's inner growth. But one cannot write an entire historical novel about children. Hugo needs other modes of representation to create a fictional context in which the children's actions can gain symbolic meaning—and here some serious problems arise. We have already mentioned the allegorical nature of his main characters. This aspect of the novel reaches a climax in the scenes following the "Massacre," in which Gauvain as mediator sacrifices himself to save his royalist uncle, the honor of the Revolution, and by inference, hope for a future filled with the creative energy the children symbolize. The significance of Gauvain's act is expressed through an operatic duet about the future between him and Cimourdain, which leaves human speech far behind, descends rapidly from the heights of the "Massacre" scene, and tries my own great admiration for Hugo's novel severely.

Yet it is not true that the novel divides itself between one great symbolic scene and a mass of abstract allegory. A kind of representation closely allied to the symbolism in "The Massacre of St. Bartholomew" pervades the novel and explains the inclusion of material which seems extraneous, yet which, at the same time, clearly reflects Hugo's genius more successfully than do its allegorical parts. Anyone who has read *Quatrevingt-treize* will remember, for instance, the vivid depiction of the havoc wreaked by a cannon that breaks loose on the gun deck of an English warship early in the novel. Here is a brief sec-

California Press, 1977), pp. 42–72. Mehlman discusses the massacre scene, in which a book is destroyed; he reaches the level of generality at which his methods operate best by quickly dismissing the depiction of the children as sentimental.

tion of that scene, describing the efforts of a crew member to immobilize the cannon: "Then something savage began; a titanic spectacle; the combat between the cannon and the cannoneer; a battle between matter and intelligence, a duel of the thing against the man" (p. 44). What unifies this passage with the rest of the novel is the basic rhetorical structure it so vividly embodies, a trope we might call "dynamic polar opposition," which appears in such words as "combat," "battle," and particularly "duel." The scene's insistent personification of the cannon promotes this effect, which is also reflected in the chapter heading "Vis et Vir" (p. 41). The next chapter is entitled "Les deux plateaux de la balance" and depicts a polar opposition in rewards for the sailor who finally conquers the cannon. He is given the Cross of St. Louis for his bravery, but is then shot because his negligence allowed the cannon to break loose in the first place. Everywhere one turns in the novel there are "duels." The labyrinthine division of the work into parts, books, and chapters itself conveys a strong sense of Hugo's presence as artist, moving into position and opposition the various blocks of his story.[13] All novels involve conflict; what is unusual about *Quatrevingt-treize* is that the process of conflict itself seems to be the focus of Hugo's interest. The content of the opposition fluctuates. We have already noted that the initial conflict between England and France, reaction and revolution, gives way in the St. Bartholomew scene to a different opposition in which revolution and reaction become "one man" and are both opposed to the innocence of the children. The historical confrontation later in the novel between Robespierre, Danton, and Marat, which we perceive as largely superfluous to the novel's action, is an extension of this central trope, and the list could be extended almost indefinitely. Such a symbolic structure is ideally suited to express Hugo's conviction that 1793, the year of the Terror, ought to be seen as the possible prelude to, and initial expression of, an ideal society of the future. As he wrote to Edgar Quinet: "Like you and with you, I want to separate the revolution from its horror . . . in this book I make innocence dominate it; I try to throw on the terrifying number 93 a subduing ray of sunshine; I want progress to continue creating law and to cease creating fear" (p. i). In his novel, Hugo attempts with remarkable success

13. Boudout puts it thus: "The entire first section of the novel establishes in our minds the idea of an implacable duel" (p. xxxi).

to resurrect the violence of the year 1783 but then to pierce beyond it to a timeless vision in which destructive energy is transmuted into creative energy.

At their best, Hugo's polar oppositions seem to enact the movement of historical process itself. They support the energetic paradoxes of the "Massacre" scene, and by their very antithetical structure add a saving negativity to what could easily have been too swift a transcendence "into the clear blue sky." As Victor Brombert has demonstrated, the ringing affirmations Hugo produces never quite silence the equally insistent negations against which they clash, even in the "Massacre" scene itself.[14] Yet there are problems with Hugo's central trope. Sometimes the oppositions seem forced and mechanical.[15] As we read *Quatrevingt-treize*, we encounter moments in which Hugo appears to be creating historical analysis and detail for the express purpose of fitting it into his chosen rhetorical form. His Tainean speculations about the effect of living in the forests of the Vendée, for instance, immediately generate two striking oppositions, first between the Vendean cities under the forest floor and Paris, and then between life in the Vendée and life in the Alps (pp. 219–40). Such unmediated oppositions are simply the obverse of the unmediated identities in *Romola*: both tend to destroy our sense of the richness, diversity, and cunning of historical actuality. Perhaps more telling is the abstraction inherent in the novel's symbolic enactment of historical process. The problem with Hugo's fascination with history as pure process is that it allows too much into the novel on an abstract level. Virtually anything can become symbolic or allegorical content for this form: hence

---

14. Victor Brombert, "Victor Hugo: History and the Other Text," *Nineteenth-Century French Studies*, 5 (1976–77), 23–33. For Guy Rosa, "*Quatrevingt-treize* ou la critique du roman historique," *Revue d'histoire littéraire de la France*, 75 (1975), 329–43, the novel demonstrates certain contradictions inherent in the very notion of historical fiction.

15. Hugo's use of what I have called dynamic polar opposition has been noticed and criticized by Erich Auerbach, *Mimesis: The Representation of Reality in Western Literature* (1946), trans. Willard R. Trask (1953; rpt. Princeton: Princeton University Press, 1968), p. 468, who believes that it produces effects that are powerful, but "improbable and, as a reflection of human life, untrue." Auerbach's reservations about this technique seem right in regard to *Notre-Dame de Paris*, to which he is primarily referring and in which Hugo's clashing antitheses produce mainly exotic effect. I would argue that *Quatrevingt-treize* is different: in it, Hugo's dominant trope has found a subject for which it is an ideal expressive vehicle.

our feeling that the cannon scene belongs yet does not belong with what surrounds it. At such a level of generality, we must wonder whether we have not left the historical world altogether, well before the novel's attempt at transcendence.

In the end, whatever we believe about the nature of historical process, I think we must respect Hugo's attempt to capture it in *Quatrevingt-treize*. It may be that a fascination with history as pure process forgets that history is irreducibly impure; it may be that a wish to redeem history forgets that history is irredeemable.[16] We may also feel that Hugo's symbolism carries with it important limitations in representing life as a truly historical phenomenon. But precisely because we do not expect historical fiction to represent all levels of human generality at once, we should value a novel which functions with such brilliance on a level of abstraction that defeats even so great a writer as George Eliot, instead of collapsing back into the familiar, important areas of representation in which nineteenth-century fiction is most comfortable.

War and Peace

In *Les dieux ont soif, Romola,* and *Quatrevingt-treize*, history is the primary subject, and all three works represent and comment upon historical process through symbolic characters and scenes. Historical representation in the greatest historical novel, *War and Peace*, is significantly different. Tolstoy is capable of producing rich and resonant symbolic moments: one recalls Pierre's visions of humanity as a pulsating globe and the soldiers coalescing into a living stream of humanity as they retreat from Moscow. But these moments occur in a representational context that alters their significance profoundly. One problem with using symbolic scenes and characters in historical fiction, as we have seen, is that symbols tend to bypass the difficulty in representing the entire spectrum of human existence. The kind of symbolism at issue here valorizes certain parts of the spectrum and ig-

16. Herbert Marcuse, *Eros and Civilization: A Philosophical Inquiry into Freud* (1955; rpt. New York: Vintage Books, n.d.), p. 216: "Even the ultimate advent of freedom cannot redeem those who died in pain. It is the remembrance of them, and the accumulated guilt of mankind against its victims, that darken the prospect of a civilization without repression."

nores others, because it views the world through what Kenneth Burke calls the "master-trope" of synecdoche; it assumes that certain privileged parts, existing at certain levels of generality, can perfectly represent the whole, because they contain the whole, acting as microcosms of it.[17] Few authors could be further from subscribing to such a view than Tolstoy is. His sense of discontinuity in human existence penetrates everywhere, even into his depiction of individual character. Tolstoy's characters constantly find their actions and even their spoken words directed by internal forces of which they are consciously unaware and which surprise them when they find expression. Napoleon suddenly screams at an envoy for no reason; Princess Mary suddenly finds her manner transformed and her social diffidence gone when she meets Nicholas Rostov; Pierre and Kutuzov say apparently meaningless things during the abandoning of Moscow, which nevertheless seem full of a significance we cannot quite grasp. In Tolstoy, human personality itself seems to exist at discontinuous levels, some of which break into consciousness only rarely and dramatically.

Tolstoy employs synecdoche in *War and Peace*, but with a difference: beings who can be adequately represented in synecdochic terms are often spiritually trivial or spiritually dead; they are always incapable (or unneedful) of change or growth. Hélène's plump white shoulders and Napoleon's plump white hands sum the two people up perfectly, because they are static and perfectly depraved; "roundness" sums up Platon Karataev because he has a finished, inaccessible perfection of a higher order. Such images are of course also associated with the constantly growing, constantly changing characters we care most about—Pierre, or Andrew, or Natasha—but they do not begin

17. Kenneth Burke, "Four Master Tropes," in his *A Grammar of Motives* (1945; rpt. Berkeley: University of California Press, 1969), pp. 503–17. Paul de Man, "The Rhetoric of Temporality," in *Interpretation: Theory and Practice*, ed. Charles S. Singleton (Baltimore: Johns Hopkins University Press, 1969), pp. 173–91, believes symbolism to be based on the trope of synecdoche; he also attacks symbolism as embodying a certain kind of nineteenth-century self-mystification which ignores man's "authentically temporal destiny" (p. 190). I believe that Scott's characteristic mode of representation could be shown to embody the trope of metonymy as Burke and certain others describe it. Graham McMaster, *Scott and Society* (Cambridge: Cambridge University Press, 1981), p. 142, who believes that the Waverley Novels are primarily about Scott's present, takes the opposite view: "Whenever metaphor replaces metonymy as the principal mode of [a Scott] novel, this is the place to try to find its real significance."

to provide an adequate way of summing them up. Of all historical novelists, Tolstoy comes closest to capturing the total spectrum of human existence in history. His success, I believe, results largely from his unwillingness to solve too easily what I have called the problem with historical novels. The characteristic narrative presence in *War and Peace* is that of a mind trying to connect different levels of experience but refusing to connect them in too simple or conclusive a manner. Characterization, thematics, structure, even philosophy of history stem from, support, and are supported by this basic stance. The reason why we feel as we read *War and Peace* that we are in the presence of history itself, as well as of human beings living in history, is that Tolstoy relentlessly compels us to share this stance.

Tolstoy refuses to reduce history to symbols because he recognizes the difficulty of uniting the various levels at which human beings exist. This refusal takes the form of a simultaneous emphasis on the particularity of individual characters and on historical process at its most general.[18] Tolstoy's critics have often noted the presence of this unreconciled opposition in his works, though they naturally formulate it in different ways to fit their different purposes. Isaiah Berlin gives a classic diagnosis of Tolstoy as both hedgehog and fox. In more purely literary terms, the great Russian Formalist critic Boris Eikhenbaum demonstrates that Tolstoy's two characteristic stylistic devices are "detailed description" and "lyric and philosophical digressions," which he reduces to the opposition between "minuteness" and "generalization."[19] Tolstoy's recognition of the difficulty of uniting different levels of human experience makes itself felt not only in the representational texture of *War and Peace*, but also as an explicit thematic concern. There are moments when characters try to create an identification between themselves and history, but such attempts usually turn

---

18. Tolstoy would thus appear to be part of a general cultural movement that links up with the "individualist" criticism I discuss in Chapter 1, but he differs from such "individualist" critics as Aldous Huxley because he does not find any easy transition from the most particular to the most general.

19. Isaiah Berlin, *The Hedgehog and the Fox: An Essay on Tolstoy's View of History* (London: Weidenfeld and Nicolson, 1953); Boris Eikhenbaum, *The Young Tolstoy* (1922), trans. Gary Kern (Ann Arbor: Ardis, 1972). Some critics believe that they have plucked out the heart of Tolstoy's mystery: thus Edward Wasiolek, *Tolstoy's Major Fiction* (Chicago: University of Chicago Press, 1978), pp. 115–28, rebukes Berlin for creating dilemmas that do not really appear in Tolstoy's text.

out to be absurd or destructive. Prince Andrew's attempt to merge with the Napoleonic legend nearly brings on his death, and it leads him to recognize Napoleon's triviality and to value other levels of existence besides the political. Pierre's number mysticism, by which he erroneously deduces that he is "L'russe Besuhof" who is destined to destroy Napoleon, is patently ridiculous.

When a merging of the individual and the historical succeeds, it does so momentarily, and it is shot through with doubt and irony. A remarkable moment of this sort, involving Natasha Rostov, occurs before the fall of Moscow. Natasha is slowly recovering after her unsuccessful attempt to elope with Anatole Kuragin. An ardent religious faith has been a central part of her recovery. One church service she attends unexpectedly includes a long prayer for the deliverance of Russia, full of pleas that the French share the fate of the Philistines and that Russia, God's new Jerusalem, escape destruction. With a subtlety and complexity that would repay an analysis considerably more detailed than is appropriate here, Tolstoy shows how Natasha's private concerns intermingle with the public meaning of the service and the special prayer, often through a partial misunderstanding of those meanings. Throughout the scene, we feel a movement toward identifying the personal, social, and historical levels of existence, accompanied by a recognition of the irreducible differences between them, which reaches a climax in the final paragraph:

In Natasha's receptive condition of soul this prayer affected her strongly. She listened to every word about the victory of Moses over Amalek, of Gideon over Midian, and of David over Goliath, and about the destruction of "Thy Jerusalem," and she prayed to God with the tenderness and emotion with which her heart was overflowing, but without fully understanding what she was asking of God in that prayer. She shared with all her heart in the prayer for the spirit of righteousness, for the strengthening of the heart by faith and hope, and its animation by love. But she could not pray that her enemies might be trampled under foot when but a few minutes before she had been wishing she had more of them that she might pray for them. But neither could she doubt the righteousness of the prayer that was being read on bended knees. She felt in her heart a devout and tremulous awe at the thought of the punishment that overtakes men for their sins, and especially of her own sins, and she prayed to God to forgive them all, and her too, and to give them all, and her too, peace and happiness. And it seemed to her that God heard her prayer.[20]

This paragraph and the scene as a whole could easily descend into satire, especially in the hands of the writer who opens *War and Peace* by dissecting Anna Scherer's salon, but they in fact are considerably more complex and interesting than satire. Throughout the scene, we badly want Natasha to be swept up in a moment of vision, because we want to see her lose her guilt and reenter life. And partly as a result of this wish, we come to feel that in her humility and faith, Natasha has become the representative of all that is most worthy to be saved in the Russian character, of the Russian people itself. Her incomprehension purifies the prayer of its jingoistic elements; for this reason the prayer deserves to be heard and God will indeed hear it. The culture that produces people like Natasha deserves to be saved; God will redeem Russia, just as Natasha's sin with Anatole is at this very moment being redeemed. For an instant, the gap between personal, historical, and cosmic closes. But only for an instant. When in the next chapter we encounter Pierre's equally naive, equally sincere, but simply ludicrous attempt to discover the fate of Russia through the mystical significance of numbers and names, we quickly reenter a world in which the connection between the different levels of generality on which we live is problematical indeed.

In Tolstoy's depiction of public figures, the same pattern persists, even more clearly. He consistently exemplifies the doctrine he states directly in the first chapter of Book Eleven, that "the sum of individual wills is never expressed by the activity of a single historic personage" (p. 918). His negative view of the place of "great men" in history is well known. He takes a grim pleasure in allowing Napoleon, or Alexander, or Count Rostopchin to prove their littleness as they attempt to represent their countries and direct the course of history. Kutuzov is a more complex case. It is clear enough that as the novel progresses, he becomes in a certain sense the symbol of the Russian nation, in part because Tolstoy draws a fine (and perhaps philosophically indefensible) line between directing history, which Kutuzov

---

20. Leo Tolstoy, *War and Peace*, trans. Louise and Aylmer Maude, ed. George Gibian (New York: Norton, 1966), p. 736; subsequent references appear in my text.

does not aspire to do, and guiding history, which he is sometimes said to do. Lukács boldly and predictably sees Kutuzov as a "typical" character, asserting that the general's "most personal and intimate qualities are concentrated wonderfully—precisely because they are often contradictory, indeed paradoxical—round" the source of his greatness, his wish to be "nothing else and nothing more than a simple, collective, executive organ" of the popular will in Russia.[21] It seems to me more accurate to say that Kutuzov's personal life, with its French novels, sentimentality, and lechery, has nothing whatever to do with his greatness: his personal life is, so to speak, what he does with the part of his existence that is irrelevant to the Russian nation. That Kutuzov does not try to force an equation between his private life and his public role demonstrates his lack of Napoleonic megalomania, but it does not make him "typical" in the full Lukácsian sense of lighting up all details at all levels of his existence with historical meaning: it would be difficult indeed to find even the most subtle dialectical relationship between his public and private selves. It is precisely because Tolstoy does not try to unify Kutuzov's personal life and his historical role that we believe in the latter.

Few characters in the novel of whom we approve share Kutuzov's ability to rest content with his discontinuous life, and we do not share it as readers, either. For us, for Tolstoy's characters, and for Tolstoy as narrator there is always a pressure to make connections, to put things together, though success is always temporary and is usually undercut even as it occurs. Before Borodino, life for Prince Andrew is full of "senseless things, lacking coherence"; afterward, when he is wounded and delirious, he is able to answer the question of what "connection" there is between him and Anatole Kuragin, who lies wounded a few feet away from him, in a rush of forgiveness based on a perception of their shared humanity. The moral nobility of this scene is profound, yet we know that Andrew is delirious and probably dying; he achieves a sense of the wholeness of life precisely by giving up his part in the world of the living. This aspect of the novel finds its emblem in the last moments of a dream Pierre has after Borodino:

21. Lukács, *The Historical Novel*, p. 87.

"The hardest thing [Pierre went on thinking, or hearing, in his dream] is to be able in your soul to unite the meaning of all. To unite all?" he asked himself. "No, not to unite. Thoughts cannot be united, but to *harness* all those thoughts together is what we need! Yes, one *must harness* them, *must harness* them!" he repeated to himself with inward rapture, feeling that these words and they alone expressed what he wanted to say and solved the question that tormented him.

"Yes, one must harness, it is time to harness."

"Time to harness, time to harness, your excellency! Your excellency!" some voice was repeating. "We must harness, it is time to harness. . . ."

It was the voice of the groom, trying to wake him.   [pp. 941–42]

The ending of Pierre's dream thematizes the central dynamic of *War and Peace*, directly in its content, and indirectly in the way it momentarily rises to a spiritual discovery but then clouds the validity of that discovery.

The notion that *War and Peace* is centrally concerned with the problem of uniting the disparate levels of human existence, a problem which it knows to be insoluble but feels compelled to solve, provides an answer to what is probably the oldest and most persistent controversy concerning it. What are we to make of Tolstoy's philosophical discussions? Readers have disagreed about what Tolstoy's theory of history actually is, about whether it is borne out by the action of the novel itself (the novel here taken to be something essentially separable from the discussions), and indeed about whether such discussions belong in this novel (or any novel) in the first place. R. F. Christian seems a representative spokesman for those who consider the discussion neither useful nor ornamental, when he asserts that "from an artistic point of view, there is little to be said for the digressions. . . . They are structurally unfortunate in that they lay too heavy an emphasis on what should emerge naturally from the course of the fictional narrative. In fact Tolstoy's conclusions, while they can in retrospect be applied to the behaviour of the fictitious characters in his novel and can be made to seem not inconsistent with this behaviour, do not strike the reader spontaneously as he reads the stories of the Rostovs and the Bolkonskys."[22] Our analysis of the problem with

22. R. F. Christian, *Tolstoy's* War and Peace: *A Study* (London: Oxford University Press, 1962), p. 146. Lukács makes a more subtle version of the same complaint. He

historical novels, however, implies that Tolstoy knows precisely what he is doing when he includes the discussions. They flow from his recognition that an understanding of the workings of history simply cannot be expected to "emerge naturally" from the concrete presentation of individuality at which he so excels, that particularities will not flow effortlessly into generalities. Tolstoy's repetitiveness and dogmatism as an expounder of historical theory stem from his acute awareness of this problem: we feel him striving to bend to his purposes a form he knows is recalcitrant. Some of the more perverse and unexpected aspects of his philosophy of history also find their source here. His vision of history as calculus depends on reducing each human integer to the same level of importance, whereas he depicts such "integers" as Pierre and Natasha and even Anatole Kuragin with an unrivaled grasp of their individual uniqueness. Both in form and in content, Tolstoy's philosophizing is best understood as a necessary part of, and one moment in, his novel's overall attempt to achieve a general vision of historical process without falsifying its particularities. It makes a basic contribution to the concrete individuality of his characters, for it sets them free from having to embody directly large and abstract historical meanings. And it also urges us as readers to engage in the process of integrating historical particularities into a general schema, though without hope of any final success. Tolstoy's extreme philosophical positions concerning free will and determinism in the Second Epilogue are reflections of his knowledge that history cannot be reduced to either the personal or the cosmic, the concrete or the abstract, and perhaps they reflect a certain frustration this insight produces.

To say that Tolstoy knows what he is doing when he incorporates the philosophical discussions is not to suggest that he thereby solves what I have called the problem with historical novels, only that he confronts it directly and with a characteristically ruthless disregard for conventional literary forms. (In one of his defenses of *War and Peace*, Tolstoy stated that he had not produced a novel, and he meant it.) Nor is it to suggest that reader discomfort with the philosophical

---

recognizes that Tolstoy includes his philosophical discussions because literary characters cannot act as direct representations of Tolstoy's philosophy of history (p. 43). But for Lukács, this proves the incorrectness of Tolstoy's theory: through the agency of typicality, a true philosophy of history can be so represented.

discussions is simply misguided. The question here, as throughout this study, is not to explain away the anomalies that different attempts to represent history create in literary forms, but to account for them, to understand their origins and their nature.

That Tolstoy grapples with the problem with historical novels helps to explain why *War and Peace* contains more of the spectrum of human existence than any other work of historical fiction. But even for him, certain areas of that spectrum are more faintly present than others. Tolstoy cares most about the individual and the cosmic. In this, I believe, he resembles many other nineteenth-century realists after Scott, especially those who depict the recent past or achieve a vision of the present as history in their works. He does not begin to have the interest in depicting limited historical milieux that an author like Scott has, though his prodigious mimetic powers and his brilliant grasp of certain aspects of the aristocratic social milieu he chooses mainly to depict in *War and Peace* obscure this.[23] In general, Tolstoy distrusts man as a social animal. Instinctive, immediate, and mysterious bonds like those at "Uncle's" country estate or, more generally, those that bind true Russians together please him best. In other respects, he tends to view social milieux with the eyes of a satirist, not a historicist. John Henry Raleigh has rightly noted how much richer Scott's depiction of the great and powerful is than Tolstoy's, and the reason is surely that (as we shall see more fully in a moment) Scott, unlike Tolstoy, is keenly interested in the positive ways in which societies function, conceiving of personality itself almost entirely in social terms.[24] Tolstoy grapples with the problem with historical novels, but even he is subject to it.

The distinction I have drawn between mimetic modes in Scott and Tolstoy is part of a larger difference in the way in which they imagine historical process, as we recognize if we compare Kutuzov with the Duke of Argyle, a nobleman and general in Scott's greatest novel, *The Heart of Midlothian*. The disjunction between Kutuzov reading

23. Christian, p. 176, goes so far as to say that "nothing" about Tolstoy's aristocratic major characters is "specifically representative of their own age, which is not also representative of Tolstoy's own generation. They are the products of a class and a way of life which had not materially altered when Tolstoy began to write."

24. Introduction to *The Heart of Mid-Lothian* (Boston: Houghton Mifflin Riverside, 1966), p. xxi.

French novels and Kutuzov as the representative of the Russian spirit is, as we have seen, absolute. The Duke of Argyle has his own contradictions, but they exist in a sphere more public than Kutuzov's private life and less cosmic than his ability to represent the spirit of a nation. Argyle embodies a cultural transition: he moves, sometimes uneasily, between his role as a Scottish patriot, still in contact with Scottish culture, and his role as a refined courtier and politician at the court of St. James. Scott's judgment of the relative worth of these two roles recalls Tolstoy's judgment of Kutuzov. Argyle's latent human greatness appears only when he is in contact with Jeanie Deans and hence with his cultural roots, just as Kutuzov is great only as the representative of the Russian spirit. After his moment with Jeanie has passed, Argyle maintains a general kindliness and decency, but he is sadly diminished, as his silly, condescending, foppish remarks about Effie Deans's "Doric" traces of a Scottish accent show. (After Kutuzov's historical moment has passed, he simply dies.) Scott's interest in Argyle's contradictions is, however, quite different from Tolstoy's interest in Kutuzov's. Tolstoy turns Kutuzov's known personal habits into a means of rendering even more striking his mysterious ability to represent the Russian spirit. Scott, by contrast, sees and explains Argyle as part of an inevitable historical progression, simple and uniform in outline, though complex and subtle in its local operations. Instead of an essentially synchronic juxtaposition, he creates a diachronic story. Argyle is part of the long, slow, inevitable process in which Scottish society is being worn away by contact with England. Argyle still values Scottish culture, but a man who continually must append to his conscious Scotticisms the words, "as we say in the North," is a man in whom the supplanting of the old by the new has reached an advanced stage.

The differences between Kutuzov and Argyle imply that Tolstoy and Scott differ significantly in their views of historical process. In Tolstoy, historical process involves movements of great complexity and on a large scale, as they impinge on individual perception. The pattern and direction of these movements are unknowable when they are occurring and hardly knowable, much less explicable, even in retrospect. Tolstoy's visions of grand folk migrations from one end of Europe to the other are devices to make his vision of historical process vividly concrete, not to explain it, for it cannot be explained except in the most general and formal terms. For Scott, with his eye more on social milieu than on the individual, the general outlines of historical process are clear, simple, linear, and knowable, and when history does not fall into such a pattern for him, his interest in historical process yields its dominant place in a novel's structure to some other historical interest, as we shall see in the chapters that follow. His viewpoint is not that of an individual in the historical stream, but of an onlooker who, to his sorrow, knows the outcome.

Tolstoy's vision and means of representation lead directly to much of the best historical fiction of the twentieth century, while Scott's moment, philosophically and artistically, seems much more distant from us. Tolstoy's recognition of the difficulties inherent in depicting history can easily shift the problem of understanding history from ontology to epistemology: in authors less committed to discovering truth than he, the question of how we can know the past at all can easily replace the question of what the past means. And his depiction of historical process as a powerful but mysterious and ultimately unknowable force can, if pushed farther, turn history into myth. We can see both these possibilities at work, though in very different ways, in William Faulkner's *Absalom! Absalom!* and in the novels of Thomas Mann. In my opinion, the movement from history to myth represents a falling off from the difficult task of sustaining a vision like Tolstoy's: it is a way of giving history a pattern for those who are unwilling that its pattern be rational, an illegitimate return to Scott's security about the shape of history. Whatever other virtues it may possess, myth can never be an adequate vehicle for registering historical life. But the literary theory and practice of our own century stand heavily against such a valuation. However that may be, though *War and Peace* contains certain potentialities more fully exploited by subsequent authors, it holds these potentialities in check. The novel's supreme achievement is precisely that it does not succumb to a number of temptations to produce a less strenuous vision of history. It does not reduce history to epistemology or myth, and it does not attempt to depict historical process through making its characters symbols. They may differ in other ways, but in these decisive respects Scott and Tolstoy are united, though we would have to add that in Schiller's terms Scott's antisymbolic art results from a "naive" view of the irreducible particularity of history, Tolstoy's from a "sentimental" view.

HISTORY AND CHARACTER IN SCOTT

For all its greatness, even *War and Peace* does not and cannot encompass the entire spectrum of human existence. It leaves relatively undeveloped the depiction of that area of the spectrum in which individual behavior shades over into social and cultural norms and practices, seen as a specifically historical phenomenon. This is where Scott is at his best. His solution to the problem of representing the spectrum of human existence is simpler than Tolstoy's. He shifts the primary focus of attention away from the individual and toward the social, and this allows him to concentrate on that area of human experience where history is most likely to reveal its influence—on the forces that bind together individuals into historically distinctive societies. There are obvious disadvantages to Scott's mimetic mode, but they are necessary disadvantages, inseparable from the strengths of his project. No work of art can represent all levels of human experience at once: some will recede from view or disappear altogether when we concentrate on others. The historical novelist is consistently faced with a choice between compromises. In *Les Chouans* Balzac achieves a powerful portrayal of individual passion, but as he does so, the representation of history fades into the background. In *Quatrevingt-treize*, Hugo makes several of his characters luminous symbols of historical process, but in doing so he sacrifices interiority and individuality. A great strength of Scott's own literary criticism is that he is keenly aware that certain esthetic virtues tend to exclude others. In discussing Walpole's *The Castle of Otranto*, he points out that its characters "are indeed rather generic than individual; but this was in a degree necessary to a plan, calculated rather to exhibit a general view of society and manners during the times which the author's imagination loved to contemplate, than the most minute shades and discriminating points of particular characters" (*MPW* III, 321). The relevance of this comment to his own works is striking. Critics are too hasty when they assume that he might have added psychological and moral depth to his characters like an extra layer to a cake, had not greed, haste, Toryism, a bad theory of art, or some other moral or artistic failing prevented him from doing so. In what follows, I want to indicate how Scott's handling of character promotes his depiction of this area of life and in other ways adds to his works' historicity. And I shall also mention the personal and cultural conditions that promote his mode of representation.

Scott's works are rarely organized around the principle of dramatizing his characters' inner lives. His characterization points outward toward historical milieux and events; milieux and events are not symbolic of the spiritual development of the individual. There is change in Scott's characters, but it is generally depicted either as instantaneous or as a fait accompli, and rarely involves a substantial depiction of moral growth. Some of his heroes, particularly Waverley and Nigel, may seem exceptions, but actually they are not. Waverley's feelings do not cut very deep. He does not so much change his views as adopt one set for the moment and then discover that they are illusory. If we feel change in Waverley, it is because of the great efficiency with which he acts as our representative in the novel: what we feel is the change of our own viewpoint as we are immersed in but then withdraw from the past. Because of their special function, Scott's heroes are special cases anyway, and I shall be treating them more fully later. More typical of Scott's fictional norms is the change that takes place in Margaret Ramsay in *The Fortunes of Nigel*. Margaret is begging help from the Lady Hermione:

> "Rise—rise, maiden," said Hermione; "you affect me more than I thought I could have been moved by aught that should approach me. Rise and tell me whence it comes that, in so short a time, your thoughts, your looks, your speech, and even your slightest actions, are changed from those of a capricious and fanciful girl to all this energy and impassioned eloquence of word and action?"
>
> "I am sure I know not, dearest lady," said Margaret, looking down; "but I suppose that, when I was a trifler, I was only thinking of trifles. What I now reflect is deep and serious, and I am thankful if my speech and manner bear reasonable proportion to my thoughts."
>
> "It must be so," said the lady; "yet the change seems a rapid and strange one." [pp. 227–28; ch. 20]

The reader can only agree. One admires Scott at points like this. He manfully faces a narrative situation where he is at a disadvantage, makes a quick attempt to forestall our criticism, and passes on to other things.

Scott's novels may lack convincing portrayals of moral and spiritual growth, but this does not mean that he fails to understand human nature or that his characters do not seem real. There has always been a countercurrent to the criticisms about Scott's characterization. Balzac was unhappy about Scott's portrayal of love, but he found his characters impressive in other respects: "Scott gives you, wherever you are, a brilliant company of human beings," he tells us.[25] Scott understood human motivations, and this perceptiveness makes his characters seem real to us. Margaret Ramsay's interview with the Lady Hermione is a good example. Margaret wishes to borrow money she desperately needs to help Nigel, and the change in her character has persuaded Hermione to help her. While they wait for Monna Paula, Hermione's companion, to fetch the money, Scott takes the opportunity to let Hermione confide her own dark secrets to Margaret (and the reader). This expedient is redeemed by Scott's description of Margaret's feelings as she listens to the story: "Even at this agitating moment, although she ceased not to listen with an anxious ear and throbbing heart for the sound of Monna Paula's returning footsteps, she nevertheless, as gratitude and policy, as well as a portion of curiosity, dictated, composed herself, in appearance at least, to the strictest attention to the Lady Hermione, and thanked her with humility for the high confidence she was pleased to repose in her" (pp. 229–30; ch. 20). Margaret's impatience and her sense of the necessity of "policy" are humanly right if slightly chilling, but the masterstroke is Scott's recognition of the part that mere curiosity would play in a scene like this.

Scott's shrewdness about human motivation is not always apparent, because he consciously leaves a great deal for his readers to infer. He wants us to take an active role in creating his fiction.[26] One characteristic device involves giving us two or more tentative explanations for an action or a trait of character, as in this excerpt from the description of Meg Merrilies in *Guy Mannering*, which precedes her famous denunciation of the Laird of Ellangowan:

25. *Scott: The Critical Heritage*, ed. John O. Hayden (New York: Barnes and Noble, 1970), p. 377.
26. In his criticism, Scott repeatedly makes the point that good authors leave room for the imagination of their readers, particularly if they are trying to achieve pictorial or supernatural effects. Scott praises this quality in Byron (*MPW* XVII, 353) and in Ann Radcliffe (*MPW* III, 379–83); he elsewhere compares it to the *"touch and go"* method of acting," which does not "satiate" our curiosity "by distinct, accurate circumstantiality of detail" (*MPW* XVIII, 100).

We have noticed that there was in her general attire, or rather in her mode of adjusting it, somewhat of a foreign costume, artfully adopted perhaps for the purpose of adding to the effect of her spells and predictions, or perhaps from some traditional notions respecting the dress of her ancestors.   [p. 49; ch. 8]

As we attempt to use these hypotheses to explain Meg's mode of dress, we find ourselves recognizing that both probably have some validity. We are left in a situation where we can go far, if we wish, in meditating on how, and at what level of self-consciousness, such motives might work in the mind of a character like Meg.

The inferential stance that Scott leads his readers to adopt is analogous to the stance of a historian before his materials. The analogy is significant but incomplete, because Scott does not leave the job of drawing inferences from his characters and scenes entirely up to us. There is much direct authorial comment in the Waverley Novels, and Scott guides our judgments in more subtle ways as well. The inferential stance is a tendency in Scott's works, not an invariable rule, but it is an important tendency.

Such a stance leads the reader to react in a particularly appropriate way to actual historical characters in a novel. We are likely to resent the intrusion into the minds of actual historical figures of thoughts we suspect are placed there because they serve the ideological or novelistic needs of the author. We want, in other words, no more information than can be inferred from the historical record, and this is just what Scott gives us. In most fiction, the author's direct depiction of the inner life is the most important evidence that we can have about a character. In many novels, it *is* the character. With actual historical figures in historical novels, by contrast, the direct portrayal of consciousness can never have such a significance. It most properly serves as a summation of what we learn about the character by other means.

In *A Legend of Montrose*, Scott comes close to representing directly the mind of an actual historical figure, but even here we observe a strong bias toward external depiction of character. Scott presents with great insight the various considerations the Marquis of Montrose must have weighed when he decided to attack his old enemy Argyle during the English Civil War, instead of moving out of the Highlands and on to Edinburgh. Scott describes the feelings of Montrose's followers, his own conflicting desires, and his ambivalent attempts to dissuade his council of war from the course of revenge against his personal, political, and clan enemy. When Montrose is alone in his tent after the council of war has ended, his decision still unmade, Scott expresses his thoughts, not in the form of interior monologue or in one of the soliloquies spoken in similar circumstances by such heroes as Nigel or Waverley, but in the form of a series of "pictures":

> In one moment he imagined himself displaying the royal banner from the reconquered Castle of Edinburgh, detaching assistance to a monarch whose crown depended upon his success, and receiving in requital all the advantages and preferments which could be heaped upon him whom a king delighteth to honour. At another time this dream, splendid as it was, faded before the vision of gratified vengeance and personal triumph over a personal enemy. To surprise Argyle in his stronghold of Inverary; to crush in him at once the rival of his own house and the chief support of the Presbyterians; to show the Covenanters the difference between the preferred Argyle and the postponed Montrose, was a picture too flattering to feudal vengeance to be easily relinquished. [pp. 295–96; ch. 16]

But, as so often with Scott, the actual process of decision results, not from the thoughts of an individual, but from the interaction of thoughts, prejudices, and the pressure of events. At this moment Dalgetty arrives with letters stolen from Argyle, full of contempt for Montrose and his military forces. Argyle's letters sting Montrose into speaking his mind aloud, and Dalgetty is there as historical observer: "'Does he not fear me?' said he; 'then he shall feel me. Will he fire my castle of Murdoch? Inverary shall raise the first smoke. O for a guide through the skirts of Strath Fillan!'" (p. 299; ch. 16). Dalgetty has escaped from Argyle with the help of just such a guide; he so informs Montrose, and the die is cast. The moment when Montrose actually makes the decision is not depicted internally at all. It does not need to be. Scott's implicit argument about historical causation here is that the force of events themselves, acting upon historically created prejudices, has made the decision: this is the point of Dalgetty's dramatic entrance just when the information he brings will consolidate the workings of clan hatred in Montrose's mind. The schematic and external depiction of Montrose's decision has little to recommend it as a representation of the ebbs and flows of consciousness. But the very lack of an emphasis on the inner life forces us out into the world, to see how history results from the ways in which men and women mesh with their physical, social, and historical environments.[27]

Scott's ability to place his characters in their larger social and historical contexts is evident from the first pages of his first novel. A deft, understated example of this kind of representation occurs when Scott describes the effect of the eighteenth-century mail service on Sir Everard Waverley, who represents North of England Jacobitism in *Waverley*. Sir Everard's younger brother, it transpires, has made a series of moves to accommodate himself to Hanoverian rule, in the hopes of obtaining governmental favors:

> Although these events followed each other so closely that the sagacity of the editor of a modern newspaper would have presaged the two last even while he announced the first, yet they came upon Sir Everard gradually, and drop by drop, as it were, distilled through the cool and procrastinating alembic of Dyer's Weekly Letter. For it may be observed in passing, that instead of those mail-coaches, by means of which every mechanic at his six-penny club may nightly learn from twenty contradictory channels the yesterday's news of the capital, a weekly post brought, in those days, to Waverley-Honour, a Weekly Intelligencer, which, after it had gratified Sir Everard's curiosity, his sister's, and that of his aged butler, was regularly transferred from the Hall to the Rectory, from the Rectory to Squire Stubbs's at the Grange, from the Squire to the Baronet's steward at his neat white house on the heath, from the steward to the bailiff, and from him through a huge circle of honest dames and gaffers, by whose hard and horny hands it was generally worn to pieces in about a month after its arrival. [p. 7; ch. 2]

This description is a perfect example of the sort of thing that can be taken as "local color" in Scott. He offers it to explain why Everard, Jacobite though he was, did not disinherit his younger brother on the spot when he learned that he had turned Whig. On the simplest level, this was because the element of drama was lacking in news that reached him in a fragmentary form several weeks after the event: "had the sum total of his enormities reached the ears of Sir Everard at once, there can be no doubt that the new commissioner would have

---

27. Lukács, p. 59, shows how much the depiction of Montrose's decision implies about the nature and depth of Scott's historical vision.

had little reason to pique himself on the success of his politics" (p. 7; ch. 2). But the description explains Sir Everard's hesitation to disinherit his turncoat brother on a more profound level as well. Everard Waverley's character, we see, has been shaped by his geographical and ideological distance from the seat of power, which distance also allows him to maintain his Jacobitism in a safe limbo, since it guarantees that he will never do anything quickly and decisively. The slow and circuitous mail service, then, is not (as a setting in a Gothic novel might be) a metaphor, much less a symbol, for Everard's mind. Instead, his mind and the mail service are both parts of a complex metonymic whole in which personality, history, and even geography and technology all play a part. The same is true of Scott's architectural descriptions in *Waverley*. The decaying country house, Tully-Veolan, and the squalid village that lies outside its gates interest Scott because they represent the actual physical results and embodiments of a set of historical forces, the same forces that also help to produce the Baron of Bradwardine. A source of great pleasure in reading Scott is to see such systems come alive, not as metaphors for truths about the human heart, but as things that in very truth existed in the past.

Speech is the natural meeting place for the individual consciousness and public structures of thought and feeling. In the Waverley Novels, spoken language can be a powerful element in Scott's external depiction of character. David Deans in *The Heart of Midlothian*, the most fully developed vehicle for the Covenanters' dialect Scott so loved to write, is a character whose spoken language enacts his culturally determined consciousness with great success. Deans is not to everyone's taste, and his long harangues can be tiresome, but they have much to offer. As he discusses whether his future son-in-law can in good conscience accept a church preferment from the Duke of Argyle, for instance, he reaches an unwelcome conclusion and then must retrace his steps without ever quite realizing what he is doing. In his meandering casuistry, subconscious desire is at work in a complex, amusing, and culturally significant way, modifying his conscious allegiance to a rigid set of doctrines with a logic of their own.[28] At their best, his

28. Scott produces this effect in an interesting way. He gives David's arguments for and against Butler's taking the preferment mainly in the form of a summary; this saves the comic side of David's rhetoric from obtruding itself and allows the complicated issues at stake to emerge more clearly. But we have heard so many examples of David's

long speeches show how values slowly transform and refresh themselves in an individual and a culture. There are limits to this mode of characterization; its techniques could never substitute successfully for those George Eliot employs to depict the evolving moral consciousness of her characters. Nonetheless, such rhetoric is a deft solution to the problem of suggesting psychological complexity in a character whose primary purpose is to function as a historical representative.

Scott's external characterization aids his historical representation in another way. It allows him to simplify certain characters for analytical purposes. Since we do not tend to make the same mimetic demands of characters we experience externally as we do of characters we experience internally, we are willing to accept a certain schematization in his characters. This is obviously true of the allegorical manner in which his heroes' love stories sometimes comment upon the course of historical process. Walter Bagehot, probably Scott's best nineteenth-century critic, suggests another way in which this acceptance of schematic characters is useful when he tells us that in Scott, religious beliefs are fixed: "Creeds are *data* in his novels: people have different creeds, but each keeps his own."[29] Scott actually goes further in this direction than Bagehot suggests. Often his characters embody merely one aspect of a religious creed or political stance. *Waverley* is full of such characters. In Flora MacIvor, we see the purely idealistic side of Jacobitism; in her brother Fergus, its tainted, opportunistic side. Callum Beg, taking potshots from behind trees at anyone he imagines to have offended clan dignity, represents one aspect of the Highland character as Scott found it recorded in his sources; Evan Dhu, shaming the English by his simple nobility when he offers his life for his chief's, quite another.[30] Though it precludes a full and convincing representation of individual psychology, Scott's technique of dividing the components of a social or political movement among different characters is useful as an analytical tool, and

---

speech on such topics that there is a carry-over: we hear his characteristic turns of phrase ringing in our ears, even though we are reading only a summary of their content.

29. *Scott: The Critical Heritage*, p. 413.

30. Callum Beg derives from an anecdote in Edward Burt, *Letters from a Gentleman in the North of Scotland* (London: S. Birt, 1754). For Scott's use of Burt, see James Anderson, "Sir Walter Scott as Historical Novelist, Part II," *Studies in Scottish Literature*, 4 (1966), 68–70.

also as a means of persuasion. In *Old Mortality*, for instance, he provides a full range of Covenanters: each of them reflects an aspect of the Covenanting tradition; together, they allow him to express a nuanced judgment upon it.[31] At the end of the novel, we have great sympathy for Ephraim Macbriar's heroic suffering at the hands of the British privy council, precisely because the inhuman, terrifying, and ignoble aspects of his cause have been represented by other characters. By bringing different representative characters to the fore at appropriate moments in his novels, Scott is able to drive us toward certain conclusions about the shape of the past, while still allowing us to honor the nobility of those causes we are persuaded to reject.

A final way in which Scott's external characterization helps to create the historical texture of his novels is by leading us to focus on the intricate workings of historical causality. A sequence from Edward Waverley's youth may serve as an example. Waverley, who is living with his uncle while his father pursues a political career in London, is in danger of falling in love beneath his station. His aunt decides to put him on a more socially acceptable course, a tour of Europe. She proposes this to Waverley's uncle, who suggests it to Edward's father, but for a variety of historical and political reasons, the ultimate effect of her efforts is that Edward receives a commission in the army. This is not at all what she had in mind, "but she was under the necessity of submitting to circumstances; and her mortification was diverted by the employment she found in fitting out her nephew for the campaign, and greatly consoled by the prospect of beholding him blaze in complete uniform" (p. 27; ch. 5). The depiction of the chain of causality that brings Waverley into the army is a good example of how history occurs on a concrete, day-to-day basis in Scott's novels, creating their characteristically historical feel, as human motivations intersect with each other and with social and historical forces as well. It illustrates an eighteenth-century doctrine that pervades Scott's works—the notion that history proceeds through the unintended consequences of humanly willed actions. In another kind of work, we would process this sequence and others like it differently: we might, for instance, be interested in it as a stage in Waverley's moral education or

---

31. Scott's inclusion in *Old Mortality* of the whole spectrum of Covenanting types has often been noted; perhaps the best discussion is A. O. J. Cockshut, *The Achievement of Walter Scott* (London: Collins, 1969), pp. 141–51.

that of his aunt. But precisely because Scott's characterization raises little curiosity about inner lives, we concentrate on the chain of causality itself and the social and historical forces that determine its ultimate shape. Here as elsewhere, Scott's external characterization, for all its limitations, turns out to have great virtues in a fiction that explores the historical aspects of human existence.

Scott's characterization is an important enough aspect of his craft to make profitable an inquiry into its sources. A broad range of influences shaped his depiction of character; they include the state of the novel in his day, his own psychology, and his intellectual milieu. What we are asking, at base, is why the historical novel should have flowered in the age and person of Scott, and why it takes the particular form it does in his works. I would be the last to deny the important part the rise of historicism played in Scott's creation of the historical novel as a serious form. I believe, however, that in Scott this general cultural phenomenon was mediated in ways which deserve our attention.

Scott lived before the full development of techniques for depicting individual consciousness in novels. That he was in his own day sometimes regarded as a great creator of characters, not merely for the purposes of historical fiction but in general, is a measure of the changes in novelistic technique and in the very conception of personality that have occurred since his time. A lack of the devices for depicting the inner life now available to a third-rate novelist promoted his external depiction of character and hence helped him to create a distinctively historical kind of historical fiction. He was also fortunate to live in a time when ideas about the novel allowed for a good deal of what James was later to call "bagginess," a quality hard to avoid in historical fiction. Critics of the time, including Scott himself and even Coleridge, tended to think of novels as collections of characters. With all their respect for the plotting of Fielding, they did not expect such formal virtuosity in general. Scott was nagged by doubts about the strength of his plots, and reviewers chastised him for hasty construction, but in his day such faults were not considered fatal.

Scott's own psychology also influenced his external depiction of character. He considered introspection a dangerous pastime, likely to lead to morbid results. In his essay on Byron, he asserts that "he who shall mine long and deeply for materials in his own bosom will encounter abysses at the depth of which he must necessarily tremble" (*MPW* XVII, 359). Preoccupation with our inner life necessarily leads to unhappiness, for "our ideas of happiness are chiefly caught by reflection from the minds of others, and hence it may be observed that those enjoy the most uniform train of good spirits who are thinking much of others and little of themselves. The contemplation of our minds, however salutary for the purposes of self-examination and humiliation, must always be a solemn task, since the best will find enough for remorse, the wisest for regret, the most fortunate for sorrow" (*MPW* XVII, 358). In another essay, Scott describes John Bunyan's inner struggles against the "foul emotions" and "phantoms of guilt" which "not only without our will, but in positive opposition to our best exertions" intrude themselves into our thoughts (*MPW* XVIII, 79). Bunyan escaped from such mental defilement by turning to the outside world. Preaching the Gospel "necessarily fixed his attention upon the minds of others, instead of permitting him to indulge in his own reveries"(*MPW* XVIII, 89).

These may seem bleak words from the genial, sociable Scott, but they could be paralleled by other comments in other places. His very sociability, his almost compulsive letter writing, his need to fill Abbotsford with guests, his love of public occasions—all these may well reflect a conviction that human beings are at their best in society and at their worst in the privacy of their studies, alone with their thoughts and their egotism.[32] The son of a Calvinist father, he tells us on more than one occasion that the heart of man is desperately wicked.[33] The beliefs of his intellectual mentors also play a part here. Like Scott's own novels, the writings of Adam Ferguson (the father of one of his best friends) and Dugald Stewart (who taught him Moral Philosophy at the University of Edinburgh and with whom he subsequently became "very intimate") place great emphasis on the importance of a benevolent temperament.[34] But Dugald Stewart also in-

32. The necessity of escaping from egotism is a constant theme in Scott's fictional and nonfictional prose; selfishness is the great human sin for him. In particular, he defends the power of love to lead us beyond our selves and thus ennoble us (*MPW* III, 56; IV, 61). For attacks on selfishness in politics, see *MPW* XVIII, 379–84; XVI, 322–32; XXI, 74–76.

33. Sir Walter Scott, *Letters on Demonology and Witchcraft, Addressed to J. G. Lockhart, Esq.* (London: Murray, 1830), p. 214; *MPW* XVIII, 79.

34. *Letters*, VI, 175.

forms us that men probably admire benevolence so much because it is so rare a quality, and that "such is the influence of self-deceit, that few men judge with perfect fairness of their own actions."[35] There are parallel passages in Scott. It is hardly surprising that he did not devote large sections of his novels to exploring the inner lives of his characters, and was not driven to create new artistic means for pursuing such inquiries. Instead of probing such matters, how natural for a man of Scott's views to be interested in public codes of action, which from one point of view seem superficial, but in which it might also be argued our truest approach to a full humanity resides.

There is an even more important area in which we can see a parallel between Scott's opinion as voiced directly and indirectly throughout his works, his practice as a creator of fictional characters, and the intellectual tradition of which he was one of the last really vital expressions. Ferguson, Stewart, and Scott held similar views concerning man's relationship to society. The men of the Edinburgh Enlightenment could not praise a cloistered and fugitive virtue; indeed, they could hardly conceive of such a thing. For Ferguson, the most interesting and important fact about human beings is that they can mold themselves, as a potter molds a vessel, through an intelligent use of their propensity to form habits. But society is the necessary ground on which human nature unfolds and takes shape. "Human nature no where exists in the abstract," Ferguson tells us: the social aspects of human nature are as intrinsic to men and women as their bodily dimensions.[36] According to Gladys Bryson, whose pioneering account of these thinkers has still in many respects not been surpassed, the Edinburgh Enlightenment held that "man is not born human, but becomes human by virtue of his societal life," since society is "in large measure, a maker of men."[37] In discussing Adam Smith and Hume, she also mentions an important consequence of such a view: "We acquire from other persons our first notions of ourselves as selves, and we are constantly molding and remolding ourselves to win their ap-

35. *The Collected Works of Dugald Stewart*, ed. Sir William Hamilton, 11 vols. (Edinburgh: Constable, 1854–60), VII, 241; VI, 21.

36. Adam Ferguson, *Principles of Moral and Political Science*, 2 vols. (Edinburgh: Creech, 1792), I, 225; II, 419.

37. Gladys Bryson, *Man and Society: The Scottish Inquiry of the Eighteenth Century* (Princeton: Princeton University Press, 1945), pp. 146, 171.

proval. . . . Indeed, in these discussions . . . there sometimes seem to be no individuals at all, so organic is the relation of person to person conceived to be."[38] Thus personality itself seems to reside in the network of human relations which become embodied in political institutions, and not in an individual center of self. Scott's assertion that "our ideas of happiness are chiefly caught from the minds of others" reflects this view, which has an obvious usefulness for a writer who employs characters to represent historical process.

Recognizing that Scott conceived of personality itself in social terms can clarify a confusion latent in some recent discussions of Scott's view of history and the place of the individual within it. It has been wisely remarked that Scott's novels demonstrate that political ideologies and structures can distort or destroy the humanity of those who subscribe to them in too rigid a way.[39] It is also true that Scott loved to portray brief, often wordless moments when fellow feeling emerges in defiance of social custom and ideological difference: one remembers, among many other possible examples, the moment in *The Antiquary* when impending financial ruin breaks through Sir Arthur Wardour's pride of birth, and he grasps Oldbuck warmly by the hand. Yet it does not follow that Scott distrusted codes of belief inherently, or thought that men could live without them, or placed any lasting trust in an inner humanity existing apart from or in opposition to the social forms that have developed over time.

38. Bryson, p. 160. Stewart nervously warns against taking such a view too far. Despite recent discoveries of new nations, which have shown us how much of man's nature is the result of "accidental situation," we should not go to the extreme of "considering man as entirely a factitious being, that may be molded into any form by education and fashion" *(Works,* VI, 233–34).

39. Karl Kroeber, *Romantic Narrative Art* (Madison: University of Wisconsin Press, 1960; rpt. 1966), pp. 185–86, provides a fine statement of this view in regard to law: "Scott was . . . too intelligent and too experienced to doubt that law is the sturdiest pillar of civilized life. But as he matured he . . . came to desire law based not on simple, abstract, and arbitrary principles but upon the complex realities of human life, realities discernible only to an historical vision." Scott's favorite teacher at the University of Edinburgh, Baron David Hume, warns strongly against excessive reliance on "systematical views," which are useful to a lawyer only after extensive experience in the world, since "the inconveniences and distresses which mankind would suffer if their affairs and intercourse were uniformly governed, according to the same invariable rule in all cases, without regard to specialties and circumstances, is mere matter of fact—which no force of genius, before actual practice of business, can enable a young man to discover": see *Baron David Hume's Lectures, 1786–1822,* ed. G. Campbell H. Paton, I (Edinburgh: Stair Society, 1939), 4–5.

When the notion of man's natural goodness apart from society is raised directly, as it is by Robert Bage's long-forgotten novel *Hermsprong*, Scott reacts with the scathing contempt of a principled conservative:

> Hermsprong, whom [Bage] produces as the ideal perfection of humanity, is paraded as a man who, freed from all the nurse and all the priest has taught, steps forward on his path, without any religious or political restraint, as one who derives his own rules of conduct from his own breast. . . . But did such a man ever exist? or are we, in the fair construction of humanity, with all its temptations, its passions, and its frailties, entitled to expect such perfection from the mere force of practical philosophy? Let each reader ask his own bosom, whether it were possible for him to hold an unaltered tenor of moral and virtuous conduct, did he suppose that to himself alone he was responsible, and that his own reason, a judge so peculiarly subject to be bribed, blinded, and imposed upon by the sophistry with which the human mind can gloss over those actions to which human passions so strongly impel us, was the ultimate judge of his actions?   [*MPW* III, 458–59]

Scott concludes this attack with the assertion that though modern freethinkers may imagine they have transcended history and traditional values, whatever true morality they possess in fact reflects the moral climate created by a Christian society.

Scott found it difficult indeed to conceive of human beings, good or bad, without reference to some set of social norms or beliefs. A telling example of his tendency to think in terms of social and cultural types is provided by a comment on Robert Burns. Burns, Scott tells us, was a difficult man to deal with in polite society, because he demanded respect from his social superiors and enforced that demand through biting, overpowering rhetoric, yet felt no obligation to answer the challenges to duels his behavior sometimes elicited. This was not due to cowardice on Burns's part, Scott continues—and here, if anywhere, we might expect a reference to Burns's inner spirit, to the poetic greatness which lifted him above social boundaries, his individuality, his spiritual uniqueness. Instead, we learn that "the dignity, the spirit, the indignation of Burns was that of a plebian, of a high-souled plebian indeed, of a citizen of Rome or Athens, but still of a plebian untinged with the slightest shade of that spirit of chivalry which, since the feudal times, has pervaded the higher ranks of European society" (*MPW* XVII, 252–53). With Scott, the appeal to historical and social setting as a means of explanation is inevitable, even automatic. He is aware of the potential dangers in codes and beliefs because he recognizes their necessity, not because he views them as deformations of an eternal human nature. This quality of insight forms the basis of his most important limitations as a novelist, but also of his greatness.

I have been arguing that Scott's mode of depicting character is exceedingly useful to him as a historical novelist. But doesn't his external characterization mean that, however strong his representation of historical milieux might be, he is cut off from a crucial aspect of history, "the mind of the past"? Some critics think that it does, particularly in light of the important place Edinburgh Enlightenment ideas concerning man, society, and history have in his works. Duncan Forbes, the first to document in a systematic way Scott's debt to his eighteenth-century predecessors, believes that a major part of what he learned from them was that men and women throughout history are uniform: their differences from one age to the next are superficial overlays created by the successive stages through which all societies pass. This familiar Enlightenment conception of man, the argument continues, prevents his depiction of character from being truly historical. Because of his belief in the essential uniformity of man throughout history, the Waverley Novels "are not 'historical' at the deeper levels of thought and feeling." Scott barely creates and certainly fails to sustain "the *frisson historique*," since a truly historical representation of the inner life depends upon the assumption, which Scott manifestly does not share, that human beings in the past were, in the depths of their souls, entirely different from those in the present. In the words of Taine, whom Forbes quotes with approval, "Walter Scott pauses on the threshold of the soul, and in the vestibule of history."[40]

40. Duncan Forbes, "The Rationalism of Sir Walter Scott," *Cambridge Journal*, 7 (1953), 31. Forbes quotes Taine on this page, and also in *The Liberal Anglican Idea of History* (Cambridge: Cambridge University Press, 1952), p. 190, n. 202. The extent to which Scott believed in the uniformity of human nature over time has been a much discussed question: see, for instance, David Brown, *Walter Scott and the Historical Imagination* (London: Routledge & Kegan Paul, 1979), pp. 173–94; and D. D. Devlin, *The Author of Waverley: A Critical Study of Sir Walter Scott* (London: Macmillan, 1971), pp. 44–50.

In a sense, Forbes and Taine are entirely correct. As we have seen, Scott was relatively uninterested in depicting the ebbs and flows of consciousness, in either past or present. He held a social, perhaps a sociological, view of what our essential moral being amounts to, not the Romantic notion of a deeply individual consciousness set over and against society, which would lead one past "the threshold of the soul." But the larger issues of whether Scott's external characterization can shed light on the mental worlds of human beings in the past, and whether, given the influence of Edinburgh Enlightenment ideas on him, he is interested in doing so, are worth pursuing. Without doubt the doctrines Forbes so usefully draws to our attention were important to the Edinburgh Enlightenment. Among other things, they are the basis for what Dugald Stewart calls "conjectural history," a mode of historical analysis that allows a historian to plot the course of historical development even in the default of direct evidence, by drawing upon a knowledge of the various stages through which all societies necessarily progress and an understanding of the unvarying human nature which underlies all social forms. Nor can we deny that Scott was familiar with these doctrines and employed them in his works, particularly in his essays, reviews, and histories.[41] But Enlightenment ideas about history were not intrinsically so antihistorical as Forbes suggests. A belief in human uniformity over time vitiated Enlightenment historiography primarily because it was habitually used as an ideological and political weapon, often to debunk religious "hypocrisy" (no one could *really* have believed what medieval churchmen said they believed), not as a tool for historical research. Then too, the doctrine of human uniformity is less far-ranging than it might appear to be. When Enlightenment philosophers said that at base men were the same in every age, they meant *at base*; in the eyes of the Enlightenment, "only the fundamental passions . . . were uniform and universal; customs, religions, institutions, forms of social

41. The best study of Scott's contact with the ideas of the various generations of Edinburgh Enlightenment thinkers is Peter D. Garside, "Intellectual Origins of Scott's View of History" (Diss., Cambridge University, 1970), which also discusses Scott's place in the Scottish antiquarian tradition; see also his "Scott and the 'Philosophical' Historians," *Journal of the History of Ideas*, 36 (1975), 497–512. McMaster, pp. 49–77, gives an interesting account of Scott's debt to the Edinburgh Enlightenment; in some respects, particularly in emphasizing the social nature of identity in Scott, his analysis and my own agree.

organization, and styles of life were susceptible to almost infinite, almost unimaginable variety."[42] Man's fundamental passions are thus rather like the primary qualities in Hume's psychology, which are everywhere the same but come to us only in bundles; they are the simple materials from which arise complex and unique wholes. Freed from its use as a political weapon, there is much to be said for the assumption that sufficient uniformity exists between us and our ancestors to allow us to reconstruct the mental horizons their historical circumstances created in them. Such an assumption acts as a useful tool, a step toward understanding the past instead of being intimidated or intoxicated by its strangeness.

If we turn to Scott's writings as a whole, we find contradictory evidence concerning his interest in the mind of the past. In the Introductions written for the first editions of *Waverley* and *Ivanhoe*, he makes a great point of stressing our shared humanity with the men and women of the past. But these passages are not so unequivocal as they are sometimes made to appear, and their stress on human uniformity over time is sharply qualified by other passages in the Waverley Introductions.[43] *Waverley* and *Ivanhoe*, it is worth adding, appear at crucial points in Scott's career. In *Waverley*, he began to write historical novels; in *Ivanhoe*, he made a radical change of historical setting, from Scotland to medieval England. In both instances, Scott's invocation of the idea that though clothing and manners may change, human beings remain the same beneath them, serves a rhetorical purpose. He is trying to convince his readers, and perhaps himself, that a novel about the past need not simply be a collection of historical bric-a-brac and antiquated speech, as in Joseph Strutt or Jane Porter, that it can have an interest for mature men and women. Scott's comments

42. Peter Gay, *The Enlightenment: An Interpretation, II: The Science of Freedom* (New York: Knopf, 1969), pp. 380, 383. The classic refutation of the notion that the Enlightenment was antihistorical is Ernst Cassirer, *The Philosophy of the Enlightenment* (1932), trans. Fritz C. A. Koelln and James P. Pettegrove (Princeton: Princeton University Press, 1951).

43. S. Stewart Gordon, "*Waverley* and the 'Unified Design,'" *ELH*, 18 (1951), 107–22, points out that in the opening chapter of *Waverley*, Scott talks in terms of giving a picture of men, not manners, but in the closing pages, he informs the reader that his purpose has been to preserve for coming generations the manners of a bygone age. Similarly, Scott claims in the Advertisement that accompanied the first edition of *The Antiquary* that "the present Work completes a series of fictitious narratives intended to illustrate the manners of Scotland at three different periods" (p. v).

as an essayist fall into the same contradictory pattern. He tells us that basic human emotions never change and that the manners of an age are like clothing, and he asserts that the purpose of plays and novels is to penetrate the intricacies of the human heart, intricacies he conceives of as combinations and permutations of the basic emotions common to us all. But he also makes many comments suggesting that the idea of human uniformity is the first word, not the last word, about human beings. He is very hard on the French, for instance, because their literature depicts foreign characters who are foreign only in their external dress and mannerisms: in their modes of thinking they remain Frenchmen (not, in Scott's view, a desirable status).[44] He also betrays a continued interest in alien states of mind. He recognizes that Greek tragedy affected its original audiences much more powerfully than it can modern audiences, because the Greeks felt themselves to be in the presence of their gods *(MPW* VI, 234), and he believes that ballads had a comparably strong effect in the warlike Scottish Borders.[45] In a similar vein, he responds to the seventeenth-century Gaelic scholar Robert Kirk's belief in witches and elves by reflecting that "it is indeed curious to consider what must have been the sensations of a person who lived under this peculiar species of hallucination, believing himself beset on all hands by invisible agents" *(MPW* XIX, 11–12). The rationalistic ring of the word "hallucinations" should not obscure Scott's fascinated recognition that such hallucinations were real enough to Kirk and his contemporaries.

In his review of Walpole's *The Castle of Otranto*, Scott claims literature can have the power of transporting us for a time into the past. Walpole's achievement was to "wind up the feelings of his reader till they became for a moment identified with those of a ruder age" *(MPW* III, 316). Scott's own novels reflect a rich awareness of the dis-

---

44. *MPW* XVII, 306–7; XVIII, 357.

45. Sir Walter Scott, *Minstrelsy of the Scottish Border*, ed. T. F. Henderson, 4 vols. (Edinburgh: Blackwood, 1902), I, 20. This is something of an eighteenth-century commonplace. Even Gibbon remarks that we literally cannot conceive of what their poetry must have meant to the ancient Germanic tribes: see *The History of the Decline and Fall of the Roman Empire*, ed. J. B. Bury ([New York]: Limited Editions Club, 1946), p. 181; ch. 9. David Daiches, *The Paradox of Scottish Culture: The Eighteenth-Century Experience* (London: Oxford University Press, 1964), pp. 79–81, gives examples of similar speculations by such Edinburgh Enlightenment figures as Hugh Blair and Lord Kames.

tance between the minds and emotions of different ages; at his best, he can create fictional situations where we make momentary contact with the mind of the past in a way that leaves Walpole far behind. John Henry Raleigh claims, *contra* Forbes, that in *The Heart of Midlothian* Scott is able "to recreate historically the human consciousness of an age." He substantiates this claim with particular success with respect to the lower-class characters in the novel. Their mental horizons are restricted in terms of knowledge about the outside world: Effie Deans, for instance, thinks that London is "far ayont the saut sea." Yet they possess an imagination, half-religious and half-superstitious, which endows "this same little world with an animation and a meaning almost impossible to imagine" either today or in Scott's own time.[46] It is illuminating to trace how Scott makes us recognize in such characters a mental world quite different from our own. An excellent example is the scene in which Jeanie Deans goes to meet Robertson, who she thinks may be the devil himself:

> Yet firmly believing the possibility of an encounter so terrible to flesh and blood, Jeanie, with a degree of resolution of which we cannot sufficiently estimate the merit, because the incredulity of the age has rendered us strangers to the nature and extent of her feelings, persevered in her determination not to omit an opportunity of doing something towards saving her sister, although, in the attempt to avail herself of it, she might be exposed to dangers so dreadful to her imagination. So, like Christiana in the *Pilgrim's Progress*, when traversing with a timid yet resolved step the terrors of the Valley of the Shadow of Death, she glided on by rock and stone, "now in glimmer and now in gloom," as her path lay through moonlight or shadow, and endeavoured to overpower the suggestions of fear, sometimes by fixing her mind upon the distressed condition of her sister, and the duty she lay under to afford her aid, should that be in her power, and more frequently by recurring in mental prayer to the protection of that Being to whom night is as noonday. [pp. 152–53; ch. 15]

In this passage and the scene that follows, we observe Scott's external characterization at work. He gives us a dramatic natural setting, a literary analogy, and the relevant cultural and historical background. He lists the things Jeanie thinks of to keep up her courage, but beyond that makes no attempt to depict her mental state directly. Scott

46. Introduction to *The Heart of Mid-Lothian*, pp. xiv–xv.

trusts us to complete the picture he has sketched. The technique used here is one Scott praised in Walpole: a mixture of general fictional excitement and specific historical detail leads the reader to make an imaginative leap backward in time.

There is an ultimate modesty in Scott's treatment of the minds of men and women separated from him in time. It is part of a larger fictional tact that rarely promises or attempts to execute more than it can convincingly deliver. This tact helps to save him from the exoticism Lukács deplores in many later writers, who seem so very sure that they can depict directly the mind of an earlier age, but instead merely project into it, in concentrated form, the most brutal imaginings of their own times.[47] Scott respects his characters, and he often reminds us of the gap separating us from them. Such a reminder occurs in *The Fair Maid of Perth*, Scott's best medieval novel. Simon Glover, a Perth tradesman, has taken refuge in the Highlands, since he is suspected of heresy. He finds himself sitting on a hill overlooking a Highland loch, observing the burial rites of a Highland chief who has recently died. Flotillas of boats and rafts gather on the lake, and suddenly a deafening cry of lament arises in the mountain fastness. This is an impressive scene, and Scott means it to be. But in its midst we find the following observation:

> There were even curraghs, composed of ox-hides stretched over hoops of willow, in the manner of the ancient British; and some committed themselves to rafts formed for the occasion, from the readiest materials that occurred, and united in such a precarious manner as to render it probable that, before the accomplishment of the voyage, some of the clansmen of the deceased might be sent to attend their chieftain in the world of spirits. [p. 319; ch. 27]

One might take this as proof of Scott's insensitivity to the past, as an Enlightenment joke at the expense of primitive societies and their absurdities, but I think something more important is happening here. Scott, after all, has painted the scene and created the tone from which this comment departs. The joke is really on us as readers and on Scott himself. He cannot and does not want to offer us a facile merging with the past. His fiction does not provide the chance to live in the days of yesteryear. We can only visit the past, catch glimpses of it,

47. Lukács, pp. 192–94.

wonder about what it meant to its regular inhabitants. We are different from the Highlanders. We see that the rafts are crazy and unsafe —we certainly would not trust ourselves to them. Scott has done his antiquarian, artistic, and human best, but the gap remains, and he knows it.

I would suggest, then, that though the notion that Scott believed in the essential uniformity of human nature is in a limited sense true, it can lead to mistaken conclusions about his historical insight and his artistic achievement. Our view of the Waverley Novels will be thrown sharply out of focus if we take the doctrine more seriously than Scott himself did, and hence assume that beneath their surfaces, his novels are centrally about human qualities that persist in spite of history. Such an assumption tends to degrade the historical representation at the heart of Scott's novels into mere background or local color. Instead of attending to what Scott does best, we will find ourselves driven to discover inner lives in his characters and to turn concrete historical depiction into moral allegory. If we do so in a consistent way, we will be forced to conclude, with Van Ghent, that since Scott's novels are inefficient vehicles for exploring the eternal human soul, they have little value.

Scott's novels embody a clear but not an overwhelming recognition that we are different from the men and women of the past. He has a stronger interest in historical difference than Tolstoy does, but a much weaker interest in human interiority and hence a less acute sense of the discontinuity between the levels of human existence in any age, past or present. As a result, he is fascinated by the pastness of the past, and he feels free to use his externally depicted characters as devices to explore history in ways that Tolstoy, given his representational priorities, could never have achieved and, given his spiritual priorities, would never have wanted to achieve. Tolstoy is surely the author of the greatest single historical novel, but Scott is arguably, because of the variety of things he does well with history in his novels, the greatest historical novelist.

He is at least the most historical of historical novelists. My discussion of his characterization should make this hyperbolic statement intelligible on the level of novelistic texture, since it has shown that

Scott's characterization occurs where human beings, societies, and history meet. The remainder of my book demonstrates the ways in which larger structures in the Waverley Novels are likewise designed to further essentially historical ends.

4

Form in Scott's Novels:
The Hero as Instrument

Scott did not believe in changing history merely to suit his fictional convenience, though he was willing to alter specific historical details to reveal with greater clarity fundamental historical patterns. He believed in telling the truth about history. He was often cavalier in his attitude toward novels, especially those produced by his contemporaries, Jane Austen excepted. But he was serious indeed about history and the duties of historians. Despite the low opinion he often expressed of the novel as a genre, we have every reason to think that he agreed with his friend Gifford's opinion, expressed in the anonymous review (which Scott coauthored) of Tales of My Landlord, Series One, that the successful historical novelist "takes his seat on the bench of the historians of his time and country."[1]

Scott's sense of history was based upon his sense of place. In an autobiographical sketch composed in 1808, he describes how a sense of place grew on him as a youth: "The love of natural beauty, more especially when combined with ancient ruins, or remains of our fathers' piety or splendour, became with me an insatiable passion."[2] This intense feeling for the historical associations of specific locales never left

1. [Walter Scott, William Erskine, and William Gifford], review of Tales of My Landlord, First Series, Quarterly Review, 16 (1817), 467. Martin Lightfoot, "Scott's Self-Reviewal: Manuscript and Other Evidence," Nineteenth-Century Fiction, 23 (1968), 150–60, untangles the problem of the review's authorship.

2. J. G. Lockhart, Memoirs of the Life of Sir Walter Scott, Bart., 2d ed., 10 vols. (Edinburgh: Cadell, 1839), I, 55.

Scott.[3] It made him particularly apt to take full advantage in his novels of the convenient historical fact that, until his own day, as a traveler moved from the south of England to the north of Scotland, he was on the whole moving back in time with respect to the social structures he encountered. When Waverley travels from England to the Highlands, he visits an earlier age. The usefulness of this geographical metaphor for a historical novelist is obvious enough, but it is important to recognize that it is a special kind of metaphor, one that happens to be literally true. Scott was not creating a metaphorical system he could conceivably have changed at will.[4]

G. M. Young has suggested that Scott was able to make historical documents speak in the same way that he could make a landscape yield up its historical significance. "The secret is to treat every document as the record of a conversation, and go on reading till you hear the people speaking."[5] Scott's success in this sort of historical recreation depended upon his shrewd grasp of human motivation, as well as his sociological understanding of the relationship between human beings and their historical milieux.

A sensitivity to the historical components of place, geography, and social milieu—this is the basis from which Scott's historical vision arose. We can describe such interests as representational and analytical: Scott wants us to see what the past was like and how past milieux worked. In some of his novels, he is mainly content to give a vivid portrait of an earlier time. Usually, he goes beyond this, and his vision raises issues we can describe as rhetorical and evaluative. His deepest historical interest, as all his best commentators from his own day to

3. David Daiches, "Sir Walter Scott and History," *Etudes anglaises,* 24 (1971), 459–60, discusses the topographical component of Scott's sense of history.

4. Martin Meisel discusses the influence of Scott's topographical sense in "*Waverley,* Freud, and Topographical Metaphor," *University of Toronto Quarterly,* 48 (1979), 226–44. That Darsie Latimer in *Redgauntlet* travels south, not north, to discover a more primitive level of society is further proof of the historical actuality behind Scott's geographical metaphors. At the highest level of generality, north indeed means increasingly primitive societies, as the progression London—Edinburgh—the Highlands suggests. But Edinburgh was a more civilized place than the area directly south of it, the Borders, which were in Scott's view much like the Highlands in social structure.

5. G. M. Young, "Scott and the Historians," in *Sir Walter Scott Lectures, 1940–48,* introd. W. L. Renwick (Edinburgh: Edinburgh University Press, 1950), p. 98.

the present have realized, is in historical process, its costs and its rewards. The power of his greatest works stems in large part from the intensity with which they imagine both the losses and the gains that result from progress. Attempts to decide that Scott is a pure apostle of progress, or a nostalgic obscurantist, or that he takes some definite position between these two extremes, will never seem wholly convincing. On the level of absolute value, Scott remained, with excellent results for his fiction, divided between his love of the past and his respect for the present; on a pragmatic level, he knew that progress was inevitable.

A final aspect of Scott's sense of the past often merges with the problem of the loss and gain occasioned by historical process, but is separable from it. Scott was interested in the sense of the past as a phenomenon, a sensation, a feeling and a passion. His novels explore the esthetics of the sense of history. This interest is akin to his fascination with human beliefs concerning the supernatural, and indeed with all elevated, irrational states of mind. The formal implications of Scott's interest in the historical sense as a sensation have been largely neglected.

Scott, then, believed in telling the truth about history. In his eyes, that truth took a number of forms. It included the rich historical associations of topography and the fact that in Great Britain certain movements in space were also movements in time. It included a perception that different societies in the past formed coherent systems, and a grasp of the slow process by which one state of society gives way to another. It included a dynamically divided judgment concerning the desirability of historical change, but also a moral imperative toward accepting the inevitable. Finally, it included an interest in reactions to the past as phenomena in their own right, a fascination not simply with the grand and frightening stream of history on which we are all embarked, but also with how it feels to contemplate its course.

Scott's belief in telling the truth about history opened up for him great imaginative possibilities, but also made him subject to certain constraints. The notion of historical truth, however, deserves further consideration before we can describe its workings in the novels. The explorations of historical "fore-understanding" by thinkers as diverse as H. G. Gadamer and Hayden White make it difficult to suppose that telling the truth about history could involve a simple cross-check-ing of a novel against a positive historical record. Scott himself often seems unaware that historical facts are not stones he can give a Johnsonian kick; given his position in the development of historical thought, it is hardly surprising that he makes the mistake opposite from our own, seeing too few problems in apprehending historical reality, where we tend to see too many.[6] Scott's sense of what it means to be true to history is obviously mediated, consciously or unconsciously, by the tacit cultural assumptions that inform his ideology (using the latter term, as I have been throughout this book, in a basically neutral way). His Scottish nationalism, his class position, his training as a lawyer, and his schooling in the ideas of the Edinburgh Enlightenment clearly enter in here. Such things translate themselves, by the crooked and indirect byways of ideological mediation, into a preference for depicting certain kinds of characters and finding in history certain kinds of plots. But they do not form a smooth and seamless amalgam that transforms history into their mirror image. A serious attempt to explain why Scott's novels are as they are makes abundantly clear the inaccuracy of supposing that history's intractable otherness is an illusion. It might be possible to imagine human beings or societies with ideologies so pure and consistent that they could not be transcended, even in thought, and even by the most conscientious and well-informed thinkers. But such human beings and societies have never existed and never will: they are products of Cartesian abstraction. The mental constructs by which human beings make sense of the world are infinitely more subtle and more contradictory than that; the contradictions of the past are not those of the present, and this in itself provides an opportunity for knowledge of the historically other. One might argue that class ideologies determine concrete

6. Hans-Georg Gadamer, *Truth and Method* (1960; trans. New York: Seabury, 1975); Hayden White, *Metahistory: The Historical Imagination in Nineteenth-Century Europe* (Baltimore: Johns Hopkins University Press, 1973); see also White's *Tropics of Discourse: Essays in Cultural Criticism* (Baltimore: Johns Hopkins University Press, 1978). We do not lack voices to remind us that a historicism like Scott's hovers on the brink of any number of philosophical inconsistencies, and may even tumble in. Thus we can wonder why Scott supposes that he understands how history works, while none of the characters in his novels seem to have such knowledge, and we can chip away at the facticity of what he takes to be historical facts. Instead of pursuing such issues, I shall examine what Scott erected on foundations that may well be shaky.

action and the practical use to which ideas are put in a given society, but that is another question. Products of the mind are not so bound, and for society to maintain its patterns of domination, they need not be.

Because Scott believes in telling the truth about history, his choice of the subject for a novel is crucial. His ideology may give him a set of (potentially conflicting) criteria for that which is historically true and esthetically pleasing, but it does not guarantee that he will always be able to bend a historical subject to his needs. When he makes an unfortunate choice, the result is disastrous, and the best that can happen (since he rarely abandons a project once he starts it) is that he rushes a work like *The Black Dwarf* to a huddled conclusion, and goes on to write an *Old Mortality*. He also must reckon with the public's expectations, or lack of expectations, concerning the tracts of history he chooses to depict, and with his own wish to avoid repeating himself in form or subject matter. All these things help to determine whether he can fulfill his wish to provide for himself and his readers certain kinds of imaginative pleasures: the excitement of experiencing imaginatively the structures of past societies, the catharsis of seeing history fall into a comprehensible and conclusive pattern, the heightened self-awareness of knowing what it means to experience the past.

Understanding form in the Waverley Novels means discovering the interplay between the historical subject of each novel and the esthetic and historiographical patterns Scott brings to it. In this chapter and the next, I shall argue that he devised two main strategies for giving his historical interests fictional form in the novels that center on history. One of these strategies is familiar; it is a mainstay of much of the fiction that preceded and followed him. In such novels, the protagonist serves as the substantial center: he is central both in embodying the novel's meaning and in providing the center of its structure. We have discussed the problems such a protagonist poses for the author of a historical novel. What I have called the problem with historical novels calls into question the adequacy of any character to represent the entire spectrum of human existence. But a protagonist with a substantially central structural position in a historical novel tends to be given precisely this representational function. As we might expect, Scott does not create a central protagonist often, but on two occasions the nature of his historical subject invites him to do so. The novels that result are the subject of my final chapter.

Another kind of fictional strategy, which Scott employs more frequently, involves the creation of a more instrumental kind of protagonist—or, to be more precise, a range of such protagonists. Even at their most complex, such heroes act ultimately as markers, pointing toward some aspect of history; in simpler incarnations, they are frankly utilitarian, and their fictional careers fit Scott's own description of plot as a string to hang fine things upon.

Because we tend to assume that protagonists will possess substantial centrality in novels, we lack an adequate vocabulary for discussing those lacking centrality. The terms generally used to describe such figures in Scott—the "weak" hero, or at best the "middle-of-the-road" hero—tend to imply moral or political opprobrium. The absence of more neutral terms has obscured some necessary distinctions. In the present chapter, I shall distinguish between "disjunctive" and "conjunctive" protagonists, focusing on what their fictional careers imply about historical process. The heroes of disjunctive novels imply little or nothing in this respect. Their successes and failures do not translate into propositions concerning the course of history. Their fictional careers are severed or disjoined from historical process, though they can help to create other kinds of historical meaning. In conjunctive novels, by contrast, Scott's form leads us to interpret the hero's career as a commentary on historical process, though we do not take it to be a consubstantial symbol of that process.[7]

To put the distinction in more formal terms, we can say that in Scott's conjunctive novels, our hopes and fears for the hero involve more than his individual desert and fate: the hero's action effects and comments upon Scott's exploration of historical process. The action of *Waverley*, for instance, drives us to hope that his fate will take a certain form. Since we hope that he will survive and marry the safe, loving, domestic Rose Bradwardine, we are led to wish to see history assume a shape that will allow this, and we acquiesce in the historical transition from a dangerous, heroic past to a safe, dull present. In Scott's disjunctive novels, by contrast, the action is both central and peripheral. Although it is the organizing principle for the novel, it leads to but does not embody the novel's historical meaning and effect. A disjunctive action has a function much like that which Balzac

---

7. Here as in my discussion of uses of history in historical fiction, I concentrate not on all the theoretical possibilities but on the forms Scott actually employed.

assigns to the central figures in Lethière's historical painting, *Brutus*. Balzac, as we have seen, suggests that the dramatic scene in the center of the painting exists not for its own sake but to draw us into the painting, so that we will come to know Rome. In Scott's disjunctive novels, the central action points toward more than milieu—usually, it points toward a great historical figure. When Scott employs disjunctive form, his major task, as well as his major opportunity, is to make his action more than a pretext, to give it as much independent interest as he can.

Disjunctive form in the Waverley Novels often results from Scott's wish to depict historical material too particular and idiosyncratic to fit into a conjunctive pattern. To demonstrate how historical specificity can stand in the way of conjunctive form, we may examine the opening section of *The Abbot*. In the novel's first chapters, the hero, Roland Graeme, plays the role we would expect the hero of a conjunctive novel to play. As he threads his way through successive scenes, he has a series of encounters that sum up the basic conflicts of his society and historical period. Through his eyes, we observe the life of the Avenels, a noble Protestant family in the Borders of Scotland, whom he serves as page. When he is briefly expelled from the family, his adventures lead him to a newly sacked abbey and to the scattered remnants still actively supporting Catholicism. As befits a Waverley hero, his own allegiances are divided. He has great affection for the Protestant lady whom he serves, but he remains a crypto-Catholic, and his grandmother, a ferociously loyal Catholic, periodically reappears to assert her dominance over him and to keep him true to her faith. This dominance is something he comes to resent. His problem at first seems a variation on the basic problem faced by many Waverley heroes. Where Waverley is searching for a proper father, Roland Graeme in the initial section of the novel is searching for a suitable mother, one whose heritage will enable him to grow instead of stifling him.

Ruins are a prominent part of *The Abbot*. Throughout the opening section, when Roland Graeme comes upon a scene of recent destruction, it has an easily recognizable significance. In the Cell of St. Cuthbert, for instance, he discovers a sacred statue that has been sacrilegiously thrown down and broken. He restores it to its proper place, but his piety has ironic results. His grandmother suddenly appears and devotes him body and soul to the Catholic cause. Her abject groveling before the statue seems to justify the Protestants' view that such works of art are idols. Her fanaticism poses a grave threat to his development, indeed to his life. Our hopes and fears for Roland in this scene resemble those *Waverley* evokes: we hope that he will be able to escape from the influence of his grandmother without dishonoring himself. But when the historical issues at stake in his time have been presented through such scenes as the one at the Cell of St. Cuthbert, the quality of his experience and his function in the novel begin to change. He journeys to Edinburgh with another of the Avenel retainers, and on the way he encounters a piece of ruined architecture which stubbornly refuses to fit into the general pattern the novel has created. Its significance can hardly be discussed, much less understood. When Roland asks his companion about it, he is told, in "a low and impressive whisper," to "ask no more about it; somebody got foul play, and somebody got the blame of it; and the game began there which perhaps may not be played out in our time" (p. 154; ch. 17). The ruin is in fact the Kirk of Field, where Mary Queen of Scots' second husband was murdered; it was exploded with gunpowder while he was sleeping there. Whether or not Mary herself was responsible remained, in Scott's eyes at least, an open question. After he sees the ruins of the Kirk of Field, Roland increasingly comes to play the role of a disjunctive hero, whose action serves to lead us to the novel's true center, Queen Mary. Mary becomes the mother he had been seeking, but as part of a wish-fulfilling myth about legitimacy like the one that wells up at the end of *Guy Mannering*—Roland turns out to be a nobleman and comes into his own—not in a way that leads us to draw conclusions about the general historical process surrounding these events and personages. Like her son James VI and I, Mary does not easily assume a place in the larger scheme of historical process. Scott is much too interested in her as a dramatic personality to want to view her primarily as an index or summation of historical forces. She lacks the simple relationship to historical process of Charles Edward in *Waverley*. Some of the particularities that most intrigue Scott simply cannot be explained without question, as in the case of the murder of Darnley at the Kirk of Field. The best he can do is to produce a "low and impressive whisper" about them, and he does this very well indeed in *The Abbot*, despite the tushery of the novel's spoken language. The ruined Kirk of Field exists at a level of particularity that begins to resist being made part of a larger historical pattern; it must be approached in disjunctive fashion. So must Mary herself. When she finally appears in the novel, Roland Graeme is there to show her to us. She does not become a part of his action; his action exists for her sake.

A great deal rests upon what sort of mimetic function we ascribe to the heroes of Scott's novels. If my distinctions between different kinds of Waverley heroes hold, they cast doubt on criticism that depends, implicitly or explicitly, on seeing the Waverley hero, however conceived, as the substantial center of all the novels. The implicit or explicit use of a simple Bildungsroman model for the novels becomes particularly questionable, if the heroes do not concentrate the meanings of the novels within themselves, and if not all of them create historical meaning in the same way.[8]

The most important fact about form in the Waverley Novels is that Scott brings to bear on each scene as many of his historical interests as he can, but that these interests appear at different levels of importance, creating different formal consequences in different works. Since nearly all his historical interests enter into every Waverley Novel, it is possible to provide evidence for a basically homogeneous Scott, who was really doing the same thing in all his novels, but with varying degrees of success. Because of the multiplicity and persistence of Scott's historical interests, changes in historical mode in a given novel or between novels are rarely so clear as the change of mode we discovered in *Les Chouans*, where even though the historically representative parts of the novel continue to the end, they clearly become increasingly peripheral as the novel progresses. Important and systematic differences nonetheless exist between different kinds of Waverley Novels. The categories I shall employ to register these differences—my distinctions between instrumental and central protagonists and between conjunctive and disjunctive forms—are "ideal types," never realized

---

8. If they hold, my categories of Waverley heroes tend to dilute the singular hero Alexander Welsh discusses in *The Hero of the Waverley Novels*, Yale Studies in English, 154 (New Haven: Yale University Press, 1963). It also becomes difficult to draw conclusions about Scott's view of history from whether or not his heroes survive, as Marian Cusac does in *Narrative Structure in the Novels of Sir Walter Scott* (The Hague: Mouton, 1969).

in a pure state in any given novel. They name tendencies that coexist with other formal tendencies, but that are decisive in determining form and meaning. They are thus "dominants" in the sense in which the Russian Formalists used the term.

The Waverley Novels lend themselves to univocal readings because their complexity is unobtrusive. Such readings can have great strengths. Modern critics who explore Scott's depiction of the workings of historical process are describing what is most enduringly important about his work. In another vein, David Daiches has seized upon what probably matters most about Scott to his fellow countrymen, his exploration of the problems of Scottish identity.[9] Such analyses have an enduring value. But though they see Scott steadily, they do not see him whole. To capture as much of his diversity as possible, we need coherent ways of describing how the different strands common to the novels form distinctive wholes in individual works.

DISJUNCTIVE FORM

Scott's disjunctive novels are probably his most underrated works. Identifying them as a group possessing their own distinctive problems and techniques may help to promote an appreciation of their virtues: it should also direct our attention to the things their protagonists do well, and prevent us from attaching inappropriate kinds of historical significance to their adventures. Scott's disjunctive heroes usually frame and illuminate their novels' true subjects in a rich and effective way. Beyond that, disjunctiveness itself can become a positive advantage, by promoting a contrapuntal dialogue, rich in historical significance, between the protagonist and the historical figure on which a novel centers.

Quentin Durward

The purest example of Scott's disjunctive form is *Quentin Durward*. The novel has a strongly constructed action, in which the pro-

9. This interest is perhaps most richly present in Daiches's classic article, "Scott's *Redgauntlet*," in *From Jane Austen to Joseph Conrad: Essays Collected in Memory of James T. Hillhouse*, ed. Robert C. Rathburn and Martin Steinmann, Jr. (Minneapolis: University of Minnesota Press, 1958), pp. 46–59.

tagonist, Quentin, becomes a member of the Scottish Archers of Louis XI and subsequently undergoes a series of adventures which ultimately win him the hand of a countess. During the course of his activities, Quentin fulfills many of the functions we associate with the Waverley hero. As a historical sightseer, he covers a good deal of territory geographically, politically, and socially. More important, his action is the instrument by which we come to place in historical context the true subject of the novel, Louis XI. Quentin fulfills this, his primary function, with admirable efficiency, but in a way that has little direct historical significance. Our pattern of hopes and fears for him as he wins his countess does not strongly translate into a developing set of historical propositions, and this is why the novel is disjunctive, not conjunctive. Scott makes the general outlines of form in *Quentin Durward* clear in his Magnum Opus Introduction to the novel, in which he describes Louis XI as "the principal character" in *Quentin Durward* and parenthetically remarks, as if embarrassed by the obviousness of what he is saying, that "it will be easily comprehended, that the little love intrigue of Quentin is only employed as the means of bringing out the story" (p. xvii).

To say that *Quentin Durward* is disjunctive in form is not to say that it is disorganized. In fact, the novel is among the best plotted of the Waverley series. Scott takes considerable pains to weave the elements of his story into a whole. One means he employs is to invite us to believe initially that Quentin is indeed the center of the novel, even though he is not. Scott excuses his first chapter, which contains a historical sketch of the character and times of Louis XI, on the grounds that "the passions of the great, their quarrels, and their reconciliations, involve the fortunes of all who approach them; and it will be found, on proceeding farther in our story, that this preliminary chapter is necessary for comprehending the history of the individual whose adventures we are about to relate" (p. 7; ch. 1). Unlike the description from the Magnum Opus Introduction, which gives a truer notion of Quentin's place in the story, this passage is a tactical part of the fiction itself. The appreciation of a work like *Quentin Durward* turns out to be a complex affair. On one level, we place Quentin at the center of our interest, for doing so propels us through what would otherwise be a fictionally inert portrait of Louis XI and his age. At a deeper level, we know all along that Quentin is a means, not an end, and we derive considerable pleasure from seeing the skill with which Scott so employs him.

This skill is nowhere more apparent than in the novel's opening scenes. In the first chapter, Scott has given an analysis of the character of Louis XI: now the problem is to enact that analysis. Toward this end, Scott employs a favorite ballad situation, the motif of the disguised king, which among other things promotes the external depiction of character and historical significance Scott habitually favors. Quentin falls in with a man who is dressed like a rich burgher, but whom he cannot wholly comprehend. In successive scenes the burgher seems at first ordinary, then distinctly sinister, and then, when he is praying at a shrine, almost saintly. The man, who calls himself "Maître Pierre," is Louis XI. Each of Quentin's discordant impressions underlines a facet of the king's character—his singular mixture of cruelty, deceit, brilliance, coarseness, and religiosity. Finally, the game comes to an end, and Maître Pierre is revealed to be the king. Quentin's impression of him is ironically transformed, as

> those eyes which, according to Quentin's former impression, only twinkled with the love of gain, had, now that they were known to be the property of an able and powerful monarch, a piercing and majestic glance; and those wrinkles on the brow, which he had supposed were formed during a long series of petty schemes of commerce, seemed now the furrows which sagacity had worn while toiling in meditation upon the fate of nations. [p. 88; ch. 8]

This passage and the scenes that precede it pose an implicit question—how different is this king from a burgher? When Louis meets Quentin for the first time, he is amused that Quentin takes him for a "money-broker or a corn-merchant" and replies, "My business is indeed to trade in as much money as I can" (p. 12; ch. 2). For Scott, the reign of Louis XI represents the first step in the process by which kings ultimately become if not burghers themselves, then the representatives of burghers. He is the prime example of a king in tune with the historical process that destroyed the feudal, chivalric world.

Quentin subsequently serves to illuminate the character of Louis XI in a more straightforward way. He is a hidden spectator at a dinner during which Louis XI exhibits his diplomatic genius, his scurrilous mind (Quentin is shocked at the jokes he hears), and his unscru-

pulousness (Quentin has been ordered to murder the Burgundian am-
bassador should Louis give the signal). So that Quentin can function
as a commentator as well as a spectator, Scott gives him a certain degree of modernity in outlook. He possesses a well-developed conscience and a maidenly modesty, which are made barely probable by
his having been brought up in a monastery for much of his youth. His
moral scruples throughout the novel when faced with Louis XI's ne-
farious schemes effectively emphasize the Machiavellian nature of his
employer.

After his services at the king's dinner prove unnecessary, Quentin is
sent on an expedition that puts him, physically at least, in a more independent position. Two noblewomen have come to the French court,
seeking protection from their feudal lord, the Duke of Burgundy. Instead of harboring them himself, Louis orders Quentin to conduct
them to neutral territory in Liège. One of the women is the countess
with whom Quentin falls in love and whom he eventually marries.
Determining the fictional purpose of this journey is crucial to understanding the form of the novel as a whole. Before it, Quentin has
clearly been used to illuminate the character of Louis XI; after it, except for a brief episode at the end which can be considered an extension of the journey since it ends in the marriage of Quentin and the
countess, Louis again enters the picture as the obvious center of attention. Even during his journey, I shall argue, Quentin remains a disjunctive hero, whose function is to reveal the character and significance of Louis XI.

Quentin goes into motion precisely when the portrait of Louis XI
threatens to become static. Extended portraits of great historical figures in historical fiction always run that risk, and such devices as the
"disguised king" motif can do only so much to counter it. But Quentin's adventures are nothing if not dynamic, and they enrich our sense
of Louis as well. Quentin's mission turns out to be entirely characteristic of Louis. It is antichivalric. Instead of trying to aid two damsels
in distress, Louis decides to use them to further his own political
aims. The plan is treacherous in a grand way. Louis does not inform
Quentin of his actual intent, namely that the ladies should be kidnapped by a particularly brutal robber baron, William de la Marck,
the Wild Boar of Ardennes. If all goes well, the kidnapping will em-

broil de la Marck in a war with Louis's rival, the Duke of Burgundy. Should Quentin Durward be killed, as he probably will be, so much the worse for him. The plan is politically astute, but in typical fashion for Louis XI, it verges on oversubtlety. Louis picks Durward because the latter appears too simple and honest to see through the king's plans, and in turn could hardly be suspected of being part of such a ruthless scheme. But Durward's very youth, bravery, and ingenuousness lead him to escape from the ambush that had been prepared for him. In the long run, however, the king's subtlety vindicates itself, for Quentin's sense of honor prevents him from betraying Louis, even after he has discovered what the king had in store for him. Finally, the choice of Durward for this mission betrays the strange mixture of rationalism and credulity Scott finds in Louis XI. The king employs Durward for the devious reasons already mentioned, but also because of religious superstition (Louis first met Durward on a certain saint's day) and a credulous belief in astrology (the court astrologer has predicted great things for the boy).

Quentin's adventurous journey not only reveals the character of Louis XI, it also gives Scott the opportunity to place the king in a larger historical context.[10] This is partly a matter of Quentin's function as a historical sightseer. Through his eyes we discover the unruly world Louis is attempting to tame, as well as the force that will ultimately succeed him—the middle class, typified by the burghers of Liège. The journey also allows Scott to depict the decadence of the system of chivalry, the last remnants of which Louis is doing so much to destroy. At the beginning of the journey, Quentin is attacked by two knights errant, who are interested in the countess but whom he succeeds in fending off until the king's archers arrive. One of the knights turns out to be a prince whom Louis intends for his own misshapen daughter and who is promptly taken off to prison. So much for chivalrous attempts to win fair ladies by battle. During the journey, a more comic deflation of chivalry is provided by one of Quentin's charges, the aging and still unwillingly single Lady Hameline. Her interminable stories about a tournament once held in her honor

---

10. For a discussion of the novel's vision of Louis XI's world, see Avrom Fleishman, *The English Historical Novel: Walter Scott to Virginia Woolf* (Baltimore: Johns Hopkins University Press, 1971), pp. 58–61.

make one feel that chivalry is not merely dead but well dead, especially when she recounts with scarcely concealed relish the bodily in-
juries sustained by the knights who fought for her.

Quentin's journey, then, serves primarily as a means of historical
analysis, but it has other resonances as well. Scott the moralist surfaces briefly in two ways. His belief that international politics ought
in all ages to be conducted openly is reflected when Quentin decides
to tell both King Louis and the Duke of Burgundy that the Liègeois
are planning a night attack, so that neither will have an unfair advantage over the other.[11] Scott also provides an example of how young
men ought to submit good humoredly to their elders. Quentin earns
the respect of the Count of Crèvecoeur by keeping his temper even
when taunted about his overambitious love for the countess. Beyond
that, there is a hint, though it is *just* a hint, in Quentin's pursuit of the
countess of a tacit proposition about historical process. The countess
persists in refusing to obey the Duke of Burgundy when he selects a
husband for her, and in a rage, he decides that she shall become the
wife of whoever kills de la Marck in an impending battle. In the
event, de la Marck falls by the hand of Quentin's uncle, who though
egotistical, stupid, and uncouth, is expert at removing heads and de-
livering them to his superiors. The uncle yields his claim to Quentin,
who had been fighting de la Marck before duty called him elsewhere,
but the fleeting possibility that the countess will have to marry a boor
helps us to acquiesce in the passing of chivalry. Countesses ought not
to be won by the fortunes of battle: chivalry is an attractive ideal, but
an uncomfortable reality. A further reflection on historical process,
familiar to readers of other Waverley Novels, is implied by Quentin's
finally gaining the countess—the hope that, in the modern world, the
virtues of chivalry can be preserved without its attendant brutalities
and absurdities. Quentin acts the part of a gentleman when he breaks
off fighting de la Marck to save a girl from being raped by some other
soldiers, and Providence takes care of Quentin for so doing.

If Quentin's plotted action functioned consistently to promote the
propositions about historical process I have just described, the novel
would be conjunctive in form, not disjunctive: it would be another
Waverley. In fact it does not. Even in the final scenes, where it is pos-

---

11. Scott inveighs against "Machiavellian" statecraft in the Magnum Opus Introduction to the novel.

sible to make out a propositional content in the action most clearly, there is a strong countercurrent. One lesson of the final scenes is that countesses should not be won by battle, but our interest in Quentin's "little love intrigue" throughout the novel makes us feel that this countess should be so won, and won by Quentin, who otherwise would have no chance at her. Though much about *Quentin Durward* suggests that chivalry is not merely dead but well dead, Quentin himself helps to create a countervailing feeling, if not about the realities of chivalry, at least about chivalry as an ideal and as an object of the imagination. Despite their analytical usefulness, his adventures are tinged with a strong element of self-conscious historical fantasy. This note sounds from the opening of the novel. In an early scene, Quentin first observes the countess he will ultimately marry at the hostelry where the supposed Maître Pierre takes him for a meal. Afterwards, Quentin lingers, hoping to catch a glimpse of her from his turret room at the inn:

> The turret of Quentin was opposite to another turret, and the little window at which he stood commanded a similar little window in a corresponding projection of the building. Now, it would be difficult for a man twenty years older than Quentin to say why this locality interested him more than either the pleasant garden or the grove of mulberry-trees; for, alas! eyes which have been used for forty years and upwards look with indifference on little turret-windows, though the lattice be half open to admit the air, while the shutter is half closed to exclude the sun, or perhaps a too curious eye—nay, even though there hang on the one side of the casement a lute, partly mantled by a light veil of sea-green silk. But, at Durward's happy age, such "accidents," as a painter would call them, form sufficient foundation for a hundred airy visions and mysterious conjectures, at recollection of which the full-grown man smiles while he sighs, and sighs while he smiles. [pp. 39–40; ch. 4]

Quentin watches the window closely and unobtrusively, and his vigilance is rewarded; he sees

> a white, round, beautiful arm take down the instrument, and . . . his ears had presently after their share in the reward of his dexterous management.
> The maid of the little turret, of the veil, and of the lute sung exactly such an air as we are accustomed to suppose flowed from the lips of

the high-born dames of chivalry, when knights and troubadours listened and languished. [p. 40; ch. 4]

The strength and interest of this description lie in Scott's genial
amusement at our wish for romance, his mixture of belief and disbe-
lief in what he is doing. We feel the same tone of self-amused embarrassment when he refers to Quentin's "little love intrigue" in the
Magnum Opus Introduction. Scott knows what we would like to
think about the past, and to an extent he allows us to indulge ourselves. As the novel progresses, a romantic treatment of the late Middle Ages recedes, but it does not wholly evaporate in the depiction of
Quentin himself.

Scott's recognition that the age of Louis XI was dangerous and
inhuman is abundantly clear from the novel itself, with its sinister ex-
ecutioners and its picture of men hanging by the neck from the trees
that surround Louis XI's castle. Quentin's adventures help to reveal
the character of the age, but they also provide a fantasy promise of
imaginative freedom as an alternative to the brutality of William de la
Marck, the heedless and wasteful chivalry of the Duke of Burgundy,
and the Machiavellian plotting of the antichivalric Louis XI. Late in
the novel, the Count of Crèvecoeur tells Quentin that he has been
walking in a dream to think of marrying a countess. The count has a
point. Having used Quentin so skillfully for the main historical purpose of his novel, to present a portrait of Louis XI, Scott allows himself and us to enjoy with Quentin a genial historical fantasy come
true, which is as Crèvecoeur puts it "all full of heroic adventure, and
high hope, and wild, minstrel-like delusion, like the gardens of *Mor-
gaine la Fée*" (p. 281; ch. 24). The use of a hero to serve as an instrument of historical analysis, but also to provide a counterpoint to the
historical vision that analysis reveals, characterizes Scott's disjunctive
fiction at its best.

The Fortunes of Nigel

The nature of Scott's subject in *The Fortunes of Nigel* invites him
to create a richer, less calculated counterpoint than he achieves in
Durward. An early scene in *Nigel* depicts James VI of Scotland and I
of England sitting in his study, surrounded by a welter of materi-

als—papers of state and his own amateurish poems, sermons and books of bawdy songs—which in their confusion mirror, the narrator tells us, the contradictory nature of James's own mind. The remainder of the novel uses narrative means to define the significance of this singular figure.

One way in which James's significance is revealed is through the moral education of the novel's hero, Nigel Oliphaunt, Lord Glenvarloch. This education pits the qualities of George Heriot, a character based on James's royal goldsmith, against those of the king, much to the king's disadvantage. In the course of the novel, Nigel makes a series of discoveries that help to define James's weaknesses as a man and a ruler. He learns, first of all, to transcend "the Bastile of his rank" (p. 315; ch. 27), by coming to respect the middle classes, whom Heriot represents at their best. Initially, Nigel shies away from accepting the help of a mere tradesman. When Heriot suggests that the Lord Chancellor of Scotland has secretly foiled Nigel's attempt to regain his patrimony, he replies that he "cannot believe a nobleman would carry deceit so far" (p. 45; ch. 4). By the end of the novel, Nigel has had a very full taste of how far a nobleman's deception can go, and he finds himself marrying Heriot's goddaughter, the daughter of a watchmaker, who is related, but only obscurely related, to a noble Scottish family. It is necessary to add some qualification and caveats here. Nigel may learn to appreciate the virtues of the middle classes, but he most certainly does not become in any sense a direct representative of the middle classes. The seemingly democratic side of the novel is balanced by its delight in demonstrating that people (the romantic heroine excepted) should keep to their proper stations; no one believes more firmly in maintaining class distance and decorum than Heriot himself. Heriot counsels Nigel to be true to his dead father, which means being true to his own best self as a nobleman. We must suppose that the reformed Nigel will go on to follow the course of action he himself outlines before his lapse from fidelity to his father's ideals, much to the amusement of the novel's villain, Lord Dalgarno, and of certain modern critics, who find it antiquated: he will return to Scotland, live on his country estate, take care of his vassals, teach his children virtue and self-sacrifice, and generally preserve his patrimony.

In pursuing his fortunes, Nigel learns more than the value of the middle classes: he comes to understand the reasons behind the high standard of morality to which his father had committed him and from which he is seduced by Dalgarno. This education does not come easily. In the course of the novel he undergoes a series of encounters in which he is rudely awakened to his own misconduct by no less than nine of his social inferiors. Five of these scenes involve direct, scathing attacks on his manners and morals, and the narrator is careful to point out Nigel's mental suffering in listening to them. They culminate in his being baited in prison by Sir Mungo Malagrowther, whom Scott in another context calls a speaker of "useful, though unpleasant truths."[12] Nigel has been foolish enough to draw his sword in the king's park, and it seems for a moment that he will lose his right hand for committing this crime. Sir Mungo describes for him in excruciating detail the sufferings of a previous malefactor, a member of the lower classes named Stubbs, who suffered the same fate: his hand "flew off as far from the owner as a gauntlet which the challenger casts down in the tilt-yard" when it was cut off, and his bleeding stump "fizzed like a rasher of bacon" when it was cauterized (p. 369; ch. 30). Sir Mungo himself has lost several fingers in a duel, is riddled with pride of caste, and is an altogether useless hanger-on at court. He stands as a warning of what may become of Nigel should he not mend his ways.

In moments like Sir Mungo's description of the mutilation of Stubbs, Scott takes an evident delight in giving a relatively innocent and random narrative career a sudden, threatening turn. Such darkly humorous moments demonstrate that our actions may have consequences that are frighteningly unpredictable yet, in retrospect, inexorably logical. Heriot fleshes out this perception when his turn comes to upbraid Nigel for his misdeeds, by giving this answer to Nigel's promise to undo any harm he has caused, "so far as is in [his] power":

> "Ah! my lord," continued Heriot, "that is a melancholy though a necessary restriction; for how lightly may any one do an hundred times more than the degree of evil which it may be within his power to repair to the sufferers and to society!" [p. 351; ch. 29]

12. MPW XXI, 270. The reference occurs in the "Malachi Malagrowther" letters, in which Scott employs a supposed descendant of Sir Mungo to attack a proposed change in the Scottish currency.

In his next speech but two, Nigel declares that he is in prison "because, to begin from my original error, I would be wiser than my father" (p. 351; ch. 29). Heriot, we realize, has already shown why it is foolish to try to be wiser than one's father. The web of inherited customs, traditions, and laws is so complexly interwoven that once disturbed it can hardly be mended. This is why it is so easy for a man to do more harm than he can repair, why Nigel's seemingly venial sins suddenly take on ominous proportions. By the end of the novel, Nigel has learned that at the base of his father's moral punctiliousness lies a sound insight concerning life in society.

Nigel's moral education creates an ironic counterpoint between Heriot and King James which attempts to encompass matters both moral and historical. For James abundantly lacks the central quality Heriot exemplifies and recommends to Nigel, moral "firmness"—a word that in its various forms Scott employs as a leitmotif throughout the novel. The historical and moral sides of the novel, then, appear to fall into a neat and conclusive pattern, with Nigel's moral education serving to define the meaning of the mutually illuminating relationship between Heriot and James. By stressing the dangerous absurdity of over-rigid class distinctions, Nigel's education points to the perils in James's lack of contact with the people he rules. By demonstrating the heroic firmness of the middle classes, it emphasizes how thoroughly James himself lacks such firmness, and it also suggests where the true vitality of English society lies. Finally, by allowing Nigel to take on certain aspects of middle-class probity without losing his aristocratic essence, it gestures toward defining the kind of utopian solution to class differences which James himself spectacularly fails to achieve, but which remains Scott's rather hopeless dream for history, and for his own age.

But the nature and significance of James's failings as a king, and their relationship to historical process, turn out to be considerably more subtle and complex. The plotted action in *Nigel* plays out a medley of conflicting responses to James, no Louis XI across the Channel, but a figure deeply intertwined in the historical issues about which Scott felt most passionately ambivalent—issues involving Scottish independence and the Scottish character. In the novel as a whole, there are strong countercurrents to the values Heriot embodies; seen in this context, the firm moral center Heriot provides begins to look like a willful device to force history, and our reactions to history, to have a univalent meaning and to make moral sense.

The prison scenes, which are so crucial in creating the novel's bourgeois critique of James, have other resonances concerning the king's failings as well, some of which unexpectedly measure him against standards that are anything but bourgeois. Heriot, an abstemious, chaste widower, is particularly harsh with Nigel for his alleged sexual misconduct, even when that misconduct turns out to have been slight: Nigel has allowed a false rumor that he had seduced his landlord's wife to circulate uncontradicted. Yet the prison scene itself is full of sly sexual innuendo and voyeuristic joking which involve the novel's heroine. She had disguised herself as a page, hoping to make her way to the king and beg for Nigel's freedom, but after her interview with the king, she finds herself, still in disguise, placed in Nigel's cell. Some predictable byplay follows, as Nigel offers to share his bed with the supposed page, she shrinks in horror, and the reader enjoys the dramatic irony, just as James himself is in fact doing—he has arranged the scene to "test" Nigel, and is eavesdropping, though the reader does not yet realize it. When Heriot enters the cell, he recognizes and berates the heroine for her seemingly loose behavior, but he also finds time for some sexual levity of his own. He is annoyed that she sought out the king without telling him, but he is sure that nothing immoral resulted, since King James differs from his ancestors: "Had you been closeted with his grandfather, the Red Tod of St. Andrews, as Davie Lindsay used to call him, by my faith, I should have had my own thoughts of the matter; but our master, God bless him, is douce and temperate, and Solomon in every thing save in the chapter of wives and concubines" (p. 360; ch. 29). Heriot's nickname for the heroine, "Peg-a-Ramsay," itself derives from a remarkably crude Scottish song.[13] This sort of joking may come as a surprise from the writer who purified prose fiction for Victorian consumption, but it finds echoes in the rest of *Nigel*, helping to form a backdrop against which the king is weighed and found wanting according to standards quite different from those provided by Heriot's stern moralism. When James foolishly congratulates his courtiers on their good fortune that

13. The song is collected in *Wit and Mirth: Or Pills to Purge Melancholy*, ed. Thomas D'Urfey (New York: Folklore Library Publishers, 1959), V, 139–40, and referred to in *Twelfth Night*, II, iii.

he is less ferocious than his ancestors had been, their response makes it clear that moral firmness is not the only kind of firmness he lacks. If one of James's ancestors were on the English throne, comes their reply, audible to all but James, "at least . . . we should have had *a man* to our sovereign, though he were but a Scotsman" (p. 107; ch. 9). At such moments, the Scottish past is transformed from the repository of moral virtues Heriot tries to make it in eulogizing Nigel's father. It becomes a lost world of martial prowess and sexual potency, with the ferocious, lecherous James IV ("the Red Tod of St. Andrews") replacing Nigel's dour, abstemious father as the standard from which the present has degenerated. On the surface, *Nigel* may suggest that bourgeois values are the wave of the future; it may point the way to the civilization of Scott's own day, in which the word "manly" has become a rough synonym for "repressed." But the novel as a whole does not view this process with entire equanimity.[14]

Judging a historical character to possess the virtues of neither the past, the present, nor the future betrays a certain animosity. That King James is one of Scott's greatest comic characters would be foolish to deny. But beneath Scott's evident enjoyment in bringing out the absurdities of "*Gentle King Jemmy* our Scottish Solomon" there lurks a certain impatience.[15] At one point in the novel, Nigel's servant Richie Moniplies expresses his amazement that the king should, by the tenor and wording of a proclamation forbidding Scottish suppliants from coming to England, contrive to bring disgrace on the country of his birth. Scott shares this wonder, and unlike Richie he also knows that the union of the monarchies under James was the begin-

---

14. For another reading of *Nigel* which stresses its ambivalent attitude toward "the old and new ways" (p. 4), see John E. Burke, Jr., "Scott's Views on History in *The Fortunes of Nigel*," *Clio*, 8 (1978), 3–13.

15. In his nonfictional writing, Scott refers to James in less than laudatory terms. In his edition of the *Somers Tracts*, 2d ed., I (London: Cadell, 1809), 508, for example, he calls James "the most arrant coward who ever wore a crown." He had an ambivalent grudge against James as the first king who succeeded in pacifying the Scottish Borders; we learn in *Minstrelsy of the Scottish Border*, ed. T. F. Henderson (Edinburgh: Blackwood, 1902), II, 207, that Montrose might have succeeded in rallying Scotland to Charles I's cause in 1643 if the Borders had not been previously disarmed by James. In the letter in which he first mentions his plan to write a novel about "*Gentle King Jemmy* our Scottish Solomon," he adds that "it is a pity that rare mixture of sense and nonsense pedantry and childishness wit and folly should remain uncelebrated" (*Letters*, VII, 16).

ning of the end of an autonomous Scottish culture. That such a turning point should be presided over by such a king, who threatens to
transform latent tragedy into simple farce, is a historical irony that
Scott might enjoy on some levels of his being but could only resent on
others.

The spectacle of such a king strains Scott's version of negative
capability—his patient acceptance of historical complexity, which is
accompanied by a recognition that the actions of individuals can only
rarely, intermittently, and imperfectly symbolize historical process,
and that no one individual can ever cause it. At times, *Nigel* seems to
espouse a simpler view of historical causality: it begins to appear that
James's weaknesses directly cause his own political problems and the
tragedy that befalls his son. But Scott knows better than this, and his
characteristic vision asserts itself in the novel as a whole. During the
chapters that most insistently uncover James's lack of firmness, an important fictional sequence deflates the notion that his central flaw is
the key to his place in history. Nigel has decided to seek an audience
with the king in an attempt to salvage his reputation and save his
right hand from the executioner's cleaver. As luck will have it, he encounters the king alone and on foot during a hunt. But James is too
frightened to do anything to the purpose, though he wants to. Instead, he makes himself ridiculous as he tries to clamber back on his
horse and escape: "The timidity which he showed was not the plain
downright cowardice which, like a natural impulse, compels a man to
flight, and which can excite little but pity or contempt, but a much
more ludicrous, as well as more mingled, sensation. The poor king
was frightened at once and angry, desirous of securing his safety, and
at the same time ashamed to compromise his dignity; so that, without
attending to what Lord Glenvarloch endeavoured to explain, he kept
making at his horse" (p. 329; ch. 27). Once again, James's lack of
"'firm resolve,' so well called by the Scottish bard, 'the stalk of
carle-hemp in man,'" creates a situation in which "even his virtues
and his good meaning became laughable" (p. 318; ch. 27). But
James's laughable indecision produces serious results. He jumps to the
conclusion that Nigel has designs on his life, and Nigel soon finds
himself in the Tower, accused of treason.

All of this remains on the level of a static historical portrait. But toward the end of the scene, Scott's ever-present interest in historical

process asserts itself. Nigel makes a melodramatic appeal to Prince Charles, reminding him that even he "may one day ask to be heard, and in vain" (p. 332; ch. 27). Such a flat-footedly prophetic statement concerning the future Royal Martyr does not reveal Scott at his best, but it does betray the desire to fit the hunt scene into a larger framework. A few pages later, James appears to provide the key to understanding the historical significance of his own flaws when he remarks, "I kenna how or why, the place [England] is sair changed—read that libel upon us and on our regimen. The dragon's teeth are sown, Baby Charles; I pray God they bearna their armed harvest in your day" (p. 334; ch. 27). Here again the judgments of historical process and morality seem to coincide: James's lack of firmness has sown the seeds of his son's destruction. But instead of driving this point home, Scott immediately makes the doomed Charles reply in a way that undermines it:

> "I shall know how to stifle the crop in the blade—ha, George?" said the Prince, turning to the favourite with a look expressive of some contempt for his father's apprehensions, and full of confidence in the superior firmness and decision of his own counsels. [p. 334; ch. 27]

"Superior firmness and decision," we can only hope, are their own rewards. The example of Charles, whose firmness hastens his destruction, demonstrates that the place of such private virtues in history is equivocal. History here emerges, as it always does in Scott's best fiction, as a complex dialectic involving unintended consequences and unexpected reversals, in which such qualities as "firmness" gain meaning only from specific contexts and relationships. James himself, in discussing Nigel's crime of drawing his sword on Dalgarno in the king's park, makes a relevant kind of distinction: "an action may be inconsequential or even meritorious *quoad hominem*, that is, as touching him upon *whom* it is acted; and yet most criminal *quoad locum*, or considering the place *wherein* it is done" (pp. 400–401; ch. 33). His fondness for such casuistry may be a mark of his pedantry and vacillation, but it also provides a level of complexity of analysis appropriate to the historical problem he himself presents. I think that we must respect and perhaps even share James's feeling of helpless incomprehension before a large historical movement which he senses but cannot control or understand. "I kenna how or why, the place is sair changed" may in the end be a more adequate response to history than Charles's assumption of mastery.

Scott knows better than to explain the course of history as a result of James's personal characteristics, but he is moralist and Scottish patriot enough to be unwilling simply to paint James's portrait, indicate the historical complexities that surround him, and move on to another novel. In *Nigel,* he preserves his characteristic sense of how history operates, but on a less impartial level his fiction also enacts a complex and contradictory set of reactions to James. Much of the novel evokes a sense of historical "if only." The moral categories Heriot upholds are inadequate to explain the course of history, though useful in defining James's character by negation, but they also express a wish ("If only standards like Heriot's *could* control history") and a nationalistic aspiration ("If only there were more Heriots and fewer Jameses in Scottish history"). They echo as well a moral imperative important to the Edinburgh Enlightenment and to Scott: human beings ought to act with Heriot's moral probity, whether their actions will bear fruit in history or not. Quite a different set of wishes find expression in the backward-looking, lawless, virile set of values that counterpoint the novel's official values. They reflect that part of Scott which finds the vitality and movement of earlier ages irresistibly attractive. And beneath all these contradictory impulses toward the bourgeois present and heroic past lies something simpler and stronger—the claims of Scottish insularity, of a small, self-contained, hermetically sealed kingdom, of local and particular attachment. According to such values, James's deepest sin is having left Scotland in the first place. Even James himself has an inkling of this: "I am not sure but we lived merrier in auld Holyrood in those shifting days than now" (p. 62; ch. 5), he exclaims to Heriot.

Nigel, then, undergoes the ordeal of imprisonment and the threat of mutilation for a number of contradictory reasons. On the surface, his experiences help Scott to define the strict moral standards associated with George Heriot. Indeed, Scott may threaten Nigel with ruthless punishment for venial sins precisely because he cannot discipline the king himself. On another level, however, we feel that Nigel is being punished for a quite different fault he shares with the king—the crime of having left Scotland and entered a society whose inner workings are opaque to him. Finally, Sir Mungo Malagrowther's blood-curdling description of Nigel's coming mutilation provides an ordeal that identifies Nigel with the heroic, violent Scottish past even while it threatens him. This identification is strengthened by the novel's love plot, in which the heroine, bourgeois though she may be, merges with the heroines of courtly romance by donning disguises and encountering perils to rescue her knight from his dungeon. When her true identity is revealed and Nigel leaps to her defense, Heriot underlines the decorum the two have introduced into the novel by drily calling them "a perfect Amadis and Oriana" (p. 359; ch. 29). All these levels, with their differing implications concerning James's significance, exist in the prison scene and in the novel as a whole, and none is conclusive, for they reflect Scott's own divided attitude toward James. Disjunctive form, which in a work like *Quentin Durward* functions with cool, admirably analytical efficiency, here takes on a life and energy of its own.

Nigel survives his ordeal in prison not by following the lead of any one of the characters or strands of meaning we have discussed, but because of efforts on his behalf made by Heriot, Margaret Ramsay, and the king, as well as by two historical grotesques, Nigel's servant and the daughter of a usurer. Such an outcome reflects a delight in the energetic specificities of history, not in the morals we draw from them or the ways in which we try to make sense of them. Despite its signs of gloom and moral rigor, *Nigel* remains a comic novel. Despite his anger at James's falling off from a Scottish tradition that never quite existed but should have, Scott creates in James one of his most vital comic characters. Some of the novel's comedy, to be sure, is simply punitive, and some of our delight as we read it is a simple delight in absurdity. Yet there is more to our pleasure than that.

The dilemma James and his age present echoes the two faces of historicism itself. Historicism, in Scott and elsewhere, is fascinated by men and societies as individual, unique, immediate to God, but it also seeks to understand the historical process by which one kind of society gives way to another. Tilt the balance sharply toward the individual and unique, and historical process (especially historical process as continuity and ascent) begins to dissolve, with history becoming a thread on which to string incommensurate historical moments. Tilt the balance sharply in the other direction, and historical uniqueness retreats before a vision of continuously evolving stages of the same

continuous essence; "mere" uniqueness becomes suspect if it does not
contribute directly to the present, to "our" present. Such an emphasis
can seem threatening; it can make us fear that we are the prisoners of
an irresistible force driving us in a direction we may dislike. James,
with his undignified mixture of freedom from and implication in history, gains comic power by relieving such anxieties. The spectacle he
presents is imaginable only as the product of certain historical forces,
yet at the same time it seems irrelevant to the direction in which those
forces are proceeding. A disjunctive form, which posits a disjunctive
relationship between a novel's protagonist and action on the one
hand, and historical process on the other, is ideal for capturing this
mixture of freedom and necessity.

Other Disjunctive Novels

Not all of Scott's disjunctive novels are as successful as *Quentin
Durward* and *The Fortunes of Nigel*. The problem with disjunctive
form is that it tends to break into pieces; at a certain point, an interest
in particularities can become inimical to the notion of form itself.
This happens, I believe, in *Rob Roy*, where Scott wishes to focus our
attention on a member of an exceptional clan, the MacGregors, not a
representative clan like the fictional MacIvors in *Waverley*.[16] In addi-
tion, he wants us to understand Rob Roy's predicament in terms of
the economics underlying clan degeneration and involvement in revolution.[17] This is intractable material indeed. In form, the novel extends the pattern we saw in *Nigel*, where the protagonist leads us to
another figure, who in turn helps to illuminate the historical subject.
But the hero in *Rob Roy* never really becomes an active part of the
process of illumination; he acts mainly as a mere connector of two
figures, as a kind of usher. As it turns out, this sets him free to become involved in a love story that is unusually intense for Scott but
that has little or nothing to do with Rob Roy himself, directly or indirectly, except on the level of simple causality in the plot.[18] Nonethe-

16. Scott provides a long discussion of the MacGregors' exceptional history in the
Magnum Opus Introduction to *Rob Roy*.
17. Fleishman, pp. 69–71, underlines the importance of financial matters in the
novel.
18. There has been a continuing controversy about whether *Rob Roy* is a successful

less *Rob Roy* is an energetic, attractive novel, because it fully exploits the rich possibilities in the juxtaposition the protagonist creates, between the Glasgow merchant Bailie Jarvie and the outlaw Rob Roy. The "foil" character, Jarvie, in fact overtakes in vitality and interest the actual historical character on whom the novel is intended to focus; this also occurs with Dugald Dalgetty and Montrose in *A Legend of Montrose*.

Kenilworth follows the same pattern as *Rob Roy*, rather less successfully. The protagonist here has a shady, vestigial existence at best; his presence seems almost to express a reflex need on Scott's part to have a male delegate for the reader in the novel. *Kenilworth* is based on a contrast between the pathetic, beautiful, undisciplined heroine Amy Robsart and the steely Elizabeth I. Amy Robsart actually lived; Scott's version of her tragic story is based on historical fact and conjecture. It tells us little about Elizabeth or about history, however, particularly since Scott feels compelled to modernize her husband Leicester's psychology, to prevent him from being "too disgustingly wicked, to be useful for the purposes of fiction."[19] Similarly irrelevant though less elaborate is the love story in *The Talisman*, a work which it would be ungenerous to take too seriously.

Certain Scott novels vacillate between conjunctive and disjunctive form; it might be better to speak of conjunctive and disjunctive tendencies within them. The actions of both *Woodstock* and *Peveril of the Peak* have a certain amount of direct historical significance. Both works deal with the Puritans and Cavaliers, and the opening chapters of *Peveril*, which depict the unsuccessful attempt of a Cavalier's wife to bring concord to her community after the Civil War, are remarkable and unjustly neglected. By ending with the marriage of a Puritan hero to a Cavalier heroine, or vice versa, both novels act out the unification of England after a period of civil strife. I nevertheless believe both novels to be primarily disjunctive in form. In both, Scott's use of the hero and his plotted action to point to specific, idiosyncratic ma-

---

novel and whether Frank Osbaldistone (or some other character) provides its center. An interesting recent attempt to rehabilitate Frank does so by stressing personal memory at the expense of Rob Roy and history: see Jane Millgate, "*Rob Roy* and the Limits of Frankness," *Nineteenth-Century Fiction*, 34 (1980), 379–96.

19. The Dryburgh Edition omits most of Scott's notes to *Kenilworth*; I quote from the Magnum Opus Edition, XXIII (Edinburgh: Cadell, 1831), 27.

terial weakens significantly their overarching historical import. In *Woodstock*, this involves a depiction of Cromwell; in *Peveril of the Peak*, it involves an attempt to give a kaleidoscopic picture of Restoration England.

The mixed success with which Scott employs disjunctive form can in part be ascribed to his notoriously speedy habits of composition, but it has more complex sources as well, and a larger significance. It reminds us of the power of a historical subject to resist esthetically satisfying representation. And the problematic nature of the protagonists in Scott recalls what I earlier identified as the problem with historical novels. But the partial failure of *Kenilworth* should not blind us to the virtues of *Quentin Durward* or *The Fortunes of Nigel*. These virtues stand out the more clearly when we do not expect the protagonists of such novels to fulfill the same functions that Edward Waverley or Henry Morton fulfill. By considering the disjunctive novels on their own terms, we recognize how well fitted their heroes generally are for the roles they perform. And we come to appreciate Scott's artistry in making complex judgments concerning historical individuals flow from the twists and turns of narration.

CONJUNCTIVE FORM

Scott's disjunctive novels possess strengths that usually pass unnoticed. But when we move from disjunctive to conjunctive form, we move toward the center of his achievement. In Scott's disjunctive novels, as we have seen, the hero can perform a rich medley of instrumental roles. Conjunctive heroes tend to play some or all of these roles, but they add another as well. Their careers comment upon the shape of historical process.

Waverley

The paradigmatic example of conjunctive form in Scott's novels is *Waverley*. The novel's basic rhetorical strategy is clear enough. Waverley begins as an untried, idealistic, romantic youth. As the novel progresses, his romantic dreams suddenly materialize before him in an unsettling way, as he visits Scotland and becomes engaged in the Rebellion of 1745. Because of his adventures and his connection with the hard-headed Englishman Colonel Talbot, he retreats from the world of romance to a less exciting but safer way of life. This change is figured by his choice of the domestic Rose Bradwardine for his wife, instead of the forceful, idealistic Flora MacIvor. His marriage also prefigures the consolidation of Scotland and England, since he is English and his wife is Scottish. Thus Waverley himself embodies or acts out or creates the attitude toward history that the novel as a whole expresses, a regretful acceptance of progress. Discovering the form of *Waverley* turns largely on describing exactly how he does this.

One view is that Waverley is the hero of a Bildungsroman and that the novel depicts his historical education.[20] But there are problems with this view. To begin with, the level of generality and externality at which Scott's characterization operates makes it difficult to render spiritual growth. To base the meaning of *Waverley* on the education of the hero, it becomes necessary to inject significant moral judgments and moments of moral decision in places where they do not comfortably fit. At a turning point in the novel, for instance, Waverley saves Colonel Talbot from the Jacobite troops. A Bildungsroman reading of the novel naturally wants to consider this a moment of decisive moral growth. I believe that it is nothing of the kind. In saving Talbot, Waverley acts admirably, but he does not grow at all: he remains the same well-meaning, humane young gentleman who left his home in the North of England at the beginning of the novel. When he saves Talbot, he acts as one English gentleman in war ought to act toward another. The operative contrast in the scene is not between a past and a present Waverley, but between the code of values he and Talbot share, and the savagery of the Highlanders with whom Waverley is at present engaged. What Waverley learns in the novel is that the values of the Jacobites are not his values. This is fair enough for Scott's purposes, but tepid in moral and spiritual significance when compared to

20. Francis Hart, *Scott's Novels: The Plotting of Historic Survival* (Charlottesville: University Press of Virginia, 1966), pp. 14–31; S. Stewart Gordon, "Waverley and the 'Unified Design,'" *ELH*, 18 (1951), 107–22. D. W. Jefferson, "The Virtuosity of Scott," in *Scott's Mind and Art*, ed. A. Norman Jeffares (Edinburgh: Oliver and Boyd, 1969), p. 63, makes a shrewd distinction between Waverley's function as an occasion for the description of manners in the first part of the novel, and his more active use as a "reflector" of "the direction that history will take" after he joins the Jacobites. This change in function may be what is mistaken for moral growth in Waverley.

the insights that Wilhelm Meister gains in his education. Waverley's limited education is neither the most important nor the most interesting part of the novel that bears his name. To try to make the scene where he saves Talbot a decisive moment of moral growth is to load it with a weight it cannot bear. To do so plays into the hands of Scott's detractors, by implicitly sharing their assumption that novels ought to be about the moral growth of individuals. If *Waverley* is a Bildungsroman, it is a dull one.[21]

The most tempting sequence in the novel to interpret in Bildungsroman terms, and the one which seems least amenable to the historical analysis I myself prefer, is the sequence in which Waverley is rescued from the British forces by some Highlanders, is injured in the process, and then convalesces in a cabin in the woods, attended by a romantic female figure whose face he is never able to see. We might want to take this sequence as a symbolic or mythic surrogate for the process of inner growth and change which Scott does not portray directly in the novel. It would then rank as a symbolic ordeal, an immersion in the realm of pure imagination that Waverley for a time embraces in his acceptance of Jacobitism, but then finally rejects by reacting to another more nightmarish ordeal, witnessing (though at several removes) Fergus MacIvor's death. Anthropology or psychology of various sorts could flesh out the analysis.

This sequence clearly draws upon Romance convention; further, there is abundant evidence throughout Scott's fictional and nonfictional works of his strong interest in dreamlike states like Waverley's during his convalescence, and of his identification of such states with the workings of the imagination, which he considers the highest po-

---

21. I am using the term "Bildungsroman" loosely here, as it tends to be used in Anglo-American criticism, to describe works that depict within their adolescent protagonists a substantial process of growth and change. Multiple ironies arise in applying this model to Scott. Jerome Buckley, *Season of Youth: The Bildungsroman from Dickens to Golding* (Cambridge: Harvard University Press, 1974), pp. 8–9, who more than anyone else has legitimized the notion of English Bildungsromane, himself does not believe *Waverley* to be one. But the rigorous and persuasive description of the German Bildungsroman given by Martin Swales, *The German Bildungsroman from Wieland to Hesse* (Princeton: Princeton University Press, 1978), is in form close to my own notion of how *Waverley* works, because it shifts the process of education to the reader and sees the protagonist primarily as an instrument to effect it (p. 32). The issues with which, according to Swales, the German Bildungsroman is centrally concerned are not, however, those that are central in Scott.

etic gift. Yet what seems most striking in the sequence, when taken in the context of the novel as a whole, is the way in which Scott's particularist historical imagination assimilates even such material to its own needs and interests. Even this sequence turns out to have a number of important nonmythical functions, which forward the novel's various historically based systems of probability. By the strong break it creates in the novel, it helps in an effective though entirely nonlogical way to excuse Waverley for being a turncoat. Something substantial must intervene between his dismissal from the Hanoverian army and his joining the Pretender; his convalescence provides just this space, particularly since its mode of depiction disrupts the normal logic of the novel. This mitigation of Waverley's guilt facilitates his use as a tool to explore the Jacobites, and it smooths the way for his rhetorically crucial return to the Hanoverian fold at the end of the novel.

Waverley's experiences during his abduction also make his joining the Pretender's camp probable in a more local way, for they explain why the Pretender's personal appeal for help affects him so strongly. Having spent a good deal of time in captivity makes Waverley ripe for a flattering appeal to his sense of self-worth, and the aura of romance that fills his abduction by the Highlanders vivifies for us as readers the side of his character which makes joining the Pretender's quest to regain a crown so seductive. An appeal to his self-respect also motivates Waverley to transfer his love from Flora (who humiliates him by not taking him seriously) to Rose; further, Rose's own part in Waverley's convalescence—for it is she, and not as Waverley fondly hopes, Flora, who hovers around him in the cabin—gives her a saving tinge of romance, for all her prosaic domesticity, and thus helps to promote at least the illusion that he need not abandon the romance of Jacobitism entirely at the end of the novel. Even when they are at their strongest, then, romance elements do not begin to have the power to subvert for long the dominantly historical mode in which *Waverley* is cast.[22] The simple moral paradigm by which Waverley outgrows his

---

22. Critics who stress the romance elements in the novel as symbolic ordeal include Hart, pp. 27–31, and Lawrence J. Clipper, "Edward Waverley's Night Journey," *South Atlantic Quarterly*, 73 (1974), 541–53. For *Waverley* as a "realistic displacement of romance," see David Daiches, "Scott's *Waverley*: The Presence of the Author," in *Nineteenth-Century Scottish Fiction: Critical Essays*, ed. Ian Campbell (New York: Barnes and Noble, 1979), pp. 7–8. Northrop Frye, *The Secular Scripture: A*

irresponsible dreaminess functions in the same way. It is part of a network of fictional patterns that have a primarily historical significance; it does not draw the novel's focus toward the inward development of the protagonist or toward myth.

Waverley is designed to create an experience in the reader, not to imitate in a focal way the education of the hero. In his essays and reviews, Scott habitually assumes that it is legitimate for works of literature to use a variety of different means, some realistic and some purely conventional, to create effects in the minds of audiences. He would have been the last to suppose that the only way in which a work could convey an attitude toward history is through representing internal growth in its protagonist.[23] His handling of Waverley as a hero puts the focus precisely where it belongs in a novel designed to explore historical process—on the shape of societies and events, not on individual volition. Scott involves us in his rhetorical and esthetic interests in history primarily through our hopes and fears for Waverley as we share his experience of the world around him; he involves us in his analytical interests in history primarily through our appreciation of the structure and significance of the episodes Waverley's fictional progress connects.

A brief sequence involving a minor character provides an example of how Scott builds his historical interests upon one another in *Waverley*; it also suggests how little he depends on giving his hero's inner life symbolic status to gain his rhetorical ends. When Waverley returns from an innocent but suspicious-looking trip to the Highlands, he is captured and brought before a magistrate, Major Melville, who decides that he must find some way of sending him to a secure prison in Stirling Castle, since the Highlanders may overrun the country at any moment. The only available escort is provided by one Gifted Gilfillan and his men, who are Presbyterian extremists called Cameronians. On the simplest level, Gilfillan appears in the novel to be seen: he reflects Scott's analytical and representative interests in the particu-

---

Study of the Structure of Romance (Cambridge: Harvard University Press, 1976), p. 40, finds a different dynamic in Scott, "the absorption of realistic displacement into romance itself."

23. See, for instance, Scott's comments on *The Castle of Otranto* (MPW III, 313–24) or on Henry Mackenzie's *The Man of Feeling* and *Julia de Roubigné* (MPW IV, 12–19).

larities of historical time and place. Francis Jeffrey, always alive to this side of Scott, recognizes the usefulness of setting a novel at the time of the Forty-five, since "that unfortunate contention brought conspicuously to light, and for the last time, the fading image of feudal chivalry in the mountains, and vulgar fanaticism in the plains."[24] Gilfillan represents a variety of "vulgar fanaticism" no longer extant in Scott's day, and Waverley fulfills the function of a historical sightseer by asking useful questions about him which a Presbyterian minister answers for his edification and for ours.

But in *Waverley*, even so minor a character as Gilfillan is more than a historical exhibit. His spiritual pride and political prejudice make him unwilling to listen to Major Melville's suggestions about escorting Waverley to Stirling. When he ignores the advice of one of his social superiors and begins to talk rudely to him, Gilfillan's function as a representative kind of Scotsman from a certain period in history becomes subsumed under a larger purpose, the rhetorical purpose of the novel as a whole. We are expected to sympathize completely with Major Melville's explosion of anger at him:

> "Mr. Gilfillan," he answered, with some asperity, "I beg ten thousand pardons for interfering with a person of your importance. I thought, however, that as you have been bred a grazier, if I mistake not, there might be occasion to remind you of the difference between Highlanders and Highland cattle; and if you should happen to meet with any gentleman who has seen service, and is disposed to speak upon the subject, I should still imagine that listening to him would do you no sort of harm. But I have done."   [p. 226; ch. 35]

Gilfillan is dealing with soldiers instead of cattle because impending civil war has forced the government to look anywhere it can for help. He is the sort of figure who comes out of the woodwork in periods of national turmoil, Scott is telling us. Charles Edward may be an exciting, romantic figure, but his rebellion unleashes forces in society which Scott expects any sane reader to fear and deplore. In an uncharacteristically crude and topical way, Scott tries to stack the deck further against Gilfillan through guilt by association. The narra-

24. Francis Jeffrey, review of *Waverley*, *Edinburgh Review*, 24 (Nov. 1814), 208–43; rpt. in *Scott: The Critical Heritage*, ed. John O. Hayden (New York: Barnes and Noble, 1970), p. 80.

tor informs us in a long and otherwise pointless digression that Gilfillan's drummer comes from a town that later supplied the drummer for the "British Convention"—a pro-French, reformist society of the kind Edmund Burke attacked in his *Reflections*—which met in Edinburgh in 1793. A more obvious and graceless attempt to enlist the contemporary reader's fears of lower-class unrest on the side of Scott's rhetorical purposes could scarcely be imagined. It is worth adding that the handling of Gilfillan demonstrates how Scott can educate the reader without educating Waverley. We object to Gilfillan partly because he poses a threat to Waverley, but his rudeness teaches Waverley himself nothing. At this point in the novel he has other things to think about, principally his impending imprisonment and possible death. He in fact has already begun to react to the circumstances in which he finds himself by becoming a rebel, not simply by association, but in fact. The historical and social point Gilfillan represents would be lost on him, even if there were any reason to believe that he is aware of it. Here and elsewhere, Waverley's inner life lacks the symbolic importance it might have in another kind of novel. Perhaps the oddest moment in *Waverley* occurs when Scott uncharacteristically attempts to make him symbolic in too direct and consubstantial a fashion. During a ball at Holyrood House, Waverley undergoes a strange metamorphosis; even the worldly Pretender himself remarks that the usually shy and dull Englishman has suddenly become "one of the most fascinating young men" he has ever seen (p. 276). This unlikely change appears intended to symbolize the brief efflorescence which the Jacobite cause itself is enjoying, but the choice of representational means is unfortunate.

My discussion of the limits of mimesis in historical fiction suggests that narrative sequences would be more likely than individual characters to have a directly symbolic status in Scott's works, though even here we would expect such symbolism to exist at a fairly abstract level. A recurring sequence of this kind in *Waverley* depicts something as imposing or sublime at a distance, but shabby or even ludicrous close at hand. Thus Waverley is on a hillside when he first views the Highland troops leaving Edinburgh, and he is heartened by their picturesque appearance. But his optimism fades when he joins the line of march and sees them for the rugged, ill-armed, undisciplined group they are. This pattern need not figure a simple loss of illusion. When

Waverley enters a romantic Highland cavern, he meets a Highland robber, who turns out to be not the impressive figure he had expected, but a short, sandy-haired man got up in a silly French uniform. This moment of bathos does not, however, discredit the romance of the Highlands. By rejecting a false, bookish sublime, it prepares us for the true imaginative richness the Highlands offer—the concrete social relationships they tenuously preserve. Yet we must also admit that at a deeper level of analysis, the far-near pattern has a cumulative rhetorical effect that leads away from active involvement with Highland magic of any kind. It predicts and consolidates the pattern of the novel as a whole, for Waverley and for us, as we move from spectatorship to an unsettling engagement with the past, but then make a crucial retreat to spectatorship again. The ultimate rhetorical and ideological effect of the pattern is to reinforce a stance of passivity before the process that has led to the dull but safe present.

By the end of *Waverley*, our sense that the Jacobites are doomed by historical process is so firm that Scott can include scenes in which he gives full play to his sympathy for their virtues without endangering the basic analytical and rhetorical structures he has created. The best of these is Evan Dhu's famous attempt to save his chieftain's life at their trial for treason, but among them we must also count Waverley's last meeting with Flora MacIvor. This scene has been seriously misinterpreted by critics who mistake Waverley's function in the novel and disregard the fictional rhythms he helps to create. It is inappropriate to take Flora at her word when she suggests that she is responsible for her brother's execution, because of the example her pure and consistent devotion to the Jacobite cause set him. The remarkable thing about the scene is the breadth of its sympathy, which can have full play precisely because the novel has already settled its political issues so completely. An adequate response would involve respect and admiration for Flora's consistent idealism, which makes her entertain the terrifying thought of guilt for her brother's death, relief that Waverley and Rose are not themselves subject to such idealism, but also regret at the diminishing of human possibility their safety implies. Scott doesn't need to judge Flora, though he teeters on the brink of doing so, and neither do we, though we recognize that her need to judge herself is an important fact about her character and the qualities she represents. We know that Fergus would have been what he was despite her influence, just as we know why she has to blame herself, being the sort of character she is. In her self-condemnation she is engaging in the illusory but humanly necessary process of trying to make sense of history by reducing historical causality to the terms of individual morality.

Flora's attempt to deal with history touches on another of Scott's historical interests, his fascination with the sense of the past as an independent phenomenon, a sensation in its own right. But Waverley is the main instrument Scott employs to incorporate his interest in the sense of the past in the novel. This is why the opening chapters, which deal with Waverley's childhood and youth, are as long as they are. They could suggest his romantic tendencies in short order, if their only function were to initiate a pattern of romantic illusion succeeded by realistic disillusionment. But the opening section needs to be slow paced and expansive to fulfill another purpose. It invites us to enjoy in a self-consciously indulgent way the idea of living in a world in which time seems to have stopped, and a child can amuse himself in a musty library with forgotten Romances or listen to the equally cobwebbed reminiscences of his elders. Scott's interest in the sense of the past as a feeling in its own right gains a final expression at the end of the novel. A painting in Baron Bradwardine's restored mansion depicts Fergus MacIvor and Waverley, dressed in their tartans as part of the rebel army: as the family gazes at it, it has already begun to cover their exploits with the patina of time and memory.[25]

A final way in which Scott creates historical insight in *Waverley* is through a self-reflexive thematization of his fictional devices. Such a thematization anticipates, to be sure in a less elaborate way, Tolstoy's merging of the formal problematics of historical fiction with his theory of history in *War and Peace*. Throughout *Waverley*, Scott shows a keen interest in the ways in which historical process is mediated through language. One of the first things we learn about the Baron of Bradwardine is that he hates puns and "canting heraldry" (which derives a family's crest from a pun on its name), and that he has willed his estate away from the daughter he loves for the sake of a feudal

---

25. Peter D. Garside, "Waverley's Pictures of the Past," *ELH*, 44 (1977), 659–82, contains a stimulating discussion of the use of pictures in *Waverley*; he mentions the picture of Waverley and Fergus on p. 677. He also notes the "far-near" pattern in the novel (pp. 670–71).

definition of land tenure. Later in the novel, he exhibits a comic persistence in trying to decide the exact meaning, in modern terms, of his feudal duty to pull the king's boots off after battle, raising such issues as whether the Latin word *caligae* ("boots") includes the sort of shoes Prince Charles happens to be wearing. But, as Donald Davie has shown, he is later able to achieve a truly noble and flexible kind of translation, when he applies the Latin classics to his own homeless state after the failure of the rebellion.[26] And in the final scene in the novel, he seems to have abated if not entirely forgotten his wish for linguistic univalency, as he endures Waverley's bridesman's jokes about heraldry with a good grace. In this scene, Scott has created a context in which all present can relish cultural differences, instead of fighting over them. Even Colonel Talbot, formerly an anti-Scottish bigot, enters this decorum, when he says that he had better explain how he recovered a favorite cup of Bradwardine's, so that no one will think he is "a conjuror, which is no joke in Scotland" (p. 446; ch. 71). But his comment *is* a joke, and it would not have been earlier in the novel, when its political issues still seemed open.

Scott is also sensitive to the importance of larger linguistic units for knowing and surviving in history. Waverley recovers from the horror of Fergus's execution in a characteristic way, by turning it into a story that he can tell to his wife-to-be, Rose. We have already seen the same impulse at work, containing Waverley and Fergus inside the frame of a picture that all admire at the end of the novel. A more elaborate, less obvious example involves that embodiment of Highland cunning and violence, Callum Beg, in an exploit Colonel Talbot recounts. Callum Beg, he tells Waverley,

> was playing at quoits the other day in the court; a gentleman, a decent-looking person enough, came past, and as a quoit hit his shin, he lifted his cane; but my young bravo whips out his pistol, like Beau Clincher in the *Trip to the Jubilee*, and had not a scream of *Gardez l'eau*, from an upper window set all parties a scampering for fear of the inevitable consequences, the poor gentleman would have lost his life by the hands of that little cockatrice. [p. 345; ch. 56]

This brief description occurs when Talbot is himself trying to remember to call the Pretender by the more equivocal title of "Chevalier,"

26. Donald Davie, *The Heyday of Sir Walter Scott* (London: Routledge & Kegan Paul, 1961), pp. 32–33.

because that young man has generously allowed him a parole to visit his sick wife. Why did Callum Beg whip out his pistol? Readers of "The Two Drovers" will know, though Talbot, with his literary parallel from England, does not. To submit to a personal beating was for a Highlander a disgrace that could never be eradicated, though it had to be revenged. The vignette between Callum Beg and the gentleman contains the implicit material for the kind of tragedy of cultural incomprehension Scott later created in "The Two Drovers." But instead, the incipient tragedy is dissipated by another culturally resonant action, the call of an Edinburgh maid before she empties a chamberpot into the street below. Scott has here created a compact example of local color as ideological mediation. The oldest of old jokes about Edinburgh turns out to have its uses. For Callum Beg and the gentleman, and for us as readers, it creates a shift from a potentially tragic mode of registering cultural difference to a comic one. Trivializing cultural individuality by depicting it in terms of reductive stereotypes is in this case a way of defusing its negative consequences.

Waverley is perhaps the purest example of conjunctive form in Scott. It creates in the reader a developing experience that includes all aspects of Scott's interest in history. As the center of a developing pattern of hopes and fears, Waverley drives us to accept the fruits of historical process and hence fulfills the novel's dominant intention; Waverley is conjunctive precisely because its plotted action leads us to draw such conclusions about historical process. As a historical tourist, Waverley allows us to explore a wide range of social forms and historical beliefs: through him, Scott exercises his powerful ability to make locales and documents speak. As a character much given to dreamy states, Waverley encourages us to enjoy our own dreams about the past, but with an awareness of their potential inaccuracies and dangers. These different fictional functions and interests in history coexist harmoniously in the novel for several reasons. First, the novel operates historically and fictionally at a fairly high level of generality. In Waverley, Scott is writing about the phenomenon of Jacobitism in general at least as much as he is chronicling the Forty-five. He takes from the Forty-five its pattern of descent into England followed by retreat back to Scotland, but draws upon other Jacobite risings for concrete details when it suits his purposes to do so.[27] The ac-

27. James Anderson, "Sir Walter Scott as Historical Novelist: Part II," *Studies in Scottish Literature*, 4 (1966), 65–72.

tual character of Charles Edward also promotes Scott's fictional patterning, for his resonance as an individual is minimal. He draws his significance entirely from the historical events with which he is associated. Similarly, Waverley as a fictional character has a useful simplicity of motivation and psychology. He is easily moved from one side of a historical confrontation to the other, and back again, fitting readily into a simple, integrative pattern of illusion about the romantic possibilities of life, followed by a sadder and wiser awakening to reality. Throughout *Waverley*, in short, Scott avoids treating the specific, idiosyncratic material that requires disjunctive form.

In his retrospective Introduction to *Redgauntlet*, Scott describes the Jacobites as providing a "perfect" theme for historical fiction. This comment reflects a wistful recognition of the near-perfect balance his subject allowed him to achieve in *Waverley*. The subject of *Old Mortality* was anything but ideal in this sense. Yet *Old Mortality* has a depth and daring of insight we don't quite find in *Waverley*, and this suggests that creative tensions and discontinuities may serve Scott's historical purposes at least as well as formal balance and integration.

Old Mortality

Scott employs in *Old Mortality* the same conjunctive form he had used in *Waverley*. But his conception of his historical subject necessitates a number of adjustments, which introduce certain instabilities and contradictions into what in *Waverley* had been balanced, conclusive patterns of form and meaning. Scott's response is to restabilize his fiction through some adroit tactical maneuvers, but also, at a deeper level, to allow instability and contradiction to have their say, raising questions that never approach the surface in *Waverley*. In this respect, the relationship between *Old Mortality* and *Waverley* resembles the relationship between *The Antiquary* and *Guy Mannering*. In *Waverley* as in *Guy Mannering*, Scott creates a rounded, conclusive form; in *The Antiquary* as in *Old Mortality*, he allows a louder voice to contradictions that threaten to disrupt his most deeply held social and historical ideals. The great difference between *Old Mortality* and *The Antiquary*, which helps to make the former novel a far greater work than the latter, is that in *Old Mortality* Scott makes positive, brilliant use of his protagonist, instead of permitting his action to be merely a string upon which to hang thematic concerns.

Most readers find *Old Mortality* a grim novel, despite its fine comic scenes. Scott's friend Lady Louisa Stuart, always one of his most perceptive readers, wrote to him that "it makes its personages our intimate acquaintance, and its scenes so present to the eye that last night after sitting up unreasonably late over it, I got no sleep, from a kind of fever of mind it had occasioned. It seemed as if I had been an eye and ear witness of all the passages, and I could not lull the agitation into calmness."[28] What gives the novel this kind of power? *Waverley* deals with rebellion, battle, and execution, but it does not affect us as deeply as *Old Mortality* does. Why did the novel's images linger in Lady Louisa Stuart's mind? Scott wrote so arrestingly in *Old Mortality*, I think, because of the nature of its subject. The novel is set during the "killing times," a period of intense royalist reaction against the Scottish Presbyterian Covenanters (and especially their militant, "Cameronian" wing), which immediately preceded the Glorious Revolution of 1688. *Old Mortality*'s main action chronicles the Covenanters' initially successful but finally disastrous attempt at armed rebellion.[29] One stage of society does not displace another, as in *Waverley*. Instead, we have a pointless, destructive conflict within a society, for whatever their local losses and gains, both sides will soon be left behind by the course of history, as moderation prevails in the person of William of Orange. And it is not just the bloody, pointless brutality of the times which makes them unsettling for Scott. The Covenanters represent the specter that most frightened him and his contemporary readers, especially in view of recent occurrences in France: the threat of determined, well-organized, and at least temporarily successful lower-class rebellion. To make matters the more unsettling, these rebels fight not simply against their social betters but against English domination of Scotland; in however twisted a way, they represent, as the Jacobites did, the cause of Scottish nationalism. Being made the "intimate acquaintance" of a group of predominantly lower-class religious zealots anxious to take over the state and willing to murder their social superiors in the process might well rob Lady

28. *Familiar Letters of Sir Walter Scott*, 2 vols. (Boston: Houghton Mifflin, 1894), I, 394.

29. Angus Calder's Introduction and notes to his edition of *Old Mortality* (Harmondsworth: Penguin, 1975) show how Scott "simplifies, compresses, and synthesizes" (p. 21) the actual historical events of the time to suit his fictional purposes.

Louisa of her sleep, just as attempting to master the contradictions embodied in such a movement spurred Scott on to create a novel of remarkable intensity.

For a man of Scott's class and temperament, a polar opposition between classes was more threatening and hence more difficult to mediate than the gap between different stages of society. This puts great strain on a conjunctive hero, one of whose primary functions is to act as bridge and mediator. One might have guessed that this strain would reduce Henry Morton, the hero of *Old Mortality*, to playing the purely external role of providing some order in the novel as the center of a conventional romantic plot. In fact, Scott makes Morton considerably more substantial, both as a character and in his commitment to rebellion, than Edward Waverley is. He is right to do so. It is hard to imagine how an English outsider like Waverley could be attached to the Covenanters with any probability, and harder to imagine a Scotsman who could shuttle as Waverley does from one side to the other without losing the reader's sympathy. Scott's treatment of Morton respects the historical dynamic toward unyielding polarization that is central to the "killing times."

Scott not only gives Morton a depth of commitment Waverley lacks, he attempts to depict directly the mental and emotional processes by which that commitment blossoms. This uncharacteristic invasion of the inner life is only partially successful by the standards of later nineteenth-century fiction, but it produces remarkable results nonetheless. Understanding the form of *Old Mortality* means discovering how its uncharacteristic hero furthers Scott's esthetic, analytical, and rhetorical interests in history.

We can begin by observing that Morton is not and cannot be a suitable vehicle for representing Scott's interest in the esthetics of historical vision. Scott's depiction of Morton's own past is designed to explain why at the opening of the novel he has not taken sides in the political conflict raging around him: his instincts are moderate, but social deprivation and latent Scottish nationalism make it likely that he will join the Covenanting side. There is no room here for a dreamy childhood like Waverley's, and creating the sense of a rich and leisurely enjoyment of the past would hardly be in keeping with the historical decorum of a novel set in the "killing times." But precisely such an evocation of memory, suitably tinged with melancholy, is created by the novel's narrative frame, in which a late-eighteenth-century schoolmaster and man of feeling, the supposed narrator of Morton's story, describes how he came upon its source, one of the last of the Covenanters.[30] Here, as later in *Quentin Durward*, Scott makes extended use of the eighteenth-century convention of the fictional editor to express an aspect of his historical sense for which his hero is not a suitable vehicle.

Morton may not play a role in furthering Scott's evocation of the richness of historical memory, but as befits a conjunctive hero, he is central to *Old Mortality*'s analytical and rhetorical designs. In some ways, he is after all rather like Waverley. His place in the councils of the Covenanters is to some degree thrust upon him by the pressure of events. His spirit is clearly aristocratic, not populist; his upbringing has "frozen" some of his best attributes, but he is a member of the gentry and displays a proper horror at his miserly uncle's suggestion that he learn to use a plow. His very language puts him on the side of the genteel characters in the novel, and in so doing also performs a useful analytical and rhetorical function: it serves as a standard by which we can judge the chaos of competing languages employed by the different Covenanting factions, a chaos representing the debilitating fragmentation into splinter groups which is for Scott the inevitable fate of all extremist movements. Thus Morton's eventual marriage with the royalist Edith Bellenden, which enacts the moderate compromise between opposing factions that history creates in 1688, is probable, and we wish for such an outcome just as we hope that history will save Waverley and unite him with Rose Bradwardine.[31]

Yet there remains the critical matter of how much more deeply Morton is implicated in rebellion than is Waverley, and of the way in which his commitment is depicted. This aspect of the novel has its analytical and rhetorical uses also, in ways that are subtle and complex enough to demand detailed attention.

The sequence in which Scott effects Morton's transformation from

30. A. O. J. Cockshut, *The Achievement of Walter Scott* (London: Collins, 1969), p. 130, recognizes the affective importance of the novel's opening chapter.

31. George Goodin, "Walter Scott and the Tradition of the Political Novel," in *The English Novel in the Nineteenth Century: Essays on the Literary Mediation of Human Values*, ed. George Goodin, Illinois Studies in Language and Literature, 63 (Urbana: University of Illinois Press, 1972), pp. 14–24, explores the novel's political implications and the techniques that create them.

an alienated onlooker to an active participant in rebellion is crucial here.[32] Morton, having been arrested by the royalist forces on equivocal grounds and imprisoned in the castle in which his lover Edith Bellenden resides, is on his way to be questioned by an already legendary oppressor of Scottish dissidents, John Grahame of Claverhouse. He overhears and misinterprets Edith's attempt to save him from likely execution by enlisting the aid of his rival for her love, Claverhouse's associate Lord Evandale. Morton jumps to the conclusion that she loves Evandale. His pessimistic reaction stems from a diffidence natural enough in a Presbyterian of reduced circumstances who aspires to the hand of the daughter of a wealthy Cavalier and aristocrat; he has also just been falsely informed that Edith and Evandale will soon be married. For these reasons, the narrator informs us, hearing Edith begging Evandale for his life transforms Morton:

> That moment made a singular and instantaneous revolution in his character. The depth of despair to which his love and fortunes were reduced, the peril in which his life appeared to stand, the transference of Edith's affections, her intercession in his favour, which rendered her fickleness yet more galling, seemed to destroy every feeling for which he had hitherto lived, but at the same time awakened those which had hitherto been smothered by passions more gentle though more selfish. Desperate himself, he determined to support the rights of his country, insulted in his person. His character was for the moment as effectually changed as the appearance of a villa which, from being the abode of domestic quiet and happiness, is, by the sudden intrusion of an armed force, converted into a formidable post of defence. [p. 128; ch. 13]

At the heart of this passage lies a structure which is uncharacteristic of Scott in general but which plays a major role in *Old Mortality*—the substantial equation of public and private spheres encapsulated in the sentence, "Desperate himself, he determined to support the rights of his country, insulted in his person." Scott repeatedly blends Morton's individual predicament and the general state of Scot-

32. Any discussion of Morton's transformation must be indebted to Welsh, pp. 243–55. In his shrewd analysis of the scene, he takes as passive symptoms of Scott's discontent with his overcivilized ideology what I understand to be the result of an active probing of ideological self-mystification. Welsh's approach stems from his having drained the Waverley Novels of any self-consciously critical capacity by deciding that they are "projective" romances, not novels.

land into a single chord, but he also introduces enough dissonance to make us question this blending. The result is to thematize the problem of ideology, the part thought plays in the making of history.

One one level, Morton's attempt to equate his personal disappointment in love with Scotland's political predicament shows how otherwise reasonable people become swept up in political movements largely irrelevant to the personal grievances which in fact motivate them. A multitude of personal, social, and political forces separate Morton from Edith, and Scott takes pains to render one of the most important inexplicable in political terms. Morton angrily refers to his rival, Lord Evandale, as a "pensioned cut-throat" at the service of "the all-pervading and accursed tyranny which afflicts at once our bodies, souls, estates, and affections" (p. 126; ch. 13). But a prime reason for Morton's difficulties with Edith and the world in general is his lack of a gentleman's education, a lack only partly balanced by his visits with his dead father's old friend Miles Bellenden, Edith's uncle. His own uncle and guardian, Morton of Milnwood, has depressed and "frozen" his abilities, not in the service of a repressive regime, but because he is a miser unwilling to support Morton as he should and could. Scott does not connect Milnwood's greed with politics or history in any substantial way: he is as unhistorical a figure as Scott is capable of imagining. He is intended to be taken as a Scottish "character," but the difference between him and a figure like the Baron of Bradwardine in *Waverley* could hardly be more striking. The Baron is historically typical; Milnwood is merely a probable member of his historical milieu.[33] While the Baron lives in a decaying manor house next to a decaying village and is himself decaying intellectually and socially, all because of the stagnant situation of Scotland in the early eighteenth century, Milnwood is a miser because he likes money— and because the reader must know that Morton's attempt to fuse his personal wrongs with the state of Scotland is questionable.

Morton's attempt to force an identity between his personal concerns and the problems of his country does not end with this scene. Its problematic nature is clear in a darkly comic interchange between him and the unscrupulous Covenanter Burley later in the novel. At the very instant when public interests are forcing Morton to leave

33. For the distinction between "typical" and merely "probable" characters, see my discussion of Lukács and typicality, Chapter 1.

Edith and her family to Burley's tender mercies—he is besieging them in their castle—Morton warns Burley that he is "as constant" to his "private affairs and personal attachments" as he is to his "political principles" (p. 241; ch. 26). But of course the movement, structure, and closure of the novel, not to mention Morton's imminent trip to Glasgow, his eventual survival, and his marriage to Edith, all depend upon his separating and compromising these dual allegiances continually. Morton's actions repeatedly demonstrate that it is as hard to be equally constant to one's private and public roles as it is to be at two places at the same time. Scott, like Siegfried Kracauer, realizes that history is not homogeneous.

Our recognition that Morton joins the Covenanters for questionable reasons furthers Scott's rhetorical strategy in the novel—to examine the nature of and the justification for the Covenanters' rebellion, but also to disown it. (For Scott's conservative contemporary readers, creating tacit ways of disowning the rebellion from the start was probably the only way in which Scott could win a hearing for the Covenanters in the first place.) The imagery that describes Morton's transformation into a revolutionary supports this end. The picture of a peaceful cottage being turned into a post of defense is hardly reassuring. And Scott goes out of his way to make the characters who surround Morton at this point comfortably knowable types. Morton in his former incarnation is a typically bashful country lover. Edith is conventionally proper as well as conventionally embarrassed at the unmaidenly forwardness required in her attempts to save Morton's life. Her maid is described as and acts like a "true-bred serving-damsel" (p. 125; ch. 13), and the list could be extended. The studied effect of all this conventionality is to make Morton's transformation particularly startling, almost uncanny, as it breaks the rules of the fictional decorum into which it intrudes.

Morton's inadequate attempts to knit his private and public concerns into a seamless whole alert us to expect that those around him may also be victims of ideological self-mystification. The self-deception of the Covenanters is reasonably obvious from the excesses of their different styles of biblically-based rhetoric. The case of their enemy, Claverhouse, is more subtle, and more like Morton's, whose genteel rhetoric Claverhouse shares. Claverhouse has a telling conversation, concerning the death of his nephew and only heir during the defeat at Drumclog, with the heroine's uncle, Major Bellenden:

"Colonel Grahame," said the affectionate veteran, his eyes filling with tears, "I am glad to see you bear this misfortune with such fortitude."

"I am not a selfish man," replied Claverhouse, "though the world will tell you otherwise—I am not selfish either in my hopes or fears, my joys or sorrows. I have not been severe for myself, or grasping for myself, or ambitious for myself. The service of my master and the good of the country are what I have tried to aim at. I may, perhaps, have driven severity into cruelty, but I acted for the best; and now I will not yield to my own feelings a deeper sympathy than I have given to those of others."

"I am astonished at your fortitude under all the unpleasant circumstances of this affair," pursued the Major.

"Yes," replied Claverhouse, "my enemies in the council will lay this misfortune to my charge; I despise their accusations. They will calumniate me to my sovereign; I can repel their charge. The public enemy will exult in my flight; I shall find a time to show them that they exult too early. This youth that has fallen stood betwixt a grasping kinsman and my inheritance, for you know that my marriage-bed is barren; yet, peace be with him! the country can better spare him than your friend Lord Evandale, who, after behaving very gallantly, has, I fear, also fallen." [pp. 188–89; ch. 20]

These few sentences imply a subtle and coherent view of Claverhouse, explaining his contradictions and at the same time forwarding Scott's larger inquiry into the nature and perils of ideology. We see a figure of heroic proportions who has indeed escaped selfishness of any common kind, but only by merging himself, as Morton can never successfully do, with ideas of honor and the state, and who has consequently attained a chilling abstraction from normal human concerns. But with the jump from the first to the second of his speeches, we observe a dialectical progression in which his selflessness becomes a new kind of selfishness: precisely because he identifies himself with the state, maintaining his influence at court becomes the focus of his attention. Yet this subtle egotism is not the simple appetitive self-seeking of his fellow politicians and soldiers, eager to gobble up what possessions the Covenanters still retain. Claverhouse clearly deserves the place among the Cavaliers he is accorded in "Wandering Willie's Tale" in *Redgauntlet*: they are all in Hell (Wandering Willie is the descendant of Covenanters), but he sits apart from the rest of them, beautiful as he was in life, in disdain of their brutality and venality. The way in

which Morton's ideological self-mystification attunes us to Claverhouse's anticipates the disjunctive form Scott uses later in his career,
in novels like *Quentin Durward*, which center on famous rulers.
The maneuvers by which Scott adapts Morton to fulfill the rhetorical and analytical functions of a Waverley are deft. But the amount of
interiority he gives to Morton has implications these maneuvers never
quite contain. Morton reveals limits and contradictions in Scott's
most fundamental beliefs concerning humanity, society, and history,
particularly as they involve the crucial matter of class relations.
   Through much of *Old Mortality*, Scott's view of the proper relationship between classes seems clear. By giving Morton a lower-class
double, Cuddie Headrigg, Scott suggests that upper and lower classes
are inherently complementary; this suggestion implicitly condemns
both upper-class repression and lower-class rebellion by implying that
the only good society is one in which the salient aspects of different
classes are maintained intact, in a state of mutual, organic interde-
pendency.[34] A conversation between Morton and Cuddie, held when
they are tied together on the same horse as prisoners of the Cavaliers,
reinforces this suggestion:

> "I will resist any authority on earth," said Morton, "that invades
> tyrannically my chartered rights as a freeman; and I am determined I
> will not be unjustly dragged to a jail, or perhaps a gibbet, if I can pos-
> sibly make my escape from these men either by address or force."
>   "Weel, that's just my mind too, aye supposing we hae a feasible op-
> portunity o' breaking loose. But then ye speak o' a charter; now these
> are things that only belang to the like o' you that are a gentleman,
> and it mightna bear me through that am but a husbandman."
>   "The charter that I speak of," said Morton, "is common to the
> meanest Scotchman. It is that freedom from stripes and bondage
> which was claimed, as you may read in Scripture, by the Apostle Paul
> himself, and which every man who is free born is called upon to de-
> fend for his own sake and that of his countrymen."
>   "Hegh, sirs!" replied Cuddie, "it wad hae been lang or my Leddy
> Margaret, or my mither either, wad hae fund out sic a wise-like doc-
> trine in the Bible! The tane was aye graning about giving tribute to
> Caesar, and the tither is as daft wi' her Whiggery. I hae been clean
> spoilt, just wi' listening to twa blethering auld wives; but if I could get

34. John P. Farrell, *Revolution as Tragedy: The Dilemma of the Moderate from
Scott to Arnold* (Ithaca: Cornell University Press, 1980), pp. 73–86, lays heavy stress
on the importance of organic community in Scott.

a gentleman that wad let me tak on to be his servant, I am confident I wad be a clean contrary creature; and I hope your honour will think on what I am saying if ye were ance fairly delivered out o' this house of bondage, and just take me to be your ain wally-de-shamble." [pp. 139–40; ch. 14]

Both characters in this passage, and not just Cuddie, are placed in a specific, limited, and limiting historical context. Morton is very much in character as a seventeenth-century Presbyterian, when he draws on biblical chapter and verse to support his belief in the inalienable rights of a freeman. He is performing the same kind of operation the extreme Covenanters perform with scripture, although in a more liberal and humane spirit, and this historical mediation calls into question our natural assumption that as protagonist he represents in a direct way the values of the novel. Cuddie's suspicion of Morton's class bias, which crystallizes in his question about whether "charters" apply to the likes of him, is entirely to the point.[35] Equally shrewd is his motivation for putting himself at Morton's disposal, which bypasses political issues, involving instead personal admiration for Morton's martial skills and a canny intuition that Morton, just because his rhetoric lacks the bite of the Covenanters' rhetoric, is not likely to make a martyr of himself or his servants. The point here is not so much to deflate Morton or Cuddie by revealing hypocrisy in the one or opportunism in the other; the point is to suggest that both of them need each other, as servants and masters tend to need each other throughout Scott's works. Even though Morton is penniless, Cuddie is right to ask to be his servant, and Morton is right to accept.

Throughout most of *Old Mortality*, this idea of a symbiosis between classes persists, as genteel notions of "honor" are balanced and brought down to earth by pragmatic peasant shrewdness and allegiance to the moderate, local, immediate, and physical. Lady Bellenden tells interminable stories about the breakfast Charles II took in her baronial hall. She needs to do this; she has lost a husband and two sons to the royal cause. But her stories cry out for deflation, and they get it. One of her maids, for instance, extends and thereby sub-

---

35. Hart, pp. 77–78, believes that the novel calls on us to distinguish sharply between Morton's principles and Cuddie's opportunism. Robin Mayhead, *Walter Scott* (Cambridge: Cambridge University Press, 1973), p. 105, seems closer to the truth in suggesting that Morton is "playing the same sort of game" as Cuddie is.

verts her wish to entertain Claverhouse precisely as she had entertained Charles II by remarking that "if everything is just to be as his Majesty left it there should be an unco hole in the venison pasty" (p. 105; ch. 11). The famous scene toward the end of the novel in which Edith Bellenden sees what she takes to be the ghost of Henry Morton shares the same comic decorum, as those who object to it because it is "unbelievable" fail to recognize. As Edith, in completely good faith, speaks the rhetoric of honor and self-sacrifice, promising to renounce the memory of Morton (who she thinks is dead) and reward the faithful Evandale with her hand, the image of her desires (such as they are—Morton is pale when he looks in the window) rises before her in ironic negation of what she has just said.[36] Instances of this pattern in Old Mortality could be greatly multiplied; those whose idealism is not so tempered perish.

The social and ideological balance Cuddie and Morton maintain depends upon a vision of human personality in dynamic relationship to society as a whole; or to put it another way, the basic unit here is society, not the individual. But forces in the novel—chiefly the social contradictions contained in its subject matter and the emphasis on individual interiority created by the depiction of Morton's identification with his country—threaten to disrupt this social balance, particularly in the final scenes.[37] In those scenes, peasant shrewdness begins to look like mindless appetency; aristocratic notions of honor threaten to become "mere" ideology, which either masks or perverts the same appetitive drives.

The most brilliant and unsettling moment in Old Mortality occurs when Cuddie Headrigg, at the instigation of his wife Jenny, betrays Morton by refusing to pierce through the transparent disguise he

36. This scene is thus a variant of a scene in Tom Jones (Bk. 7, ch. 9), in which Sophia Western's pride at the thought of sacrificing herself for her father nearly leads her to abandon Tom, until she glances at a muff she associates with him and remembers her own healthier desires.

37. Most commentators see the novel's ending as a problem. The best discussions are Welsh, pp. 255–64, and Robert C. Gordon, Under Which King? A Study of the Scottish Waverley Novels (Edinburgh: Oliver and Boyd, 1969), pp. 55–66. David Brown, Walter Scott and the Historical Imagination (London: Routledge & Kegan Paul, 1979), p. 90, points out that the ending of the novel is bound to be problematical, because only the Glorious Revolution can resolve its political dilemmas, and "to properly explain the events of 1688, a Scottish focus is not sufficient."

adopts when, having been exiled after the defeat of the Covenanters, he revisits Scotland in semiconscious pursuit of Edith Bellenden. This betrayal is unsettling because it is the logical outcome of what have seemed the novel's deepest values. We have consistently admired Cuddie's immunity to ideological excess. We appreciate his cunning and flexibility. Above all, we respect his love of the local and familiar, and sympathize with his dismay at the prospect of being forced to go "to a far country, maybe twall or fifteen miles aff" when his mother's Cameronian fanaticism leads to their eviction from Lady Bellenden's estate (p. 61; ch. 7). Yet it is precisely his attachment to land, peace, and stability, to all that the Glorious Revolution itself triumphantly represented to Scott and his readers, which makes Cuddie betray Morton. Jenny reminds him that they stand to lose all that peace has brought them, if he allows his loyalty to Morton to overcome his own self-interest. She fears, with some justification, that Morton's sudden reappearance will break off the impending marriage between their landlord Lord Evandale and their protector Edith Bellenden, in which case they may lose their "ain bit free house, and the kale-yard, and the cow's grass" (p. 343; ch. 38). Cuddie cannot resist such logic. As he ruefully acknowledges, her arguments, the arguments of possessive individualism, have replaced the fanatical ideologies of the women who guided him in the past, his mother and Lady Bellenden.

When Cuddie betrays Morton, the values of moderation and local attachment which most of the novel celebrates begin to seem questionable and subhuman. Earlier scenes in the novel, in which devotion to the local and immediate cancels out wider sympathies, take on new meaning; we find more than comedy in Alison Wilson's wish that she hadn't mentioned the impending execution of Lord Evandale (which Morton is in a position to stop now that he knows about it), since having done so has spoiled Morton's dinner. But if our enjoyment of such concrete, "natural" correctives to finespun notions of aristocratic honor and fidelity begins to sour at the end of the novel, that ideology itself ceases to provide much of an alternative. Throughout the novel's final scenes, ideological concerns are in danger of being reduced to simple veils for desires and ambitions. The gallant Claverhouse, with his compelling speeches about honor and immortality and his highly refined selfishness, is indeed dead in the Scotland to which

Morton returns after his banishment. Lord Evandale, who tries to become Claverhouse's successor, appears absurdly quixotic in his attachment to the cause of the Stuarts. He knows that the men he must depend upon are radically untrustworthy, and yet he persists. We wonder if he is not motivated by a death wish to escape his impossible relationship with Edith. His sister explains his determination to support the Stuarts as the result of "family connexions and early predilections" (p. 346; ch. 38). In the same breath she urges Edith to provide him with the same sort of excuse for ignoring the cause that Jenny uses to render Cuddie inactive. If Edith will only marry him, perhaps he will remain at home. In the new order, only the displaced, disappointed, and unloved need opt for loyalties that extend beyond themselves and their families.

Morton himself provides the clearest example of the superficiality that characterizes conscious intentions and beliefs in this part of the novel. He avoids letting his right hand know what his left hand is contriving, with a thoroughness that leaves his earlier self-mystifications far behind. When he returns to Scotland, he feels an overwhelming desire to be seen, recognized, accepted, reincorporated into a community in which his place had always in fact been equivocal, and he wants to marry Edith as well. These subconscious desires subvert his conscious intentions and values repeatedly, as he performs action after action designed to break through the disguise he has assumed to help him act with "honor" toward Edith by not reviving his claims on her when she again appears to have chosen to marry Evandale instead. At times the elaborateness of his actions verges upon comedy, and in one instance, Morton himself nearly becomes conscious of what he is doing. As he approaches Niel Blane's inn in a "disguise" consisting of the clothing he wore when he last visited it, it occurs to him "more than once . . . that his resumption of the dress which he had worn while a youth . . . might render it more difficult for him to remain incognito" (p. 374; ch. 41). In the previous scene, Morton's wish to be recognized by his uncle's housekeeper despite another disguise involves him in a series of increasingly elaborate expedients, until he finally calls his old dog by name. Alexander Welsh has argued, with some plausibility, that Morton's subconscious motivations also take a darker turn: he goes for reinforcements when he learns his rival Evandale is in danger instead of joining him, because in fact he wants him dead.[38]

In its closing scenes, then, *Old Mortality* is on the verge of reaching an unexpected and uncongenial conclusion—that ideologies are either destructive perversions of humanity, or mere blinds for unconscious appetites, or both at once. The notion that concrete, "natural" peasant life can provide a humanly attractive alternative to ideological excess also becomes increasingly dubious, as such natural behavior shades into simple selfishness. The one decisive exception, the superhumanly generous Bessie McClure, has a goodness so singular and inexplicable we hardly know what to make of it. And even her goodness coexists, in schizophrenic fashion, with an abstract set of beliefs concerning the church every bit as unyielding as those possessed by the Covenanters who would have killed Morton for being an "Erastian."

The split between ideology and "natural" appetency I have been tracing, which debilitates both, rests upon a split between classes, figured in Cuddie's betrayal of Morton, a disruption of the organic social relationships that the novel posits as an ideal. It is odd that the consequences of such a division should be most profoundly explored *after* 1688, *after* class rebellion has failed. Perhaps a setting of external social calm was needed before the deepest implications of peasant revolution could be approached. Or perhaps Scott is suggesting that the compromise of 1688 itself necessarily leads to the end of organic social relations. Cuddie and Jenny may serve as forerunners of peaceful, selfish suburbia, which wishes nothing so much as to remain uninvolved. At any rate, Scott suggests at the very end of the novel that the mechanisms binding together an organic society still have some vitality. Jenny may be able to prevail upon Cuddie to betray an old master with whom he no longer has concrete ties, but when his present landlord, Evandale, is in physical danger, he runs to his aid, gun in hand, despite Jenny's shrewd, cautious, law-abiding wish that he stay in his own house and mind his own business. What seems remarkable in *Old Mortality*, however, is not that Scott ultimately reasserts the existence of organic social ties, but that he calls them into question so thoroughly before he reasserts them.

38. Welsh, p. 263.

The resonances of Morton's homecoming extend even farther. When Morton arrives at Niel Blane's inn, he is not recognized, but he has a recognition about the unchanging country life around him which is a sober, rationalistic, bitter precursor to the ecstatic visions in *War and Peace* in which humanity itself coalesces into a vibrant, pulsating globe, or a column of marching soldiers becomes a single indistinguishable stream of life:

> "Let the tide of the world wax or wane as it will," Morton thought, as he looked around him, "enough will be found to fill the places which chance renders vacant; and, in the usual occupations and amusements of life, human beings will succeed each other, as leaves upon the same tree, with the same individual difference and the same general resemblance." [p. 375; ch. 41]

With this perception, *Old Mortality* threatens to turn into a kind of fiction I have argued Scott does not write, a fiction that pits the alienated individual over and against society. Is *Old Mortality* Scott's *Père Goriot* or *Lost Illusions*? Morton's trip to Niel Blane's inn brings to the surface a potentially tragic dilemma inherent in the notion of an organic society. Morton's wish to be recognized and hence to reenter the society of his youth registers the immense attraction of belonging in a way in which members of postfeudal, postorganic societies can never belong; yet the vision of human beings as leaves on a tree betrays an awareness of how fundamentally inhospitable such a society is toward the individual *as* an individual, toward all that we value in bourgeois individuality.

By giving Morton greater interiority than Waverley, Scott anticipates the representational norms of the Victorian novel. But this creates a perspective in which his usual mode of viewing the relationship between individuals and societies suddenly looks alien, limiting, and threatening to the individuality and interiority Morton begins to possess. This shift of perspective brings to the surface other problems as well. The simple indifference of historical process to individuals is nowhere more apparent in Scott's works than it is in *Old Mortality*. A sense of human littleness, which almost amounts to a sense of existential homelessness, is one of the work's distinctive qualities. We feel it in the early description of the wild moorlands across which Morton and Cuddie are led to the Battle of Drumclog:

This desolate region seemed to extend farther than the eye could reach, without grandeur, without even the dignity of mountain wildness, yet striking, from the huge proportion which it seemed to bear to such more favoured spots of the country as were adapted to cultivation and fitted for the support of man, and thereby impressing irresistibly the mind of the spectator with a sense of the omnipotence of nature and the comparative inefficacy of the boasted means of amelioration which man is capable of opposing to the disadvantages of climate and soil.

It is a remarkable effect of such extensive wastes that they impose an idea of solitude even upon those who travel through them in considerable numbers, so much is the imagination affected by the disproportion between the desert around and the party who are traversing it. Thus the members of a caravan of a thousand souls may feel, in the deserts of Africa or Arabia, a sense of loneliness unknown to the individual traveller whose solitary course is through a thriving and cultivated country. [pp. 144–45; ch. 15]

I have said that Morton does not further the representation of the rich, genial sense of historical memory so characteristic of Scott's novels. But he does evoke a sense of history which is its opposite (and which is always hovering around its edges)—a sense of history as exclusion, loss, chaos.

Scott has an answer to the deepest dilemmas Morton's homecoming raises, just as he has an answer to the problems of social fragmentation and class antagonism. The Edinburgh Enlightenment was all too familiar with the unsettling vistas that can open out in the midst of what had seemed familiar terrain. In many ways, the moral philosophy of the men who most influenced Scott intellectually constitutes a principled attempt to close off certain possibilities opened by their friend David Hume. Morton's experiences when he returns to Scotland reduce him to thoughts of despair and suicide, but he soon exchanges them for a stoicism like Adam Ferguson's: "'I am a fool!' he said, 'and worse than a fool, to set light by that existence which Heaven has so often preserved in the most marvellous manner. Something there yet remains for me in this world, were it only to bear my sorrows like a man, and to aid those who need my assistance'" (p. 361; ch. 39). The claims of action in the world supersede individual sorrow, and responding to them contains the seeds of salvation.[39]

39. Adam Ferguson, *Principles of Moral and Political Science*, 2 vols. (Edinburgh: Creech, 1792), I, 7–8; see also Duncan Forbes, Introduction to *An Essay on the His-*

Action in history also has less high-minded attractions for us as readers. Cuddie Headrigg reacts to the Battle of Drumclog with a mixture of horror at its destructiveness and delight in its energy that we share: "Eh, sirs!" he exclaims to Morton, "yon's an awfu' sight, and yet ane canna keep their een aff frae it!" (p. 165; ch. 17).

Old Mortality is surely one of the greatest historical novels by Scott or anyone else. It reflects the depth and subtlety of Scott's insight into the past, and it shows his willingness to follow the logic of his fiction to unpleasant conclusions. The novel also demonstrates the rewards that come from paying close attention to the logic of Scott's artistic structure and particularly to the key to structure in the Waverley Novels, the manner in which each protagonist creates historical meaning.

Other Conjunctive Novels

In the period immediately following the completion of Old Mortality, Scott turns away from the conjunctive novel, toward other forms. In Rob Roy and A Legend of Montrose, he creates works which employ disjunctive heroes to present portraits of famous historical figures. In The Heart of Midlothian and The Bride of Lammermoor, he puts the protagonist at the center of things, in a way that departs from both conjunctive and disjunctive form, as we shall discover in my final chapter. He returns sporadically to conjunctive form in later years: it is important in Ivanhoe, and it touches Woodstock and Peveril of the Peak as well. But only toward the end of his career, with Redgauntlet and then, four years later, with The Fair Maid of Perth, does he employ it with the strength and inventiveness he had manifested in Waverley and Old Mortality. In the following I shall touch briefly on these later conjunctive works.

In discussing Waverley and Old Mortality, my chief concern was to define the different ways in which their protagonists help us to experience and understand history. The heroes of these novels have two main functions: their progress through the novels creates historical meanings of various kinds, and they also guide us in processing each

tory of Civil Society by Adam Ferguson (1767; rpt. Edinburgh: Edinburgh University Press, 1966), p. xxviii.

novel as a whole, alerting us to the kinds of issues each novel raises. The protagonist of *Redgauntlet*, Darsie Latimer, plays both these roles, but in an unusual way. Unlike Morton or Waverley, Darsie lacks a willed connection with the novel's historical subject: he happens upon history inadvertently, and he retreats from it as quickly as he can. His uncle, who is the chief instigator of a Jacobite uprising, kidnaps him in an attempt to involve him also. But Darsie rightly views the Jacobites as men whose historical moment has passed; he wants nothing so much as to escape from their attempt to be more than historical curiosities.

Darsie Latimer's tenuous connection with the historical events that surround him indicates the mode in which Scott wants us to view history in *Redgauntlet*: it marks those aspects of the Jacobite movement he wishes to stress, and those he wishes to keep in the background. In *Redgauntlet* as in *Old Mortality*, he is interested in the relationship between history and ideology; but whereas in *Old Mortality* he depicts a rebellion during which choices must be made quickly and under great pressure, in *Redgauntlet* he considers the more usual course of ideological change—the slow, half-conscious way in which beliefs and values adapt themselves over time to evolving historical realities. The novel contains a whole gallery of characters whose ideas and values are in disequilibrium with their surroundings, from the utter hypocrite Job Trumbull, to the mainly admirable Joshua Geddes (whose attempts to see the world through Quakerly spectacles never quite succeed), to Peter Peebles (whose madness creates a world to replace the one he unhappily inhabits), to the central case—the Jacobites who have not yet recognized that they are in fact Hanoverians. But concentrating on the *process* of ideological accommodation implies creating a certain distance between us as readers and the political and social issues that constitute the *content* of that change. Darsie's tenuous connection with the Jacobite uprising figures that distance. Scott achieves it through other means as well. He diffuses some of the issues raised by Jacobitism by depicting the movement at a moment when its defeat is a foregone conclusion. And since he realizes that a quickness to tot up rights and wrongs can make ideological accommodation seem mere hypocrisy or bad faith, he blunts our hunger to make moral judgments by depicting the present and the past as difficult to choose between: the feudal violence of the remembered past in the novel balances the soulless commercialism of its present. The question here, as so often in historical fiction, is one of emphasis. *Redgauntlet* depicts with brilliant economy the historical significance of the transition from Stuart to Hanoverian rule, so that the process of ideological accommodation will be concretely intelligible. Its final scene, the allegorical vignette in which Charles Edward takes leave of his adherents and Redgauntlet vows to sink his sword in the depths of the sea that will henceforth divide him from Scotland, sums up that process in an unforgettable way. But the novel treats the significance of such actions in a special manner. Darsie is cut off from direct involvement in the Jacobite cause so that the issues that dominate a novel like *Waverley* never become central in *Redgauntlet*.

The novel's love interest provides a good example of the special kind of conjunctive hero Darsie is. Throughout most of the novel, Darsie believes himself to be in love with a mysterious, inaccessible young woman he calls "Green Mantle," since he does not know her name. But when, toward the end of the novel, the two finally engage in extended conversation, she overwhelms him with an affection that shocks the superficially romantic but deeply conventional young man he discovers himself to be. His embarrassment at her advances continues for several pages, until finally he discovers that she is, and knows herself to be, a sister he didn't realize he had, Lilias Redgauntlet. At this point, he feels the same delighted relief that the Jacobites feel a few chapters later, when the Pretender's stubbornness about giving up his mistress (who is probably a Hanoverian spy) discharges them of the duty to imperil their lives for a cause in which the pressure of events teaches them they no longer believe.

By converting Green Mantle the mysterious damsel into Lilias the devoted sister, Scott creates a historically resonant pattern similar to Waverley's choosing Rose Bradwardine for his wife instead of Flora MacIvor—a choice of the sweet domestic reality of the present instead of the threatening, overpowering romance of the past. But the nature of this pattern in *Redgauntlet* constitutes a significant and attractive variation on the normal procedures of Scott's conjunctive form. As we have seen, the marriage in *Waverley* has considerable persuasive force. The love story in *Redgauntlet* is at once less powerfully conclusive and more imaginatively free: we delight in it precisely because of its slyness and wit in paralleling certain aspects of the history of Jacobitism. Darsie's adventures in general retain the kind of significance concerning historical process that marks the career of a conjunctive protagonist, but they also initiate a rich and intricate play of mind that informs *Redgauntlet* as a whole.[40] Throughout the novel, Scott creates a wealth of metaphorical doublings in characters, speeches, scenes, and sequences, before which a simple utilitarian metaphor like Waverley's choice of Rose Bradwardine instead of Flora MacIvor pales. He seems to enjoy giving historical resonances to the most unlikely things, through dramatic irony, metaphor, simile, and allegory. *Redgauntlet* is Scott's most elaborate defense of the play of historical imagination.

Scott's other great conjunctive novel following *Old Mortality*, *The Fair Maid of Perth*, shares *Redgauntlet*'s interest in problems of ideological accommodation. But its form is best understood as a solution to the problem of employing a conjunctive hero to explore historical transitions in the distant past. Scott's heroes normally possess a certain modernity. This helps them to function as entries for the modern reader into an older world; it also provides a defining contrast between that world and the present; finally, it can play an important role in persuading us to accept historical change. Since we wish to see the hero survive, we welcome progress toward a more modern world, to which he is better attuned. But the further back in time a novel is set, the more anomalous such a hero will be, and the greater the danger that his modern aspects will rob him of historical credibility.

The problems inherent in placing a "modern" hero in the Middle Ages account for many of the characteristics of *Ivanhoe*, Scott's first medieval novel, and generate a certain schizophrenia in Ivanhoe himself, who at one moment criticizes Richard I's knight-errantry from a recognizably modern viewpoint, but at the next reacts to Rebecca with all the bigotry of his age. This self-division takes its toll on Ivanhoe. His most effective fictional moments are spent not as a Waverley-figure but as a foil for Rebecca, whose status as a Jew sets her apart from the dominant culture, making her the believable foil

---

40. Brian Nellist, "Narrative Modes in the Waverley Novels," in *Literature of the Romantic Period: 1750–1850*, ed. R. T. Davies and B. G. Beatty (Liverpool: Liverpool University Press, 1976), pp. 56–71, describes the play of mind *Redgauntlet* elicits from the reader.

for it which he himself is not.[41] The structural dilemma that weakens Ivanhoe as protagonist weakens the conjunctive force of his action as well. In the early part of the novel, before the center of interest shifts to Rebecca, our hopes and fears focus on the possibility of a marriage between Ivanhoe and the conventional heroine, Rowena. This marriage seems designed to possess the same sort of significance that Waverley's marriage has. When he gains the Saxon princess Rowena, Ivanhoe, who has made his peace with the Normans, will have enacted a fusion of Norman and Saxon cultures. But there is something unfocused about the conflict between Normans and Saxons, as well as about its resolution. The suspensive issue between Ivanhoe and Rowena soon comes to involve violent external actions—kidnappings, sieges, and so on—which depend less on the historical differences between Norman and Saxon society than upon the generally brutal conditions of life in medieval England. In fact, the conflict between Normans and Saxons functions most successfully as a shared fiction between writer and reader which facilitates the anatomy of medieval society. The action of *Waverley* leads us to understand and accept a specific historical transition that in very fact occurred; the action of *Ivanhoe* applies a similar model of change in a generalized way to a historical situation where it may or may not fit, but where it is heuristically useful. Form in *Ivanhoe* is weakly conjunctive.

In *Ivanhoe*, finding a character whose consciousness transcends the limitations of his historical setting is a technical problem. In *The Fair Maid of Perth*, the extent to which one can transcend the mentality of one's age becomes the basic issue Scott chooses to explore.[42] He solves the problem of a hero split between past and present by making the novel's protagonist completely a man of his own times. No Waverley hero is so firmly rooted in his class and moment as is Henry Smith, with his unthinking dislike for Highlanders, his fabulous phys-

---

41. For Rebecca's function and significance, see Edgar Rosenberg, *From Shylock to Svengali: Jewish Stereotypes in English Fiction* (Stanford: Stanford University Press, 1960), pp. 73–115.

42. Peter D. Garside, "Scott, the Romantic Past and the Nineteenth Century," *Review of English Studies*, ns 23 (1972), 156, notes the importance of this problem in Scott's medieval novels: "If there is a really strong theme in the medieval novels, it is that it is necessary, to be socially effective, to act within the context of the possibilities afforded by one's age."

ical strength and martial prowess, and his proclivity for becoming involved in bloody fights at the slightest provocation. This change in the hero produces at least two other important formal changes. In the first place, because he is so firmly rooted in his own historical and social context, Henry Smith, unlike Waverley, cannot be used to join the opposing social forces in the novel. This leaves the different parts of the novel loosely connected. By the same token, Scott cannot use Smith to provide an illuminating contrast with medieval Scotland. He solves this problem by developing a series of characters who, like Rebecca in *Ivanhoe*, are out of step with their times. Ultimately, the issues these characters raise become the main concern in the novel, giving form to its three plot lines. And the fates of all three characters, combined with that of Smith himself, give the novel its conjunctive force. In each instance, the ability of a character to transcend his or her times is shown to be strictly limited. Scott seems to have taken to heart Adam Ferguson's dictum that it is better to march with the members of one's society in the wrong direction than to march alone.[43]

Despite its radically different hero, *The Fair Maid of Perth* is a recognizable descendant of Scott's great conjunctive novels, both in its form and in its central concerns. Like *Old Mortality*, it exemplifies his ability to seize upon and use creatively the formal problems that result when he applies his preferred fictional techniques to material that resists them. In *The Fair Maid of Perth*, instead of glossing over the problem of "necessary anachronism" which is so apparent in *Ivanhoe*, or dealing with it in a way which makes us accept it simply as a necessary convention, Scott thematizes it and discovers in it his historical subject.

The categories of conjunctive and disjunctive form possess, as I have tried to demonstrate, considerable heuristic value: they help us to form appropriate expectations as we approach the great majority of Scott's novels. But they also have a substantial basis in Scott's own sense of history, for they correspond to the two poles of Scott's his-

---

43. Ferguson, *Principles*, I, 218. Ferguson later concludes that "although men of reflection may distinguish what is arbitrary in the manners of those with whom they live, they are not on this account by any means entitled to neglect the observance of them" (II, 384).

torical vision and indeed of historicism itself. Conjunctive form throws the emphasis on historical process, about which the protagonist's career creates an argument. Disjunctive form employs the hero primarily as an access to historical particularities that are esthetically irreducible to larger movements. The existence of these two forms as Scott's favored vehicles for historical fiction recalls the central theoretical concerns with which this study began. Are there disjunctions between different levels of historical generality, and if there are, are these disjunctions necessary and unbridgeable, or do they instead constitute different aspects of a continuous essence? And what are the consequences for the representation of history in historical fiction? The importance of conjunctive and disjunctive form appears to result from just the sort of necessary discontinuity between levels of historical generality that is the keynote of Siegfried Kracauer's "side-by-side" philosophy of history. But we have yet to see if a similar dynamic is at work in two of Scott's most distinguished works, *The Bride of Lammermoor* and *The Heart of Midlothian*.

5

Form in Scott's Novels: The Hero as Subject

Although they followed one another in rapid succession and represent Scott at the height of his powers, *The Bride of Lammermoor* and *The Heart of Midlothian* are radically different novels. *The Bride* is full of gloom, pessimism, and a hallucinatory Gothic power; *Midlothian* is as celebratory and affirmative a work as Scott ever wrote. Comparing the protagonists of the novels underlines their differences. Ravenswood, the doomed aristocrat, is moody, sometimes arrogant, but always brimming with passionate interiority; Jeanie Deans, the unself-consciously heroic peasant, has few thoughts and fewer passions. Beside her quiet strength, his flamboyance threatens to turn into rant; beside him, she seems a trifle dull. Yet in one respect the two characters are after all alike. Both serve as the substantial centers of the works in which they appear.

Scott, as we have seen, generally creates an oblique relationship between the central interests of a novel and its protagonist. Conjunctive and disjunctive form describe two ways in which he handles this relationship, neither of which gives the protagonist substantial centrality. Both kinds of works respond to what I have called the problem with historical novels—their inability to represent simultaneously all levels of human generality—by avoiding it in its fullest form. They employ a hero who shifts the part of the human spectrum they treat toward the social and historical, and away from the personal and internal matters a substantially central protagonist is ideally suited to explore. We have, it is true, observed one of Scott's most interesting conjunc-

tive heroes, Henry Morton, edging toward the inwardness of the substantially central protagonist. But Morton is exceptional, and this aspect of his characterization creates significantly problematic results.

With Jeanie Deans in *Midlothian* and Ravenswood in *The Bride of
Lammermoor*, the centrality toward which Morton fitfully reaches
becomes dominant. One purpose of the present chapter is to describe
the special conditions that make possible this centrality. Beyond that,
Scott's success in putting his protagonist at the center of these two
great novels recalls with some urgency certain questions that lie at the
heart of this study. First, there are the limits of representation in standard historical fiction. Do Edgar Ravenswood and Jeanie Deans solve
the problem with historical novels? Might they not at least solve the
local version of that problem reflected by the split between conjunctive and disjunctive form? Do they bridge the aspects of Scott's historical vision those forms embody—his interest in historical process on
the one hand, and historical particularity on the other? Certain critics
have sought to give Ravenswood and Jeanie Deans precisely such a
healing power, but I shall be at pains to deny it to them. Despite their
unusual structural roles, both characters confirm the notion that in
standard novel form, it is possible to concentrate on certain aspects of
human existence only at the expense of others. Even Scott never
solves the problem with historical novels, though his response to it
creates particularly rich and varied results.

Second, there is the question of evaluation and the ideological presuppositions that underlie it. I have not hesitated to call *The Bride* and
The Heart of Midlothian "great" Scott novels, even though their protagonists are uncharacteristic of Scott. Or is it *because* they are
uncharacteristic? A major purpose of this study has been to demonstrate that the expectations created by the standard novel tradition as
a whole may be unhelpful in approaching works of historical fiction.
One such expectation is that a protagonist who, like the Waverley
protagonists, appears to be at the center of structure ought to embody
a novel's meaning as well. Yet I myself am willing to give very high
marks indeed to the two Scott novels where this state of affairs comes
closest to existing. In such a judgment, conventional expectations
concerning protagonists seem to be reasserting themselves with a vengeance. With *The Bride*, they probably are: Scott is here working with
the one subject he can imagine deeply and intensely in terms of indi-

vidual interiority, his own deepest personal rejection, and the result is
a novel easily assimilable to a familiar form of standard fiction—the
Gothic novel. But *Midlothian* is different. With Helen Walker, Jeanie
Deans's historical prototype, Scott found for once a historical figure
who could serve as his protagonist without violating his sense of what
matters in history. Jeanie Deans is central to her novel in a way
Waverley never is to his, and Morton is only at certain moments. Yet
she remains a typical product of Scott's usual modes of characterization, reflecting the ways in which his assumptions concerning the relationship between human personality, society, and history differ from
those of the main novel traditions that follow him.

It is hardly surprising that the formal values implicit in standard fiction should assert themselves in the judgments of a critic who is writing in the twentieth century but who has a bias toward the fiction of
the nineteenth, and a conviction that, for good and ill, the values implicit in the form of that fiction remain central for the way in which
our society imagines itself. Whence arise our judgments of value—the
ones we feel on our pulses, I mean, not those we may manufacture in
attempts to transcend or negate our selves and our society—if not
from cultural traditions? Self-conscious, tentative complicity with tradition seems the most we can hope for. Attempting to take seriously a
writer like Scott can be useful in achieving such a stance. As we attempt to account for the contradictions in our reactions to his novels,
the biases on which our judgments depend begin to come into focus.

The Bride of Lammermoor

The Bride of Lammermoor has a power to excite and disturb the
imagination unique in Scott's fiction. The novel's hero, Edgar Ravenswood, is an exception to the rule that Waverley heroes are not
ends but means, existing to mediate between historical forces, or to
see historical sights, or to press us toward certain conclusions about
the shape of historical process, but not to have deep souls or interesting minds. With most Waverley heroes, our interest lies in what they
see: with Ravenswood, the focus shifts toward his mode of seeing,
which in the strongest moments of the novel becomes hallucinatory
despair. Any reader of *The Bride* will recall scenes in which Ravenswood faces visions of the supernatural which overwhelm him

even though he disbelieves in them. At such times, he gains a heroic stature, strangely at variance with his irresolute passivity in other parts of the novel. This heroism stems from his willingness to look despair in the face without flinching and to persist in hopeless resistance. Most Waverley heroes have, to be sure, a rhetorical dimension: they rouse and explore feelings concerning historical process or historical particularity. But Ravenswood's affective side is of another order of intensity and significance, for us and for the novelistic structure that surrounds him.

The Bride has a unique power to fascinate and disturb us because it expresses a complex of personal emotions with less historical mediation than any other of Scott's works. As it happens, we can identify in Scott's biography the source of these turbulent feelings, and this knowledge supplies the most convenient way to describe them. It has long been recognized, though sometimes resolutely ignored, that the novel reflects Scott's unhappy love affair with Williamina Belsches. The story of their relationship is well known. As a youth, Scott grew increasingly attached to Williamina over a number of years; finally, he more or less proposed to her. Exaggerating what seem to have been her ambiguous replies to his advances, he grew to believe that she had pledged herself to him at the very time when she had fallen in love with another man, more nearly her social and economic equal than Scott. When their engagement was announced, Scott was shattered and angry; the scars from this affair remained with him to the end of his life, as his *Journal*, written during his fifties, reveals. On a number of occasions in his writings he refers to the dangers involved in forming strong early romantic attachments, pointing out that social forces nearly always thwart them and lifelong suffering results. As a critic, he betrays a weakness for literary works depicting thwarted love, perhaps because they allow him to relive a trauma he never entirely mastered, forgave, or forgot.[1] Edgar Johnson has shown that this material makes sporadic appearances in a number of Scott's novels.[2] What sets *The Bride* apart from such works, I shall argue, is that

1. For the importance to Scott and to *The Bride* of one such work, Henry Mackenzie's *Julia de Roubigné*, see my "Scott, Mackenzie, and Structure in *The Bride of Lammermoor*," *Studies in the Novel*, 13 (1981), 349–66, which treats more fully certain points raised in the following discussion.

2. Edgar Johnson, *Sir Walter Scott: The Great Unknown* (New York: Macmillan, 1970), pp. 124, 469.

its central formal principle reflects the wish to revivify these emotions and transmit them to the reader. Ravenswood is the substantial center of *The Bride* so that he can focus and express a rejected lover's sense of horror, loss, and betrayal, and above all his violent ambivalence concerning himself and the woman who rejected him.

Ambivalent feelings about things lost, of course, characterize Scott's novels as a whole. It may be that Scott's vision of the past itself derives from his feelings about the loss of Williamina Belsches. Or it may be that his reactions in both cases stem from a third, irrecoverable source, even more deeply engrained in his psyche. Scott may have been one of those people to whom a Williamina Belsches rejection was bound to have happened, just as a Brookfield affair seems bound to have happened to Thackeray. It is entirely possible that *The Bride* derives from an ultimate psychic source that informs his other novels as well, but literature does not derive its shape from ultimate sources. It matters a great deal how directly such material enters into a work. We discover here another version of Kracauer's "law of perspective": the fictional results of expressing the same emotions at different levels of mediation may be strikingly different. In *The Bride* relatively unmediated feelings modify and even reverse the function and meaning of Scott's characteristic fictional devices.

The Bride transmits feelings of radical ambivalence which Scott is usually careful to rationalize. An ironic calculus of loss and gain pervades Scott's novels, but their form generally prevents the irony from collapsing into simple despair at the loss of the past: it controls what might otherwise become an irresistible atavism. Narrative itself works to this end: its very momentum leads us past moments that could be overwhelming, such as the execution of Fergus MacIvor in *Waverley*. Narrative allows Scott to break up potentially overwhelming totalities into their constituent parts, and it suggests ways of arranging those parts into comprehensible wholes. In this way discrimination and judgment counter the demands of simple emotion, preventing the mind from freezing in despair or horror. The multilayered nature of most of the novels, in which analytic, rhetorical, and esthetic levels coexist, works toward the same end.

The idea of a redeeming conflict between narrative judgment and unmediated emotion is not simply an analytical device of my own construction: an attempt to adjudicate between the two provides the subject for the extended fictional introduction to *The Bride* itself. In this introduction, Scott creates an imaginary dialogue between the supposed author of *The Bride*, Peter Pattieson, and his friend the painter Dick Tinto, who is not entirely satisfied with Pattieson's previous novels, *Old Mortality* and *The Heart of Midlothian*. The debate at first seems simply a genial, predictable exercise in the familiar eighteenth-century pastime of comparing the merits of the sister arts. Tinto naturally prefers his own art, painting. But as he tries to convince Pattieson that his fiction should attain to the pictorial by incorporating more action and less dialogue, it becomes clear that larger issues are at stake: his suggestion implies a radical suppression of narrative in favor of immediate, atemporal perception. He accuses Pattieson of being insensible to one of his paintings because his narrative cast of mind prevents him from registering its full meaning:

> You have accustomed yourself so much to these creeping twilight details of yours, that you are become incapable of receiving that instant and vivid flash of conviction which darts on the mind from seeing the happy and expressive combinations of a single scene, and which gathers from the position, attitude, and countenance of the moment, not only the history of the past lives of the personages represented, and the nature of the business on which they are immediately engaged, but lifts even the veil of futurity, and affords a shrewd guess at their future fortunes.   [p. 12; ch. 1]

Pattieson laughs at the apocalyptic pretensions of this sort of representation, but at the end of the introduction, he tells us that in *The Bride* he has decided to follow his friend's advice "in part, though not entirely" (p. 13; ch. 1). The debate between Pattieson and Tinto enables Scott to pass off as a technical experiment suggested by someone else his creation in *The Bride* of the immediate, overwhelming imaginative moments he elsewhere uses narrative to diffuse.

Some of the strongest expressions of ambivalence in *The Bride* occur precisely when the novel is at its most pictorial—in the stagy, hysterical vignettes that punctuate the fated visit of Sir William Ashton and his daughter to the tower of Wolf's Crag, for instance. But radical ambivalence, which substitutes for Scott's usual irony an irony close to oxymoron, pervades *The Bride* at all levels of its structure. The extent to which it dominates *The Bride* is perhaps most clearly

reflected in a radical change it produces in one of Scott's most important fictional techniques, his creation of "split" and "doubled" characters.

A good deal of splitting and doubling of characters occurs in the
Waverley Novels, but it is usually schematic and unproblematic, as
we have repeatedly seen. Edward Waverley's duality of character is
clearly part of the machinery necessary to transfer him from one side
of a historical confrontation to the other: his dreamy side involves
him with the Jacobites, while his realistic side brings him back to the
Hanoverian fold. It is more characteristic of Scott to double characters than to split them. Waverley contains light and dark heroines as
well as light and dark heroes, and it divides the Highland character
between two characters, Evan Dhu and Callum Beg. The purpose of
such doubling is analytical and rhetorical: it allows Scott to embody
certain historical characteristics in a highly visible way, and to manipulate our feelings about the direction history has taken. When he
wants us to think well of the Highlanders, he brings in Evan Dhu;
when he wants to make us remember their latent anarchy and destructiveness, he brings in Callum Beg. And when he leads us to accept Waverley's marriage with the light heroine, Rose Bradwardine,
not the dark heroine, Flora MacIvor, we have also acquiesced in the
passing of the old violent heroic life and its replacement by dull safe
modernity. Similarly, the disjunctive novel Quentin Durward divides
the positive and negative aspects of the medieval lady between the
countess Quentin ultimately marries and the vain, absurd, and la-
tently blood-thirsty Lady Hammeline.

Such analytical splitting and doubling of characters plays no significant role in The Bride. Instead, single characters in themselves possess
dual natures of a deeply problematic kind. Francis Hart has noted
that Caleb Balderstone is a simultaneous mixture of pathetic and
tragic, absurd and noble.[3] But the novel is full of such characters.
Ravenswood himself is a prime example, and not just in his alterna-

---

3. Francis Hart, Scott's Novels: The Plotting of Historic Survival (Charlottesville:
University Press of Virginia, 1966), p. 332. With respect to the question of "split"
characters, certain aspects of Frank McCombie, "Scott, Hamlet, and The Bride of
Lammermoor," Essays in Criticism, 25 (1975), 419–36, take on a special interest.
McCombie asserts that Lucy Ashton is a combination of two characters from The
Heart of Midlothian, Madge Wildfire and Effie Deans; if he is correct, he has revealed
the mechanism by which Scott created one of his "split" characters in The Bride.

tions between heroism and indecision. Readers are often puzzled about the extent to which he is guilty of bringing about his own tragedy. Such confusion is engendered by the narrative voice of the novel itself, which chides him for a number of contradictory shortcomings, but also paints him as a blameless victim of the machinations of others. He seems guilty for following the dictates of his own passions, which call for revenge, but also guilty for abandoning a just revenge and making friends with the enemy of his father. He is called an infatuated fool for allowing himself to be taken in by his enemies, the Ashtons; yet in his very gullibility he seems admirable, too simple and true for this world. Such contradictory characterization would be hard to account for in *Waverley* or *Old Mortality* or *Quentin Durward*, where it would make for simple confusion. But it ceases to surprise us when we recognize how different Ravenswood's function is from *Waverley*'s. *Waverley* balances values against one another in an ambiguous fashion, but they are known and definable values, and they fit into a recognizable pattern. The dynamics of *Waverley* require that we know where we are; hence it contains characters whose stable identities lend them a stable historical significance, characters like the charming, limited, safe heroine whom Waverley ultimately chooses for a wife. In *The Bride*, Ravenswood's split characterization is part of a novelistic structure expressing a qualitatively different kind of ambiguity, the ambivalent mixture of love and hatred which an unsuccessful lover feels both for himself and for the woman who rejects him.[4] The novel would betray itself if it offered even the stably ambiguous closure *Waverley* offers.

The contradictory emotions that inform Ravenswood reflect themselves in other characters as well. Lady Ashton is an example. She is a parvenu, who hates Ravenswood because he is the descendant of an ancient family. Naming her elder son in compliment to the founder of one of Scotland's premier families, the Douglases, is a piece of comic presumption and bad taste; Ravenswood himself turns out to be more closely related to the principal Douglas line than either she or her husband. Yet at moments she seems their true representative in her strength of will and singlemindedness. Her reliance on Puritanism and

---

4. Sigmund Freud, "Mourning and Melancholia," in *Works*, ed. James Strachey, XIV (London: Hogarth Press, 1957), 243–58, is the classic discussion of the kind of ambivalence I am arguing *The Bride* expresses.

witchcraft further identifies her with Scotland's horrifying, heroic past. Like Ravenswood, she seems not one character but two characters superimposed.

Her duality has a particularly subtle relationship to Ravenswood's central ambivalence about Lucy. He hates Lady Ashton because she comes between him and Lucy. Yet Lucy is, after all, her daughter, and both aspects of Lady Ashton's split characterization promote the expression of hatred not simply toward her but toward Lucy as well. In her role as social climber, Lady Ashton is uncomfortably close to the set of values Lucy herself embodies—a member of the new, seemingly civilized but potentially duplicitous order that Ravenswood as a Ravenswood ought to despise. In her incarnation as a true Douglas, Lady Ashton resembles someone else even more closely and uncomfortably—Ravenswood's own father, and hence the part of him that subscribes to the values of revenge, violence, clannishness. As a parvenu, she helps to justify the thought, "I wanted to lose Lucy, since she was unworthy of me." As a representative of Ravenswood's ancestral values, she justifies the thought, "I ought never to have loved her in the first place: I deserve to suffer." The complications here become dizzying—Ravenswood as complicit in the torture of Lucy by her mother; Ravenswood's hatred of Lady Ashton as an attack both by and on his own true, older self before he met and succumbed to Lucy; Lady Ashton as the mother Ravenswood lacks in the novel. But it is precisely this sense of fatal vertigo and claustrophobia that the novel itself expresses and that a more moderate critical commentary seems likely to diffuse. In the end, to be sure, Scott successfully transforms much of the energy his ambivalent mourning generates into pity—pity for Lucy and Ravenswood as victims of forces they cannot be expected to control. But there is more to the novel than that.

A final dichotomy, closer to the surface of the novel's action, is provided by Lucy herself. Through much of the novel, Scott employs a characteristic device to control his rage at his loss, as he splits the idea of woman itself into two parts. He drains off his negative feelings about Williamina/Lucy and projects them onto her mother in a manner that, for all its covert complexity, is overtly straightforward. But at the end of the novel this scheme breaks down. Lucy suddenly becomes not a weak, pale, loving girl, but a harpy. After she tries to murder the man whom she married instead of Ravenswood, she is discovered crouching in a chimney, her clothing spattered with blood, gibbering and pointing and apparently out of her mind. Clearly enough, she has been reduced to a state that renders a rejected lover's further revenge superfluous. The characterization of Lucy Ashton provides a striking example of the radical ambivalence that dominates *The Bride* and gives it its power.[5]

But as Scott transforms his normal fictional practices so that his novel can express relatively unmediated emotions and create its powerful effect, what happens to *The Bride* as historical fiction? Scott's insight into historical process and particularity does not simply disappear when he writes *The Bride*, but it does assume different roles and promote different ends from those characteristic of his fiction as a whole.

Scott's depiction of politics in *The Bride* is masterly, and the political machinations he describes are entirely appropriate for the period in which the novel is set, the time of demoralization and confusion surrounding the Union of England and Scotland in 1707, with its disruption of traditional political forms.[6] The novel presents a gallery of politicians of various ranks: the old privy councilors in Edinburgh, gaping for political spoils; the Marquis of A—, whose concern for his young kinsman Ravenswood is almost as genuine as his concern for his own political success; the wily but timid and oversubtle Sir William Ashton, whose one moment of nearly honest sentiment brings such terrible consequences; and even Caleb Balderstone, Ravenswood's servant, who apes his betters' political double-dealing in his commerce with the villagers of Wolf's Hope. But how does Scott

---

5. Scott's treatment of the supernatural in *The Bride* might seem the supreme example of the duality I have been tracing, answering as it does to Tzvetan Todorov's definition of the "uncanny" as a hesitation between belief in the laws of nature and the supernatural: see *The Fantastic* (1970), trans. Richard Howard (Ithaca: Cornell University Press, 1975). But Scott had independent theoretical grounds for choosing this mode of dealing with the supernatural, as his essay on Ann Radcliffe makes clear (see *MPW* III, 370–73), and he employs it in other works, though not with the intensity of *The Bride*. Perhaps we can say that the dominant intention of *The Bride* makes Scott's preferred mode of depicting the supernatural uniquely forceful and appropriate.

6. *The Bride* in fact gives contradictory signals concerning whether it is set immediately before or immediately after the Union: Jane Millgate provides a valuable discussion of this problem in "Text and Context: Dating the Events of *The Bride of Lammermoor*," *Bibliotheck*, 9 (1979), 200–213.

use this material in the structure of his novel? Caleb provides a clue when, after congratulating himself on the success of his latest maneuvers in the village, he laments his master's ignorance of "the ways of this warld" (p. 243; ch. 25). The same gesture of setting the protagonist over and against "the world" occurs at the end of the novel, when we learn that the Marquis of A—, after hearing that Ravenswood has disappeared in the Kelpie's Flow, hurried back from his political concerns "to mourn his loss; and, after renewing in vain a search for the body, returned, to forget what had happened amid the bustle of politics and state affairs" (p. 312; ch. 35). Scott creates a vivid, historically based sense of political life in *The Bride*, but he does so ultimately to show the world's insufficiency, venality, and callousness, not to examine it as a historical phenomenon. If Ravenswood seems too simple and true for the world, it is largely because he is placed against this backdrop. A certain amount of adolescent anger at adult compromise, a fierce repudiation of resignation that can speak sadly and elegiacally about the loss of first loves as "inevitable," informs *The Bride*. This grimly ironic depiction of the ways of the world gives an edge to the novel's sense of tragic waste; thus the final sentence informs us that Lady Ashton's "splendid marble monument records her name, titles, and virtues, while her victims remain undistinguished by tomb or epitaph" (p. 313; ch. 35). If this vision opens out into a deeply pessimistic view of history, it does so to provide a metaphor for the emotional complex that forms the basis of the novel as a whole.

History plays another role in *The Bride*. In certain scenes, the appearance of Scott's more normal historical vision provides a moment of refuge from the central tragedy. This occurs in Scott's depiction of the village of Wolf's Hope. R. C. Gordon believes that the villagers of Wolf's Hope, who have begun to assert their rights against the decayed house of Ravenswood, provide yet another example of the moral decay that sets in when new ways replace old ones, yet another indication of Scott's underlying historical pessimism.[7] About Scott's ultimate pessimism I would agree, but I think there is more to be said for the villagers. Scott uses a significant metaphor to describe their gradual emancipation from the influence of the Ravenswood family:

7. R. C. Gordon, *Under Which King? A Study of the Scottish Waverley Novels* (Edinburgh: Oliver and Boyd, 1969), p. 103.

They resembled a man that has been long fettered, who, even at liberty, feels in imagination the grasp of the handcuffs still binding his
wrists. But the exercise of freedom is quickly followed with the natural consciousness of its immunities, as the enlarged prisoner, by the
free use of his limbs, soon dispels the cramped feeling they had ac-
quired when bound. [pp. 115–16; ch. 12]

Scott does not blink at the fact that, in the good old days under the
Ravenswoods, the villagers were in a real sense prisoners. Will their
future prove any better? For a while it seems that it will not. The villagers' leader, a cooper named John Girder, may begin by declaring
his scorn for the mere idea of continuing to pay feudal dues to the
Ravenswoods. But when it appears that Ravenswood can help him to
the post of queen's cooper, Girder sings a different tune, promising
that in the future Ravenswood will find him "as pliant as a hoop-
willow in a' that he could wish of him" (p. 131; ch. 13). Such an
about-face suggests that John Girder, lately emancipated from feudal
servitude, has merely found a new kind of bondage in which patron-
age has replaced habit based on the memory of physical coercion.
However true this may be, the quality of his prison has at least im-
proved. Late in the novel, in a scene that has been neglected by critics,
Girder entertains in his own home Ravenswood and the Marquis of
A—, Ravenswood's kinsman and powerful political ally. Scott paints
a careful picture of the cooper's house, down to the hangings in the
best room, which are made of stamped leather, in imitation of the
way in which the lesser gentry imitate the nobility's tapestries. In
other hands, this description might imply a simple condemnation of
the decay of old standards, but Scott gives it a more complex significance. He admires the solidity, comfort, and half-comic dignity of a
man like John Girder. Entertaining a nobleman in one's own house is,
after all, preferable to being forced to supply food and drink for his
entertainment at the castle of one's feudal lord. Girder also has the
distinction of being able to keep the women in his household in
check, something that Scott intends to come as a relief after his depiction of Lady Ashton's tyranny over *her* husband. Girder's house is a
place of warmth and comfort, where christenings take place, families
gather, and ample meals are served. It comes closer to embodying the
spirit of community than anything else in *The Bride*. Scott does not
reduce Girder's imitation tapestries to mere satirical props, for they

are part of the historical record, amusing in certain respects but richly evocative of the particularities of a certain class, time, and place.

Wolf's Hope and its inhabitants, in short, provide a significant if muted counterweight to the pessimism that pervades the rest of the novel. Even more important for our purposes, Scott's depiction of the gradual evolution of class and consciousness in the village embodies a complexity of historical vision which the dominant strand of the novel, particularly as it gains momentum, lacks and must lack. The terms in which we need to discuss the village, and the issues it raises, are simply different from those evoked by the novel's central action. Though I cannot agree with Gordon's negative view of the villagers, I find his concluding remarks on the novel as a whole extremely suggestive as a description of how, at its deepest affective level, *The Bride* leaves behind Scott's usual concern with the particularities of history in its vision of personal loss: "In the two stark concluding chapters Lucy dies insane, Edgar rides into the Kelpie's Flow, and the three hags gleefully intone the Fate *motif*. Incidents like these reveal Scott in a realm of his own, far beyond facile categories of acceptance or escapism." And far beyond history itself, I would add. Scott's comic, complex, characteristically historical depiction of Wolf's Hope reminds us of what his novels usually are, and what *The Bride* predominantly is not.[8]

In the Wolf's Hope episodes, Scott's characteristically complex historical vision promotes a sense of control and distance. I earlier suggested that his usual narrative techniques themselves serve as a means of temporalizing and breaking into manageable parts potentially threatening totalities. That the central action of *The Bride* does not follow these norms carries with it certain dangers and temptations for the reader, especially the reader well-versed in Scott's other novels. We may wish to control and make sense of the novel's disturbing and

8. Gordon, p. 109. Scott's characteristic creation of a complex relationship between character, action, and concrete historical situation is also richly present in his depiction of Sir William Ashton. Critics who approach the novel with the norms of *Waverley* in mind attempt to show that Ashton plays an integral part in it, rightly sensing that the mode in which he is depicted is of a piece with Scott's usual fictional practices. E. M. Forster, feeling no such allegiance to Scott's usual methods, came to a different conclusion, deciding that Ashton is superfluous because "the tragedy would occur in almost the same form if he did not exist": see *Aspects of the Novel* (1927; rpt. New York: Harcourt, 1954), p. 33.

at times uncanny effect, in a way Scott himself refuses to do, by taking Ravenswood and the experience that centers on him to be translatable into propositions concerning historical process or survival in history. It is comforting to escape the novel's effect by turning against the hero and heroine, proclaiming them weak and barren, consigning them to the rubbish heap of historical failure, and drawing an appropriate moral. But if we are to respond adequately to *The Bride*, we need to resist such temptations. Judging Edgar Ravenswood is a procedure that the novel simply does not ask us to carry out; sharing his sense of horror, guilt, anger, and radical ambivalence is a more appropriate response.[9]

The Bride thus turns out to be the only major novel by Scott in which history does not function as the primary subject.[10] Instead, the novel gives a predominant place to the two other major uses of history in historical fiction we earlier discussed. In drawing on an atmosphere of historical crisis, *The Bride* employs history as a source of drama, but with hints of a complex historicity uncharacteristic of this use of history. In this respect, *The Bride* recalls but surpasses the generalized, unnuanced use of history as drama that energizes *Les Chouans* and Scott's own *St. Ronan's Well*. In creating a blank, despairing view of politics and history, which ultimately acts as a vehicle for personal feeling, Scott produces a version of history as pastoral which resembles Thackeray's defensive degradation of the past in *Henry Esmond*, though it again possesses more truly historical resonances. *The Bride* demonstrates that a novel can reflect a rich sense of historicity, even if its subject is not historical process or historical par-

---

9. Hart, *Scott's Novels*, p. 333, judges Ravenswood harshly, as a character who has failed in his historical *Bildung*. His more recent work on *The Bride* downplays its historicity, finding in the novel timeless Gothic archetypes: see *The Scottish Novel* (Cambridge: Harvard University Press, 1978), pp. 19–22.

10. David Brown, *Walter Scott and the Historical Imagination* (London: Routledge & Kegan Paul, 1979), pp. 129–50, makes an impressive attempt to show that *The Bride* is at once "Scott's most 'Romantic' novel" and also "his greatest essay in historical realism" (p. 150). Brown's central argument is that the side of the novel I impute to Scott's ambivalence over a personal loss in fact constitutes a dramatization of "the demise of the feudal order . . . as the traditional, feudal consciousness would see it—that is, not as a materialistic struggle, but as an inexplicable, fatal decline" (p. 136). I find this an attractive argument, but in the end, both for the theoretical reasons I have given in Chapter 1, and also because of my experience of the novel as a reader, I do not believe that the novel can be reduced to such terms.

ticularity; in doing so, it provides a notable exception to the norms reflected in most historical fiction in the nineteenth century. But even here, Scott's radically historical sensibility creates only a partial exception, for as we have seen, the novel's vision of despairing ambivalence finally leaves history behind. Even in *The Bride*, the different levels of human generality do not coalesce into a seamless whole: to obtain certain fictional virtues, Scott must sacrifice others.

The Heart of Midlothian

The Heart of Midlothian is as firmly centered on history as *The Bride of Lammermoor* is centered on personal experience. In all respects save their structural roles, Jeanie and Ravenswood are polar opposites. Ravenswood is at the center of *The Bride* so that he can serve as a subjective vehicle by which Scott allows us to enter a fictional world full of ambivalence and despair. In *Midlothian*, nothing is more important about Jeanie Deans than her status as historically other from Scott and from us. Perhaps Scott's success in making Jeanie Deans a structurally central protagonist utterly different from himself, coupled with his constant search for formal variety, suggested to him a further possibility, which *The Bride* realizes: to keep a protagonist at the center, but reverse his nature. However that may be, this line of experimentation quickly ran its course; after *The Bride*, he returned to his more usual methods of construction.

Why Scott abandoned the central protagonist after obtaining such remarkable results is a question worth pausing over. It is hardly surprising that he did not try to repeat *The Bride*: one such moment of personal catharsis is more than we might have expected from as repressed an author as Scott. But why did he not attempt to create another *Midlothian*? It is well to remember that Scott, unlike most novelists in the English tradition, has no special interest in central protagonists; indeed, as I have argued, his assumptions about the relationship between human beings, society, and history militate against their use. Beyond that, he may simply never have found another Jeanie Deans. Only a special kind of protagonist indeed could stand at the center of a novel and still allow him to explore the historical issues that interest him most. An obvious solution, of course, would be to employ a figure from public history, a Cromwell or Louis XIV, as a central protagonist. But Scott wisely refuses to do this: such a choice would violate his sense of how history works and would also involve a variety of representational problems that Lukács and others have described.[11] Another tack would be to create an imaginary character to act as a consubstantial symbol for a cultural movement or historical transition, but as we have seen, this is not Scott's way either. He thus requires a protagonist who is neither a world historical figure nor a historical symbol, yet who can be rendered historically significant. A perfect solution, especially given his habit of representing characters externally, would be a figure from private life who actually performed a historically eloquent action, yet who rests in an unremembered grave. Jeanie Deans, excluded from historical notice both as a woman and a member of the lower classes, is precisely such a figure, but how many other such characters could Scott hope to uncover? Finally, Scott may not have returned to the central protagonist because even Jeanie Deans does not allow him to explore his historical interests in a way that makes for a unified, well-shaped novel. To be sure, Scott is hardly obsessed with producing unity and grace in his works. But except for its central action, *Midlothian* is disorderly even for a Waverley Novel. In abandoning the central protagonist, he may simply be turning back to forms that serve his interests more directly and efficiently, though perhaps with less brilliant results.

Jeanie Deans, like the other Scott protagonists, is the key to the structure and meaning of the novel in which she appears—to its strengths, its weaknesses, and even its lack of unity. I want first to define the sort of heroine she is, and then to consider the ways in which the other parts of the novel relate to the heroic action she performs.

Like many other Waverley protagonists, Jeanie Deans has been measured against irrelevant critical models. Dorothy Van Ghent, as we discovered earlier, demonstrates that a preoccupation with eternal values can blind a critic to Jeanie's essential historicity. But Jeanie has posed problems even for more historically minded critics, especially if their interest is primarily thematic and does not extend to form. Avrom Fleishman, for instance, makes an ingenious attempt to discover in Jeanie an inner change that figures a larger cultural transition. According to Fleishman, Jeanie begins as "a figure of high ideal-

11. Georg Lukács, *The Historical Novel* (1937), trans. Hannah and Stanley Mitchell (London: Merlin, 1962), pp. 37–49.

ism and unvarying dedication to moral principle, but since that principle excludes all others that conflict with it, her consistency becomes inflexibility, her high principle priggishness, and her idealism destructive pride. Like Shakespeare and (at least by implication) Sophocles, Scott will lead his admirable but limited heroine to a broader conception of morality." According to Fleishman, the change Jeanie undergoes is emblematic of a gradual civilizing process occurring in Scotland. He recognizes that Scott does not directly depict any change whatever in Jeanie's inner life. He thinks however, that Scott does so indirectly, using the madwoman Madge Wildfire both to "humanize" Jeanie by placing her in embarrassing positions and to indicate Jeanie's moral growth by acting as a kind of Greek chorus. When Madge leads Jeanie to the church of which the elder Mr. Staunton is rector, she sings a variety of songs, among them these verses from *The Pilgrim's Progress*:

> He that is down need fear no fall,
> He that is low no pride;
> He that is humble ever shall
> Have God to be his guide.

> Fulness to such a burthen is
> That go on pilgrimage;
> Here little, and hereafter bliss,
> Is best from age to age.

[p. 318; ch. 31]

She continues in this vein, later identifying Jeanie as Bunyan's character Christiana and herself as Mercy. According to Fleishman, Scott uses this literary reference to identify weaknesses from which Jeanie must free herself. She must become more like the person described in Bunyan's song, more humble, and also more merciful. In short, an "educative relationship . . . springs up between Madge Wildfire and Jeanie," who is rendered through such means "a much more complicated moral being than she has been."[12]

---

12. Avrom Fleishman, *The English Historical Novel: Walter Scott to Virginia Woolf* (Baltimore: Johns Hopkins University Press, 1971), pp. 89–91. Fleishman's treatment of Scott as a whole does not employ the Bildungsroman model so heavily. Instead, he provides a useful discussion of the vision of historical process Scott's novels convey.

Fleishman seems right in viewing Madge Wildfire as a choric figure in this part of the novel, but in my opinion he draws the wrong conclusions from Scott's references to Bunyan. Madge is celebrating Jeanie's virtues, not her alleged faults: Jeanie is the subject, not the object of the song.[13] We feel here as in other Bildungsroman readings of the Waverley Novels a tendency toward irrelevant or misleading abstract moral judgments, and we also observe the lengths to which a critic must go in order to apply the Bildungsroman pattern to characters presented as externally as Scott's are. There simply is no convincing evidence anywhere in the novel that Jeanie undergoes an essential change.[14] Fleishman points to her decision, a few pages after the scene with Madge, not to betray George Staunton as evidence that Jeanie has been humanized. In fact, Jeanie's inner monologue concerning whether or not to betray Staunton is an excellent example of the simple, beautiful continuity in her character throughout. Scott introduces the monologue with a passage clearly indicating that Jeanie's decision is exactly what we would expect from someone in her cultural position.[15] The point of this episode, in which Jeanie must

13. Further evidence for such an identification comes from the context of the song in Bunyan. In his 1830 review of Southey's *Life of John Bunyan*, Scott quotes the song but also adds the passage that follows it: "Then said their guide, 'Do you hear him? I will dare to say, this boy lives a merrier life, and wears more of that herb called *heart's-ease* in his bosom, than he that is clad in silk and velvet'" (*MPW* XVIII, 116). Both the narrator and Madge herself make a great deal of the supposed finery she wears, which stands in sharp contrast to Jeanie's "Quaker-like" simplicity.

14. John O. Hayden, "Jeanie Deans: The Big Lie (and a few small ones)," *Scottish Literary Journal*, 6 (May 1979), p. 41, recognizes that Jeanie does not grow morally, but downgrades *Midlothian* partly as a result. His discussion illustrates how easy it is to make nonsense of Jeanie's morality, especially its casuistical side, by abstracting it from history.

15. Jeanie's motives are religious and nationalistic: "Jeanie, in the strict and severe tone of morality in which she was educated, had to consider not only the general aspect of a proposed action, but its justness and fitness in relation to the actor, before she could be, according to her own phrase, free to enter upon it. What right had she to make a barter between the lives of Staunton and of Effie, and to sacrifice the one for the safety of the other? . . . Jeanie [also] felt conscious that, whoever should lodge information concerning that event [the Porteous riot], and for whatsoever purpose it might be done, it would be considered as an act of treason against the independence of Scotland. With the fanaticism of the Scotch Presbyterians there was always mingled a glow of national feeling, and Jeanie trembled at the idea of her name being handed down to posterity with that of the 'fause Monteath,' and one or two others, who, having deserted and betrayed the cause of their country, are damned to perpetual remem-

again decide whether to save her sister with a word of her mouth, is to provide one of a series of moments on the road to London which recall her original dilemma, giving her yet another chance to show the traits of character and culture which will finally lead to her success. The most we can say for Jeanie as a transitional figure is that, from the beginning of *Midlothian* to its end, she is more humane and flexible than her father, because of a change of generations as well as an alteration in the political and social climate of Scotland. This is a far cry from saying that her action actively represents such a transition, much less that she herself becomes educated to a greater humanity as the novel unfolds.

The idea that Jeanie is really far more morally complex than we might imagine, that she is initially a moral but limited character, who subsequently becomes interesting as she grows beyond her limits, is inaccurate and pernicious. A consistent attempt to see her as a kind of heroine she is not will inevitably end in dissatisfaction with her and her creator, for it will lead us to ignore the kind of heroine she is. Jeanie is not intended to be complex in the manner of a heroine of Flaubert. Far from being moral but limited, Jeanie is moral because she is limited. She is also interesting because she is limited. If Scott had wanted to write a novel that is interesting in the sense Fleishman suggests, he would have pleased Dorothy Van Ghent by centering it on Effie Deans, not on her sister.[16]

The central section of *Midlothian* is not the story of Jeanie's *Bildung*, it is the imitation of an action. In it, a crisis occurs which is relieved in an unexpected but probable way through the very means by which it first arose. Instead of being interesting as a psychologically complex individual, Jeanie as a personality is subsumed in the culturally resonant action she performs. Georg Lukács captures precisely this quality when he describes Jeanie as a figure who is momentarily picked up by the stream of history to become the heroic representative of her people (or, as he would say, of her class), but who

---

brance and execration among its peasantry" (pp. 359–60; ch. 34). Further evidence of Jeanie's continuity of character and principle is provided by her debate with the elder Staunton concerning the relative merits of the Scottish and English national churches (p. 356; ch. 34).

16. Dorothy Van Ghent, "On *The Heart of Mid-Lothian*, in *The English Novel: Form and Function* (1953; rpt. New York: Harper, 1961), pp. 119–20.

after her historical moment has passed becomes an ordinary person once again.[17] The pleasure we derive from Jeanie's trip to London results from seeing how the very qualities that will not allow her to lie, even to save her sister, provide the strength that wins the pardon.[18] Scott uses a wide variety of fictional means to emphasize this, the crucial fact about the story he is telling. Directly before her interview with the queen, for instance, Jeanie thinks that to succeed, she may need to transform herself in some way. She wonders if she should wear more genteel clothing, and she asks the Duke of Argyle to tell her what she should say. Argyle, who at this historical moment also rises to a kind of human greatness, knows better:

> "But, sir, your Grace," said Jeanie, "if it wasna ower muckle trouble, wad it no be better to tell me what I should say, and I could get it by heart?"
>
> "No, Jeanie, that would not have the same effect: that would be like reading a sermon, you know, which we good Presbyterians think has less unction than when spoken without book," replied the Duke. "Just speak as plainly and boldly to this lady as you did to me the day before yesterday; and if you can gain her consent, I'll wad ye a plack, as we say in the north, that you get the pardon from the king." [p. 377; ch. 36]

To convince the queen, Jeanie must be herself.

Midlothian depicts a good deal more than Jeanie Deans. How do the other parts of the novel relate to its central action? A careful look at the way in which Scott transforms his source for Jeanie's story tells us much about the novel's construction.[19] Scott learned of Jeanie's historical prototype, Helen Walker, from a friend, whose brief account he reproduces in the retrospective Introduction to the novel:

> Mr.——said, there were perhaps few more remarkable people than Helen Walker. She had been left an orphan, with the charge of a sister

17. Lukács, p. 52.

18. Hart, *Scott's Novels*, p. 137, oversimplifies the issues involved in the presentation of Jeanie Deans when he states that "too much has been made of Jeanie's truth-telling as historically conditioned reflex."

19. For another, somewhat fuller examination of the historical materials Scott drew on for *Midlothian* and the use he made of them, see Mary Lascelles, *The Story-Teller Retrieves the Past: Historical Fiction and Fictitious History in the Art of Scott, Stevenson, Kipling and Some Others* (London: Oxford University Press, 1980), pp. 85–102.

considerably younger than herself, and who was educated and maintained by her exertions. Attached to her by so many ties, therefore, it
will not be easy to conceive her feelings when she found that this only
sister must be tried by the laws of her country for child-murder, and
upon being called as principal witness against her. The counsel for the
prisoner told Helen, that if she could declare that her sister had made
any preparations, however slight, or had given her any intimation on
the subject, such a statement would save her sister's life, as she was
the principal witness against her. Helen said, "It is impossible for me
to swear to a falsehood; and, whatever may be the consequence, I will
give my oath according to my conscience."

The trial came on, and the sister was found guilty and condemned;
but, in Scotland, six weeks must elapse between the sentence and the
execution, and Helen Walker availed herself of it. The very day of her
sister's condemnation, she got a petition drawn up, stating the peculiar circumstances of the case, and that very night set out on foot to
London.

Without introduction or recommendation, with her simple, perhaps
ill-expressed, petition, drawn up by some inferior clerk of the court,
she presented herself, in her tartan plaid and country attire, to the
late Duke of Argyle, who immediately procured the pardon she peti-
tioned for, and Helen returned with it on foot, just in time to save her
sister. . . .

. . . I inquired if Helen ever spoke of her past history, her journey to
London, etc. "Na," the old woman said, "Helen was a wily body, and
whene'er ony o' the neebors asked anything about it, she aye turned
the conversation." [pp. x-xi]

Scott preserves the core of this story in *Midlothian*—Walker's inability even to entertain the idea of lying and her entire lack of self-
consciousness concerning her own heroism. But he also makes two
major additions. He fleshes out Jeanie's domestic circle to include a
father, as well as two admirers, one of whom Jeanie, unlike Walker,
eventually marries. He also creates as Effie's seducer the genteel
though rebellious George Staunton, accompanying him with a set of
colorful characters who, among other things and contrary to the actual dates involved, provide a link to the Porteous Riot. Why does he
add these characters?

In the central section of the novel, both sets of characters
strengthen and define Jeanie's action in a variety of ways. As we saw
in discussing *Quentin Durward*, there is a tendency for novels that
give a portrait of a historical figure to become static, for the syn-

chronic moment of historicism to assert itself completely. The characters Scott invents counter this tendency: he uses them to transform the immediate appreciation we feel as we read Walker's story into a developing set of hopes and fears for her fictional counterpart. By serving as obstacles Jeanie must surmount, they define and celebrate her heroism, as she remains triumphantly her historical self, no matter whether she is kidnapped by outlaws, led around the countryside by a madwoman, or confronted by a suspicious English rector or a British queen.

The obstacles Jeanie confronts on the way to London also help to solve certain difficulties raised by her origins. As modern readers, we may overlook the problems Scott faced in building a novel around a lower-class heroine. When *Midlothian* was first published, *Blackwood's Magazine* noted that Jeanie Deans was "something of a new character in novel writing, and certainly a very interesting one," but added that "even with persons not very aristocratical, the attention may appear to be too long, and too diffusely called to the concerns of a cowfeeder and his daughter."[20] Scott himself greatly enjoys creating a situation in which Jeanie Deans, daughter of David Deans, cowfeeder of St. Leonard's Crags, can talk with the Queen of England in an eloquent and morally dignified way, but he cannot count on his audience to share his delight. The process by which he makes Jeanie's meeting with the queen probable begins with the Laird of Dumbiedikes. By giving Jeanie this landed-though-absurd admirer, Scott hints at the opening of the novel that she may possess more social mobility than we might expect in a cowfeeder's daughter; our impression that she has her own kind of nobility strengthens when she turns down an offer of marriage from the Laird at the outset of her journey. She climbs a rung higher on the social scale when she confronts Staunton's father, a dignified, well-to-do Anglican rector, who begins by considering her mad, then for a moment thinks her a profligate involved with his son, but ends with an admiration for her that is the more real because he cannot quite understand her. Jeanie then meets the Duke of Argyle, who begins by being politely discouraging but ends as her warm advocate. Finally there comes the interview

20. *Blackwood's Magazine*, 3 (1818), 570. Similar comments appear in "Tales of My Landlord," *British Review*, 12 (1818), 396–407; in *Scott: The Critical Heritage*, ed. John O. Hayden (New York: Barnes and Noble, 1970), pp. 165–71.

with the queen, in which the same rhythm repeats itself. Problems at first arise because of Jeanie's class status, which prevents her from knowing the intricacies of court intrigue, but in the end her simple, class-based eloquence triumphs.

Dumbiedikes's admiration for Jeanie furthers another important fictional strategy. Jeanie must have male admirers, so that her refusal to lie to save Effie will not seem to be motivated by sexual jealousy. Otherwise, the point of her journey to London would be blurred, and the novel might seem to be about individual psychology, which it is not. Yet she must not have strong and effectual male admirers, or they would go to London for her. This is why the Laird of Dumbiedikes must be comically feckless, with a wayward pony that refuses to travel any road except the one that leads from his mansion to the house of David Deans. This is also why Reuben Butler comes down ill at the moment when Jeanie is ready to leave for London.

The Laird of Dumbiedikes provides a significant contrast to the minor characters we usually encounter in Scott's novels. In juxtaposition with his ferocious father, he may suggest a growing mildness in the landowning classes. But such an analysis explains little about the specific way in which he himself is presented. The comic props associated with him, his wayward pony and his "genteel" cocked hat, tell us little about history, but they make a clear and direct contribution to Jeanie's action. In most of the Waverley Novels, we could expect a minor character like Dumbiedikes to have a strongly representative function, like the function of Gifted Gilfillan in *Waverley*. But Scott's decision to center *Midlothian* on his protagonist calls for a change from his usual fictional priorities.

The central section of *Midlothian*, then, is unified around its protagonist in a strong, solid way precluded by the very nature of either conjunctive or disjunctive form. But this action is itself flanked by episodes that seem loosely connected with it. A depiction of the Porteous Riot opens the novel, and a long description of Jeanie's married life in Argyleshire closes it, taking up nearly all of the fourth volume of the novel as originally published. Why does *Midlothian* exhibit this mixture of unity and disunity? Again, the answer involves the kind of heroine Jeanie is. We may begin to see how by considering the opening chapters.

Any demonstration that *Midlothian's* opening chapters perfectly cohere with the action that follows should arouse our suspicion, not least because it contradicts the impression of most readers. Scott takes the same sort of interest in the Porteous riot as a phenomenon as he takes in Jeanie's walk to London as a phenomenon, but the two do not entirely mesh. The riot chapters serve as a pedestal, elaborated according to its own intrinsic proportions and not those of the work as a whole, on which the rest of the novel is placed. Some have tried to find a direct thematic continuity between the hanging of Porteous and the saving of Effie Deans. The opening chapters are said to question the nature of justice, the issue which the rest of the novel supposedly explores. Jeanie's success in procuring a pardon for her sister becomes an enactment of the dawn of a more humane kind of law, replacing both mob rule and unjust statutes like the one under which Effie nearly suffers.[21] In my view, such an interpretation violates the character of Scott's representation in both the sections it seeks to unify. I would not deny that *Midlothian*, the work of a professional lawyer, betrays a keen interest in questions of law and justice, but I do not think they are thematized in quite this way or with such structural centrality. From the work's rich depiction of the mixture of violence and justice embodied in the decisions of judges and of mobs, we obtain primarily a sense of historical complexity; we are brought face to face with a web of circumstances, traditions, and conflicting desires irreducible to any univalent pattern of progress or of right and wrong. Scott clearly dislikes the child-murder statute, and he also seems to dislike certain aspects of public executions. But he goes out of his way to show us why such laws and practices come into being.[22] That the child-murder statute has been repealed is clearly a good thing, but the notion that we are approaching a utopia of just, humane laws is undercut by the studied ambivalence the narrator displays concerning public execution, a custom which, he tells us, has in his own day fallen out of use, "with what beneficial effect is uncertain. The mental sufferings of the convict are indeed shortened . . . but . . . it may at

21. Probably the most valuable discussion of justice and mercy in the novel is A. O. J. Cockshut, *The Achievement of Walter Scott* (London: Collins, 1969), pp. 171–92.

22. In his *Journal* (20 Feb. 1828), Scott gives evidence that he believed that a temporary overseverity in the law could bring good results. See his similar comments concerning severe laws in the time of James VI and I in *Tales of a Grandfather*, MPW XXIII, 335–36.

least be doubted whether, in abridging the melancholy ceremony, we have not in part diminished that appalling effect upon the spectators which is the useful end of all such inflictions, and in consideration of which alone, unless in very particular cases, capital sentences can be altogether justified" (p. 18; ch. 2).

Nor is Scott's view of the murder of Porteous simple. The mob fascinates him. Their quiet resolution, their paying for the rope with which they hang a man adjudged by Scottish law worthy of execution—these things make the act seem almost juridical. Familial piety may also figure in Scott's partial admiration of the mob. Their single-minded effort to set justice right recalls an act performed by one of Scott's ancestors, who broke the freebooter Kinmont Willie out of prison in Carlisle Castle, where he was being wrongly detained by the English, with just the sort of circumspection concerning private property that the Porteous mob used.[23] Scott was, rather surprisingly, capable of approving a certain amount of mob violence; he considered a bit of window breaking now and then a sign of healthy independence, far preferable to the good order imposed by a tyrant like Napoleon.[24] His mixed feelings about law and violence color the opening chapters of *Midlothian* to an extent that makes it impossible to abstract a simple thematic pattern from them.[25] According to R. C. Gordon, we experience Jeanie's achieving a pardon for her sister as "some sort of miracle."[26] Its full miraculousness appears only against the background the opening chapters provide, as they evoke the complexity of historical forces and their indifference to individuals.

The reason why the opening chapters of *Midlothian* seem both to fit and yet not to fit with the rest of the novel, then, is that while they depict an event that fascinated Scott but has little direct connection with the story of Jeanie Deans, they do so in a way that prepares us to

23. Scott describes this escapade in his notes to "Kinmont Willie," in *Minstrelsy of the Scottish Border,* ed. T. F. Henderson, 4 vols. (Edinburgh: Blackwood, 1902), II, 39–55.

24. "History of Europe, 1815," in *The Edinburgh Annual Register for 1815,* Edinburgh Annual Register, 8 (Edinburgh: Constable, 1817), pt. I, p. 85.

25. Compare John Henry Raleigh, Introduction to *The Heart of Midlothian* (Boston: Houghton Mifflin Riverside, 1966), p. xxviii: "There is never any sense that the author himself is taking sides on the means-ends argument, or on any of the other ironies about law and justice that are presented in the novel."

26. Gordon, p. 95.

read her story as it ought to be read. In responding adequately to the depiction of the Porteous riot, we learn how to respond to Jeanie's heroic action. The fictionalized introduction that precedes the riot works toward the same end, by insisting that true stories, especially traditional tales of actual men and women who reflect a nation's culture, are not less but more interesting than fabricated romances. In the description of the Porteous riot, we see one such tradition come alive before us. The imaginative power of the riot derives entirely from the participants' mixture of vindictiveness and discipline; it reflects the Scottish national character in its strengths and weaknesses, a topic pointedly raised in the introductory chapter.

But if Scott wishes to emphasize the importance of true stories and national character in his opening chapters, why is the man who leads the rioters not a Scotsman but a disguised Englishman, and worse, a character recognizably derived from fictional conventions entirely familiar to readers of Gothic novels and Byron? We have already touched on one answer, at the level of plot construction: Scott has compelling reasons to provide Jeanie's trip to London with a series of obstacles, which include meeting a representative of genteel English society. We must also admit that Scott seems to have felt an obligation to provide something like a conventional love story in each of his novels. But the dangers of inserting such material into *this* novel are unusually grave. Genteel, "modern" assumptions concerning the superior value of passionate interiority and individualism, as well as a certain escapism from the complexities of historical existence, are built into a character like Staunton and indeed into the Staunton-Effie plot as a whole. A similar problem exists for all of Scott's genteel plots, but is usually accompanied by advantages that more than offset it. The genteel associations of typical romance plots become, as we have seen, a positive advantage in the best conjunctive novels: in a work like *Waverley*, they help to give the protagonist a stake in the present, which makes him a useful representative in the novel for the "modern" reader and furthers the work's rhetorical aim of making us acquiesce in the loss of the past as well. Some of this usefulness remains in *Midlothian*. Staunton and Effie are in important ways our representatives. But they also threaten to undermine our appreciation of Jeanie's historically determined particularity. In *Midlothian* as in *Old Mortality* and *The Fair Maid of Perth*, Scott solves a problem his fictional devices raise not by finding different devices, but by thematizing the problem and using it to his advantage. He incorporates an upper-class, conventionally Gothic seducer into his novel, but he does so in a way that makes us reject the genteel presuppositions such a figure carries with him; as we do so, we learn to appreciate the novel's true richness. Beyond that, Staunton inadvertently helps to reveal a superior kind of romance in the fabric of history itself.

Scott begins to put Staunton in a proper perspective as soon as he appears. The presence of this English gentleman and outside agitator, disguised as a notorious Scottish madwoman, at the head of the Porteous mob, would in a more conventional novel constitute an attempt to disown the threat of disciplined and independent revolutionary action by the lower classes. The brute historical fact of the riot would dissipate into romantic cliché, just as at the end of *Les Chouans* the fact of civil war yields to eternal loves and hatreds, and skirmishes are fought so that the lovers can meet and betray one another. But in *Midlothian* exactly the reverse occurs. When Staunton tries to persuade Effie to fly with him, his romantic pleading melts away before her simple peasant refusal, accompanied by the vernacular proverb, "Better tyne life, since tint is gude fame" (p. 63; ch. 7). The genteel Staunton turns out to be effective only in the role that his lower-class compatriots give him; at this moment, they demand that he leave Effie and get on with the business of hanging Porteous. Like many another "great man" in Scott or Tolstoy, Staunton can lead those who embody national consciousness or the national will, but only where the forces of history make them want to go. Throughout the novel, Staunton accomplishes nothing significant. His efforts to save Effie wither into melodrama and bathos: even his trusted horse throws him as he gallops toward London to bargain for her life with Walpole. His few moments of substantiality are as borrowed as Madge Wildfire's name and clothing.

Staunton's failure to save Effie in the prison scene is emblematic of *Midlothian's* consistent repudiation of the values associated with him. This repudiation amounts to a rejection of the antihistorical attempt to make the external world a mere symbol of individual desires, to reduce all levels of historical generality to the timeless ego. Throughout the novel, he is given to flamboyant, symbolic gestures having only that measure of reality concrete historical consciousness gives them:

he plays at being the Devil, but for Butler and Jeanie he *is*, briefly, the Devil. In his last speeches, Staunton continues his attempts to make the external world a symbol of human interiority by insisting that the storm in which he and Butler are caught is ominous of "some important event in the world below" (p. 524; ch. 51). Butler responds, like the enlightened eighteenth-century Christian he is, that Nature follows its own laws regardless of human hopes and fears. As the scene unfolds, Staunton's view seems ironically vindicated. He dies at the hands of his own son, the child Effie was accused of murdering, but who was in fact spirited away and raised by an outlaw who attacks Staunton and Butler for their money. At this point, genteel expectations seem to have returned to the novel with a vengeance. When lovely woman stoops to folly, as Effie has, she must pay the price, either in person or by proxy. Now it is conceivable that in punishing Staunton in this melodramatic manner, Scott is simply yielding to the expectation of his readers, just as he later yielded to James Ballantyne's demand that talk of premarital sex be expunged from *St. Ronan's Well*. But given Scott's sustained attack on genteel expectations throughout the novel, it seems at least as likely that there is irony here. So the reader demands that certain crimes meet with certain punishments, described in certain literary modes? Very well. The reader shall have it all in spades—an ominous storm, fine speeches, a parricide, a gloomy hero/villain who after death is discovered to be wearing beneath his fine clothing a hair shirt, in a hopeless attempt to atone for his sins. Or perhaps Scott is doing something even more daring, creating as effective a set piece in the Gothic mode as he possibly can, in the full knowledge that his depiction of prosaic Jeanie Deans has been so strong that we will prefer her heroism to the heroics of Staunton.[27]

Whatever we make of his death, Staunton serves primarily as a means of discrediting and neutralizing prejudices Scott's audience was likely to hold concerning heroism, class status, and the proper subjects for literary representation. But *Midlothian* is not an attack on all versions of romance, however triumphantly prosaic its heroine may

27. Coleman O. Parsons, "The Influence of Grillparzer on *The Heart of Midlothian*," *Notes and Queries*, 189 (1945), 248–49, makes a convincing case that Scott's immediate source for Staunton's theatrical demise was the German drama, and especially Franz Grillparzer's Schicksalsdrama, *Die Ahnfrau* (1817).

be. *Midlothian* finds the source of true romance where it finds the source of true heroism—in the specificities of cultural beliefs and traditions as they are mediated by individuals existing at certain moments in history, and in the elements that constitute a national character. Authentic romance in *Midlothian* centers on Madge Wildfire. Scott chooses to give Madge a childhood home in England, in order to motivate her presence as an obstacle to Jeanie on her way to London, but Madge is born of Scottish parents, speaks thick Scots, and altogether represents certain aspects of Scottish culture. The "ominous" storm George Staunton expatiates about may be a stage property, but the supernatural scenes in which Madge plays a part—the scene at Muschat's cairn, or the eerie moment when at nightfall Jeanie comes upon Madge and her mother directly before she is kidnapped—have a greater authenticity. They recall the world of the Scots ballads, a folk form that finds its last vital echo in "Proud Maisie," which Madge sings as she dies. The world of the ballads is already slipping beyond reach in the period in which the novel is set: Madge's madness, conventionally motivated by her seduction and betrayal at the hands of Staunton, may on the deepest level figure its marginality. Its possibilities are still part of Jeanie's consciousness, though she has only partial, fearful, unwilling access to it, through her belief that the Devil may walk the earth, for instance. Scott makes Madge's family a kind of distorted mirror image of the Deanses: we learn that Madge's father was a member of the Cameronian Regiment, a body David Deans despises for perverting the principles of one of his own mentors, Richard Cameron, the heroic Covenanter whose name they bear. The parallels here strengthen the suggestion that Madge and Effie, seduced by the same man, are doubles: thus Madge recalls the reason for Jeanie's journey to London even as she provides an obstacle to it. But Madge is Jeanie's double as well. Together, they represent two alternative possibilities of the Scottish character, a Jekyll-and-Hyde split pitting nearly complete sublimation, discipline, and rationality against spontaneity, license, and imagination.

The most problematic aspect of form in *Midlothian*, however, involves neither the depiction of the Porteous riots nor the function of Staunton, but the relevance of the fourth volume. Readers from Scott's day to the present have loudly complained that since the novel has virtually ended after Jeanie obtains the pardon from the queen, an additional volume describing her life on the Highland estate of the Duke of Argyle is unnecessary and anticlimactic. We ought to respect the protest against the fourth volume and resist attempts to explain it away. Respecting certain explanations for the existence of the volume is another matter. Not a shred of external evidence supports the persistent view that Scott's primary motivation in producing it was financial. We have no more right to assume that Scott wrote the final volume of *Midlothian* simply for the money than we have to assume that he wrote Jeanie's speech to Queen Caroline or "Wandering Willie's Tale" in *Redgauntlet* simply for the money. The alacrity with which this pseudo-explanation has been seized upon, sometimes by otherwise excellent critics, is a measure of the problem the ending of the novel poses.[28] I believe that the formal perspective on Scott's novels I have outlined allows us to explain why Scott added a fourth volume to the novel, as well as why it does not quite fit—why it is neither totally integrated nor totally extraneous.

Volume Four of *The Heart of Midlothian* is the result of two related but distinct intentions. One reflects Scott's delight in Jeanie Deans. Having put an actual Scottish character at the center of a plotted action for the only time in his career, he finds it difficult to let her go. He continues to show Jeanie being herself, even when circumstances no longer require that she exhibit her latent greatness. His fascination with Jeanie, however, provides only part of the explanation. The

28. The supposition that Scott wrote Volume Four simply for money arose as soon as the novel was published. It is mentioned as a guess by the August 1818 review in *Blackwood's*, cited in n. 20, above. It gained modern currency, I believe, from Sir Herbert J. C. Grierson, *Sir Walter Scott, Bart.* (London: Constable, 1938), pp. 164–65. Grierson refers to it as established fact, but cites in evidence only the *Blackwood's* article and the opinion of Thomas Seccombe, "The Heart of Midlothian," in *Scott Centenary Articles: Essays by Thomas Seccombe, W. P. Ker, George Gordon, W. H. Hutton, Arthur McDowall, and R. S. Rait* (London: Oxford University Press, 1932), pp. 66–67, who in his turn cites only the "Uncanny insight of Craigenputtock!"—that is, Thomas Carlyle's assumption that financial considerations ruined Scott's art, for which see Carlyle's *London and Westminster Review* article, 28 (January 1838), 293–345; rpt. in *Scott: The Critical Heritage*, pp. 345–72. Modern critics who, like Grierson, state the supposition as if it were a fact include Van Ghent, pp. 114–15, Gordon, p. 6, and Lascelles, p. 85. It is in fact an unproven and unprovable hypothesis. For an intelligent protest against the view that Scott wrote only for money, see James T. Hillhouse, *The Waverley Novels and Their Critics* (Minneapolis: University of Minnesota Press, 1936) pp. 33–34.

main reason why Volume Four exists is to settle some unfinished
business which Jeanie herself cannot resolve. Jeanie is not and cannot
be the center of an action that represents the general movement of
historical process: she and the action she performs are too special, too
singular for that. She sums up in an unforgettable way the possibilities of a certain historical time and place, but she does not point beyond them. Yet readers who believe that the novel as a whole reflects
Scott's interest in historical process are not mistaken. Though Jeanie
is not well adapted to embody the course of historical process, other
members of her family are. The main justification for the final volume
of *Midlothian* is that in it Scott uses David Deans to demonstrate how
Cameronian fanaticism becomes softened and humanized by the passage of time, and Effie Deans to suggest some of the larger implications of this process.[29] The fourth volume is largely given over to exploring Scott's favorite theme, cultural transition, which arises from
but is not enacted by the novel's central action: hence it naturally
enough has always seemed somewhat extraneous to readers who believe, as they should, that Jeanie's action is the heart of the novel.

In an earlier chapter, I noted the masterly way in which Scott uses
David's language to enact the process of historical transition. The
narrator's own voice—an amused, tolerant voice full of insight into
human weakness and inconsistency but generously aware of their survival value—also plays a part here. Thus the narrator comments on
David's failure to ascertain whether Reuben Butler has taken the sort
of "Erastian" oath of obedience to the government which a younger
David Deans would have rejected to the death. After Butler's installa-
tion as Minister of Knocktarlitie, we learn that David's mind

> was so much occupied by considering the best means of converting
> Duncan of the Knock [who had smoked his pipe throughout the ser-
> vice] to a sense of reverent decency during public worship, that he al-

29. David Daiches, Introduction to *The Heart of Midlothian* (New York: Rinehart,
1948), p. viii, notes that "the softening of David Deans under the impact of his bitter
personal experience is indeed one of the minor themes of the story, and Scott handles
it with a delicate insight into character and his usual mastery of vernacular dialogue.
But Scott in describing this change is interested in more than the development of the
character of David Deans; as Lord Tweedsmuir [John Buchan] saw, he 'wanted to
show Scottish life passing into a mellower phase in which old unhappy things were
forgotten.'"

together forgot to inquire whether Butler was called upon to subscribe the oaths to government.

    Some have insinuated that his neglect on this head was, in some de-
gree, intentional; but I think this explanation inconsistent with the
simplicity of my friend David's character. Neither have I ever been
able, by the most minute inquiries, to know whether the formula
at which he so much scrupled had been exacted from Butler, aye or
no. [p. 463; ch. 46]

David in fact is unsuccessful in converting Duncan of the Knock to
anything, and Scott as narrator is too wise to convert David himself
completely from fanaticism to toleration. One of our last glimpses of
David reveals his keen disappointment that the Kirk Session has neglected to burn a witch and refused to ruin the reputation of a woman
whose first child arrived shortly after her marriage. But we know that
David has changed. These are essentially comic, because unavailing,
reflex actions, which the Kirk Session does well to ignore. They are
like David's own final mutterings "about right-hand extremes, and
left-hand fallings off": a servant observes that "his head was 'carried'
at the time," and the narrator adds that "it is probable that these expressions occurred to him merely out of general habit, and that he
died in the full spirit of charity with all men" (p. 491; ch. 49).

    The dominant mode of characterization in Volume Four of *Mid-
lothian* underlines the volume's difference in mode from the rest of
the novel. Everything about David Deans fits him for the role of helping to indicate a cultural transition. He is clearly one of Scott's representative characters, and these characters come into their own in this
final section of Scott's work. David's opponent, Duncan Knockdunder, is another such character. He is dressed in a way unmistaka-
bly designed to represent the half-civilized state of the Highlands.
Scott describes him as "a stout short man about fifty, whose pleasure
it was to unite in his own person the dress of the Highlands and Low-
lands, wearing on his head a black tie-wig, surmounted by a fierce
cocked hat, deeply guarded with gold lace, while the rest of his dress
consisted of the plaid and philabeg" (p. 451; ch. 44). Having made
his point, Scott proceeds to arrange an incident to relieve Duncan of
what he admits is a "ludicrous" attire: Duncan loses his Lowland hat
and reverts to a Highland counterpart.

    We recognize the difference between the representational mode of

Volume Four and the rest of *Midlothian* if we compare Duncan Knockdunder with the Laird of Dumbiedikes. Dumbiedikes's comic props, his wayward pony and his cocked hat, are fully explicable only in terms of Jeanie's action, not in terms of historical representativeness. Just the reverse is true of the dress, actions, and stage Highland speech of Duncan Knockdunder. Their only possible explanation is historical representation. Another example of the difference in fictional mode between the earlier parts of the novel and Volume Four is provided by Reuben Butler. In Volumes One and Two he first acts the part of a disjunctive hero, as an unwilling spectator to the Porteous riot; then he helps to define Jeanie's action in the same way Dumbiedikes does. But in Volume Four, he serves as the embodiment of the values that will replace those of his father-in-law, David Deans. We may measure the extent of Butler's transformation by conjuring up two images, one of him sick in bed and unable to prevent Jeanie from going to London, the other of him briskly going about his work as minister of Knocktarlitie and finding it necessary to contradict David Deans now and again in the process. These two roles reflect the two main centers of historical interest in *Midlothian*.

There remains, finally, the question of Effie Deans's place in Volume Four. Effie's transformation from a peasant and convict to the aristocratic wife of Sir George Staunton makes her an excellent foil for Jeanie, allowing Scott to demonstrate that even after Jeanie's heroic moment has passed, she remains superior to the sort of genteel lady Effie has become. Giving Jeanie a passing attack of jealousy at Effie's social success is a brilliant touch; it is humanly true, and its openness relieves once and for all any suspicion that a hidden jealousy of Effie's beauty had earlier motivated Jeanie. But Effie's most important function in Volume Four is to explore the significance of the gradual softening and civilizing of the Scottish character in a less parochial way than her father can. In her transition from the peasant girl Staunton cannot rescue to the fine lady he owns as his wife, Effie loses the historical substantiality both Jeanie and Madge possess in their different ways, and she gains wealth, social power, and an inescapable self-division. She also acquires an ability to appreciate natural landscapes, finding in them a compensation for worldly sorrows, instead of being unconsciously part of them as Jeanie and Madge are. It is appropriate that she sees "the Whistler" as part of a sublime landscape suddenly turned into threatening reality, not as the son he in fact is to her. The sorrow which Effie assuages through her love of natural beauty stems, according to the novel's use of genteel convention, from her "sin" with Staunton and its consequences. But her deepest sin is that she has become a genteel modern—one of us, or the next thing to it—whose historical fate is to lack simple cultural wholeness. *Midlothian* is a novel about a character who, because of the way she embodies certain historical forces, cannot tell a lie, even to save her sister's life. When in Volume Four Scott juxtaposes Jeanie Deans and Euphemia Setoun Staunton, a self-proclaimed "liar of fifteen years' standing" (p. 505; ch. 50) whose ultimate lie is to play the part of a woman of quality, Jeanie's "integrity" assumes a new significance. In the journey to London that constitutes the core of the novel, Jeanie's integrity leads her to express in a unique and exalted form certain possibilities of her cultural and historical moment, reflecting Scott's fascination with synchronic historical particularity. But when her heroic moment has passed and she enters the altered representational mode of Volume Four, her integrity points in another direction, toward the other pole of Scott's historicist imagination, helping to raise questions concerning historical process and its results.

Conclusion

The Heart of Midlothian is a great but disunified novel. Its disunity results in part from Scott's willingness to sacrifice certain esthetic values for the sake of a broader, richer exploration of the historical issues that most interest him. But it also results from the latent tension between the two poles of his historical vision. This tension in turn reflects what I have called the problem with historical novels, providing yet another example to support, at least with respect to standard fiction, Siegfried Kracauer's contention that the different levels of historical generality are essentially discontinuous. But disunity, however explicable and however interesting, remains disunity, an offense to certain esthetic values difficult to dismiss. Here our response to *Midlothian* becomes significant in itself, since the demand for unity in standard novels, which we can hardly avoid making, may mean that certain aspects of human existence will be represented but that others will not. Do we value certain kinds of artistic unity, and particularly unity based on the representation of human interiority, in part because they tend to exclude a range of social, economic, and political problems we can hardly formulate, much less answer? Does talk of the "eternal" values with which literature should be concerned itself rest upon a basis that is hardly eternal, the attempt of a certain class at a certain moment to deny aspects of the historical situation in which it finds itself? When read against the novelistic tradition that followed it, Scott's fiction raises such questions. It is easy to show that some aspects of Scott's ideology are bourgeois, just as it is easy to demonstrate that some aspects of historicism can degenerate into a philistine endorsement of progress. As I hope to have shown, Scott's historicist vision, taken as a whole, is much more complex than that. Almost since its first flowering, historicism has provoked a counterattack in the name of a variety of human values—freedom, creativity, authenticity, inwardness. That counterattack seems to be reaching a climax in our own day, and in certain regards it may be justified. The areas of human experience which historicism, and Scott's historicist fiction, tend to slight have an importance that is hardly negligible. But taking Scott's achievement seriously raises the possibility that the rejection of historicism may also constitute an evasion of the difficult, threatening task of coming to terms with our situation as historical beings.

The burden of historical consciousness is something Scott himself did not evade. Though we cannot wholly accept his attempts to make sense of history, they deserve our attention, particularly since they differ decisively from those made by many of his successors, and also by his contemporaries. The mainstream Romantic poets and philosophers, as M. H. Abrams has shown, believed that through historical process the past is *aufgehoben*: history takes the shape of an ascending spiral, in which despite passing vicissitudes, everything of value in the past is preserved in a heightened state in the future.[30] If there is anything that separates Scott from the other Romantics, it is his inability to believe that history takes this spiral course. In this matter, as in nearly all others, Scott is a divided soul. He yearns to believe that at least some of the best things about the past can be preserved in present-day society. Part of his rather comic disappointment at not

30. M. H. Abrams, *Natural Supernaturalism: Tradition and Revolution in Romantic Literature* (New York: Norton, 1971).

being able to engage in a duel with Gaspard Gourgaud, a French general angry about Scott's *Life of Napoleon*, surely stemmed from a desire that the modern notion of a gentleman should include in a purified form the more bellicose aspects of the ancient code of chivalry. And in the *Life of Napoleon* itself, as R. C. Gordon has recently shown, Scott appears to try to create his own version of *Aufhebung* through suggesting that the French and Spanish popular resistance to Napoleon opens the possibility of a more general resurgence of the military virtues.[31] But in his novels, which I take to embody his most profound meditations on history, things are different. The task is to prevent the sands of time and tradition from slipping through one's fingers. Though the present may be more comfortable and humane than the past, the past had its compensations, and these in the main are doomed to disappear, except in memory and artistic re-creation. The comic resolutions of the Waverley Novels that most fully represent Scott's vision of history represent a way of accepting gracefully a tragic process which destroys far more than it preserves.

Historicism for Scott, as for so many other thinkers in the nineteenth and twentieth centuries, gives only to take away. Scott can see the past in its richness only by recognizing the great gulf fixed between himself and the object of his contemplation. Part of the sadness underlying his works is surely a result of this dilemma. But the historical vision does not merely take away, separate, destroy. A vital consolation for Scott is his ability, beyond and because of the gulf, to recognize and depict men, women, and social orders with strengths and weaknesses, customs and beliefs, different from those of the present.

Scott's fictional world is more varied than has been recognized. If this book has helped to create a sense of the formal variety of his novels, it has achieved one of its central aims. Writing these richly various works answered for Scott the problem of historical consciousness in at least two ways. To begin with, the very act of narration itself provided a mode of dealing with the past in an exhilarating way. We can recall the picture Lockhart paints of seeing Scott's hand moving

---

31. R. C. Gordon, "Scott among the Partisans: A Significant Bias in his *Life of Napoleon Buonaparte*," in *Scott Bicentenary Essays: Selected Papers Read at the Sir Walter Scott Bicentenary Conference*, ed. Alan Bell (Edinburgh: Scottish Academic Press, 1973), pp. 115–33. See also his "Scott and the Highlanders: The Non-fictional Evidence," *Yearbook of English Studies*, 6 (1976), 120–40.

swiftly and relentlessly from left to right, covering line after line and page after page with re-created history. In a study like this one, we must follow, carefully and slowly, a process of artistic creation which was for Scott a rapid, spontaneous flow of artistic decisions and adaptations. It is well to remember the joy that narration afforded Scott, who insisted that his quickest writing was his best—the delight in difficulties effortlessly surmounted, problems spontaneously solved. These, the common pleasures of successful narration, had a special status in his case. Narration was a way of controlling and reliving history, in which he could identify his own creativity with the process that most fascinated him, historical change and development.

Taken to an extreme, such an identification can involve pure form without content. This possibility is realized in Victor Hugo's use of clashing dichotomies to enact his vision of historical process in *Quatrevingt-treize*. Something similar occurs with Jeanie Deans's walk to London. As we experience her journey, we feel that Lukács's notion of an individual's being picked up by the stream of history is coming to life before us: this may partly explain why certain critics, particularly those with a genuine interest in history, want so badly to see Jeanie undergo during the journey a personal change with larger historical significance. Yet a certain sleight-of-hand is occurring here. The journey to London represents more than the course of one individual, one tiny rivulet in a maze of crisscrossing destinies. But it does so purely by its texture: it provides a formal echo of historical process, not a substantial microcosm or symbolic reduction.[32] In the end, the journey turns out to be the narrative unfolding of an essentially synchronic perception about certain aspects of Scottish society and the Scottish character. The attractions of being able to identify on such a purely formal level with historical process are as strong as its dangers: one can merge with the form of the grandest, richest process in which human beings play an active role, without having to register the brutality and suffering that always accompany it. At this level of abstraction, we recognize that the complaint that Scott glamorizes the past, demonstrably false in regard to the content of his novels, has some validity; we also begin to understand how a humane, generous man could take such relish in depicting a process he knew to be

32. For an extended discussion of the problem of symbolism in standard historical fiction, see Chapter 3.

deeply destructive, and how the sense of movement underlying his narrative could so quickly degenerate into the aimless, frenetic motion that fills the novels of his less-worthy successors. On a more concrete level, narration, particularly in the conjunctive novels, gives Scott the opportunity to render historical process less terrible to the imagination by weighing its merits and giving it a conclusive shape. This tactic, too, is open to objection and to praise. The insistence that history has a shape can become a justification for passive veneration of a process whose ways are not our ways; it can also provide the basis for a revolutionary praxis that must understand what it wishes to change.

The latter move, of course, is not one which Scott himself would have made or encouraged; his political prejudices, as well as his sense of historical complexity and his instinct to conserve as much of the past as possible, were too strong for that. Besides allowing him to merge with, evaluate, and put into conclusive form historical process, creating fictional narratives afforded Scott another kind of consolation for the loss of the past: the chance to make the particularities of history live again. It may be that historical process is a bloody, wasteful business marked by some heroism, much destruction, and little justice or humanity. But the particular stages through which society has evolved have also produced individuals who could have been created in no other way, through no other process, who fascinate us because they result from a set of circumstances that neither can nor will recur. It seems a terrible mistake to allow a figure like Jeanie Deans to be drained of her specific historical value and saliency for the sake of fitting her into the kind of general moral scheme that had only a secondary interest for her creator. I do not want to see her "humanized" or to discover that she represents a general truth about "our" life. I want her to be what she is—a kind of person I shall never meet, a human being separated from me by the irresistible passage of time.

The best criticism of Scott as a historical novelist has concentrated on one pole of his historicist vision—on his depiction and evaluation of historical process. For Lukács, that is all there is, really, to admire in Scott—and it is quite enough. Such an emphasis is understandable and admirable: it is surely preferable to criticism that, under the aegis of the norms of the standard novel, fails to recognize the depiction of either historical process or historical particularity in Scott. I trust that I have not slighted the importance of Scott's representation of historical process. But an exclusive focus on historical process leads in the end to a distortion of Scott's work and significance, and I have consciously tried to right this balance. An unwillingness to allow present concerns to overwhelm the past, which reflects a grasp of historical particularities and the systematic ways in which they form historical milieux, is one of the things that separate Scott most decisively from the majority of his successors.

An insistence on the value of the particularity Jeanie Deans embodies has been a keynote of this study. My own method has been largely a particularist method: I have thought it worthwhile to make distinctions and categories, to concentrate on the workings of individual texts, and to isolate particular, sometimes conflicting strands within the fabrics of individual works. Scott's novels, like most novels that incorporate history into their forms, have priorities different from those of the works that are central to our fictional tradition. I have tried to show that Scott's kind of representation can have its own concreteness, even though it does not much deal with the specificities of the inner life or the mental process of its characters, that studies of ideology have as much validity as studies of psychology, and that "mere local color" in Scott, as it has derisively been called, can have great interest for us, if we recognize it for the concrete historical depiction it is. It seems particularly important at the present moment in intellectual history, when historical realities, past and present, seem ready to dissolve into the modalities of individual perception or synchronic codes, to insist, as Scott's novels insist, on the importance of that which is historically other from us. Scott's novels become more explicable in form and meaning, and they gain a greater significance for us, if we neglect neither pole of his historical vision, if we prize his representation of historical process but also his grasp of historical particularity.

But isn't there a hidden unity that joins both sides of Scott's historical vision? To ask this question is to raise the problem with which this book began: the problem of whether there is an inherent discontinuity between different levels of historical existence. For the purposes of analyzing historical fiction, we can bracket this problem in its most general form, and I have done so. The evidence seems overwhelming that within the confines of standard fiction, such a discontinuity operates. Even Scott's attempt to answer the problem by shifting his focus to a portion of the human spectrum which includes neither the most particular nor the most general itself tends to break apart except under the most propitious circumstances, as we have repeatedly seen. An attempt to use this property of standard historical fiction as the basis for broader extrapolation, however, evokes a teasing contradiction. We can give the fate of standard historical fiction exemplary significance only by assuming that such fiction provides a microcosm of all possible discourses concerning history. But to do this is to assume the continuity between different levels we are seeking to deny. The most we can do is to make the example of standard historical fiction one moment in a hermeneutical inquiry into the nature of historical understanding. At the end of such an inquiry, I believe, we would conclude that ultimate judgments concerning the nature of historical process are not susceptible of proof, but instead constitute the grounds of our knowledge.

This is not to say that such judgments do not matter. A "side-by-side" philosophy of history, like Scott's tolerance for disparate and irreconcilable formal elements in his novels, has its attractions and its liabilities. It promises to save at least a limited autonomy for the different levels of historical existence, without dismantling the notion of a coherent historical process altogether. Yet it can also freeze our comprehension and stultify our action. Siegfried Kracauer is surely right to suggest that in our normal lives we tend to behave differently on different levels of generality, that we are different people in our private and public roles. In some ways this is a good thing—it is probably necessary if we are to maintain our sanity—but it also helps to allow injustice to permeate every society that presently exists, as it has every past society.

Scott's work as a novelist cannot of itself ground a final judgment of whether historical existence is essentially homogeneous or essentially heterogeneous, but it seems exemplary in other ways that may be more immediately germane to our condition as historical beings. The example of his fiction can remind us that other possibilities in representation exist besides those valorized by our dominant fictional traditions. His attempts to create fictions true to both sides of his historicist vision, with their false starts, ideological dodges and distortions, and partial successes, can provide a measure of the challenge that maintaining a truly historical vision raises. And at their best, his works can remind us that historical consciousness is not simply or primarily a burden. By enabling us to imagine a broader spectrum of human possibilities and cultural alternatives, they can help us to see beyond the burdens of the present.

Index

The Forms of
Historical Fiction

Designed by G. T. Whipple, Jr.
Composed by Eastern Graphics
in 10½ point Sabon, 3 points leaded,
with display lines in Sabon.
Printed offset by Thomson-Shore, Inc.
on Warren's Number 66 text, 50 pound basis.
Bound by John H. Dekker & Sons, Inc.
in Holliston book cloth.

Library of Congress Cataloging in Publication Data

SHAW, HARRY E., 1946–
    The forms of historical fiction.

    Includes index.
    1. Scott, Walter, Sir, 1771–1832—Criticism and
interpretation.   2. Scott, Walter, Sir, 1771–1832—
Influence.   3. Historical fiction.   I. Title.
PR5343.H5S5   1983   823'.17   83–5354
ISBN 0-8014-1592-6